The Light Gray People

An Ethno-History of the Lipan Apaches of Texas and Northern Mexico

Nancy McGown Minor

D1617461

University Press of America,® Inc.
Lanham · Boulder · New York · Toronto · Plymouth, UK

Copyright © 2009 by
University Press of America,® Inc.
4501 Forbes Boulevard
Suite 200
Lanham, Maryland 20706
UPA Acquisitions Department (301) 459-3366

Estover Road
Plymouth PL6 7PY
United Kingdom

Cover: Plains Indian Girl with Melon
Credit: Friedrich Richard Petri
Friedrich Richard Petri Collection
The Center for American History, The University of Texas at Austin

Library of Congress Control Number: 2009934373
ISBN-13: 978-0-7618-4853-0 (clothbound : alk. paper)
ISBN-10: 0-7618-4853-3 (clothbound : alk. paper)
ISBN-13: 978-0-7618-4854-7 (paperback : alk. paper)
ISBN-10: 0-7618-4854-1 (paperback : alk. paper)
eISBN-13: 978-0-7618-4855-4
eISBN-10: 0-7618-4855-X

Contents

Figures, Tables and Maps

Figures

Tables

Maps

Preface

The sixty year old Lipan Apache woman calmly watched the young linguist as he opened his notepad. As Harry Hoijer studied the languages of the Mescalero and Lipan Apaches living at the Mescalero Reservation in 1939, the linguist was astounded to learn of one Lipan woman who not only carried the story of the history and customs of the Lipan people in her memory, but could recount the tale in the Lipan language. Hoijer hastily arranged an interview with the woman, Augustina Zuazua, in order to record this unique piece of oral history. As Hoijer readied his notepad, interpreter Lisandro Mendez leaned forward in anticipation of the story to be told.

If Hoijer had been looking for a dramatic tale with modern relevance, Augustina Zuazua could have told him of the Lipan history she had witnessed within her lifetime. She was born in 1879 into the *Kû 'ne tsa (Big Water)* band of Lipan Apaches living near Zaragosa, Coahuila, Mexico (Mescalero Reservation Census, 1904). At the time of her birth, her people were in the process of being driven from the Coahuilan lands they had inhabited since 1751 by military attacks launched from both sides of the Texas-Mexico border. Forcibly evicted from their Zaragosa settlement in 1903 after threats of military conscription and deportation to South America, Augustina and thirty-six Lipan men, women and children were seized by the Mexican Army and brought to the neighboring Mexican state of Chihuahua. They were imprisoned in an open cattle pen, guarded by Mexican troops and fed with raw corn which was thrown over the fence. A Catholic priest, using money raised by the Mescaleros and Lipans on the Mescalero Reservation, redeemed this Lipan remnant and reunited them with their kin in New Mexico (Carroll, 1908 and Ball, 1988: 270-272).

Once Augustina arrived at the Mescalero Reservation in 1903, she was befriended by *Nàtità-ìnìí*, an elderly Lipan woman who told Augustina the story of the history and customs of the Lipans as she had been taught by her grandmother. As the elderly woman spoke, Augustina memorized her story. Thus the history of the Lipan Apaches was passed down in a traditional oral manner, from grandmother to granddaughter, from the elder *Nàtità-ìnìí* to the younger Augustina Zuazua. But Hoijer was not interested in endings. He was interested in the origins of the Lipan tribe and its linguistic connection to other Apache groups. By preserving Zuazua's tale, Harry Hoijer not only collected an example of Lipan language but also preserved a rare recounting of early Lipan tribal history and a wealth of cultural detail (Hoijer, 1939a, 1939b).

The Lipan Apaches were once one of the largest Indian tribes of Texas and northern Mexico with a population estimated in 1778 to be at least 4,000 to 6,000 men, women and children (Juntas de Guerra, 1778: 53-54). They were equal in ferocity and exceeded in numbers only by the Comanches, their mortal enemies. The Lipan Apaches did not blaze across the grasslands, as did the Comanches. Instead, the Lipans possessed the intimate corners of the landscape. The Lipan Apaches were not eagles of the southern Plains. Rather, they were deadly rattlesnakes coiled in rocky crevices, bursting from concealment with startling velocity to rob and plunder unwary travelers and ambush military patrols. Striking with lightning precision, Lipan raiders could silently steal penned cattle and tethered horses from inside a ranch compound within a matter of minutes and be long gone before anyone noticed the theft.

For over one hundred and fifty years, the Lipan Apaches were the scourge of the southern and western expanses of Texas and northern Mexico. They made war, raided and traded with the Spanish, Mexicans and Texans, each of whom, in turn, generally considered them to be bloodthirsty, perfidious and cruel thieves. The scale of the thefts was enormous and the manner in which they were carried out so brazen and audacious that the archives still ring with the sputtering outrage of the victims. In 1762, Fr. Pedro Ramirez of the Mission of Espiritú Santo (at present-day Goliad, Texas) scorched the parchment with his anger when he wrote a letter of appeal to the Viceroy. The mission had once owned large herds of cattle, numbering at least 4,000 head, but after repeated Lipan raids the herd now numbered only 400 animals. When Ramirez tried to intervene during one robbery, Lipan raiders threatened to cut off his head while coolly driving off 100 to 200 more cattle. As they left, the raiders also took the clothing and supplies of the mission Indians who were tending the herd (Ramirez, 1762: 181-182). One hundred years later (1867), the estimated cost of Indian thefts and depredations in just five Texas counties where Lipan raiders were active totaled $64,425. In a seven-year period, twenty-one settlers had been killed, two young boys taken captive, and at least 556 horses, 2900 head of cattle and 1500 sheep had been stolen. One county (Medina) refused to even estimate the number of cattle taken and could only give a rough estimate as to the number of stolen horses. [1]

The outrageous robberies, gratuitous cruelty (why steal the clothing of poor mission Indians?) and the justifiable anger of the victims are facts about the Lipan Apaches which have colored the historical record to this day. The Lipans are portrayed as brutal thieves, sources of terror and harassment for every borderland rancher who faced constant livestock thefts punctuated by random attacks in which women and children were carried away as captives.

Of course, the Lipan Apaches saw the situation very differently. They left no written records. Their chosen medium for passing on their justifications, legends, myths and history was through the telling of a *kónä*, or story, preferably told around a fire at night by a folksy raconteur. The Lipan language contained a "felicity and peculiar aptness of native expression" which made listening to their stories a delight (Opler, 1940: 7). The rare oral histories which have been preserved show a bold, shrewd, freedom-loving people with a dry wit and an uncanny ability to turn setbacks to their advantage.

The preservation of the tribe was paramount, as the Lipan Apaches faced a formidable Comanche enemy in the eighteenth century. The Comanches and their allies sought not only to drive the Lipans from the buffalo plains of north and central Texas, but to annihilate the Lipan tribe in a conflict which lasted almost a century and a half. In order to survive, it was vital that the Lipans achieve technological parity with their enemies. Yet, the Spanish refused to arm the Lipans at a time when French traders in Louisiana and along the Red River were funneling muskets to the Wichitas, Comanches and east Texas tribes. Alliances could be made with some east Texas tribes in order to gain French weapons, but those tribes expected something more in trade than pelts. Thus the Lipan "shadow trade economy" of stolen livestock for guns was born. The Lipans stole the clothing of mission Indians because they could use that clothing as a disguise. They needed a disguise so they could move unseen among the Hispanic population in order to gain intelligence useful in planning livestock raids. They raided in order to procure large numbers of horses and cattle to trade to east Texas tribes for guns. Once Lipan warriors were armed, they needed a steady supply of ammunition, thereby fixing the shadow trade economy in a self-perpetuating spiral.

From the Lipan point of view, their livestock thefts were necessary to fuel a secondary, or "shadow," trade economy which existed concurrently with "legal" trading relationships developed with Texas Spaniards and with other Texas Indian tribes. Just as a subway rail-line, the Lipan "legal" trading track operated in conjunction with the tribe's "shadow" track of stolen livestock, with both tracks creating the framework for the powerful "third rail," which represented the Lipan over-all strategy of tribal preservation in the face of an on-going Comanche threat. By 1750, the Lipan Apaches developed an economic pattern which they would employ for the next century, as they used their dual trade economy to skillfully exploit tensions between more powerful forces for their own preservation and benefit against what they always perceived to be the greatest tribal threat- the Comanches. In the earliest instances, the Lipans exploited the geopolitical tensions between Spain and France being played out in Texas, as well as exploiting the inherent dichotomy within Spanish frontier Indian policy between the Cross (Spanish missionaries who urged a policy of Indian conciliation) and the Sword (Spanish military leaders who urged a policy of Indian conquest). As the political situation along the Rio Grande changed through war and revolution in the nineteenth century, the Lipans always sought to exploit the turmoil, playing one side against the other and stealing from both. Their goal was to outwit and outlast their adversaries.

The Lipan trade of stolen livestock for guns exemplifies the very essence of the way in which the Lipan Apaches viewed themselves. They saw themselves as the men in the middle, caught between Comanche enemies who sought to annihilate them and the Spanish (and later, the Mexicans and Texans) who sought to conquer, enslave, convert or settle them. In other words, the Lipan Apaches sought to ensure their existence by making their adversaries (the Spanish) pay for the means necessary to ensure their survival against their enemies (the Comanches). It was revenge—an Apache cultural trait woven deep into the heart of every Lipan—taken to the ultimate level.

Culturally, the Lipans were betwixt and between, as befitted their perceived status as "men in the middle." They hunted buffalo, but their culture did not include the complex rituals of other Plains tribes. The Lipans were also a mountain people, but their mythology exhibited additional elements taken from the Texas Gulf coast. Their culture reflected the vast geography of Texas and was unique, differing from other Apachean groups in interesting ways. The very name "Lipan" indicated their middle status. It means "The Light Gray People," a people who live midway between the north (as represented by the color white in Lipan color-directional belief) and the east (represented by the color black).

A comprehensive ethno-history of the Lipan Apaches has never been written which contains a full account of the rare in-depth observations by outsiders of historical Lipan culture *in situ*. Only four such glimpses exist—observations made by a Spanish priest (Fr. Diego Ximenez, 1761-1764), a Spanish military commander (Juan de Ugalde, 1780-1788), a Swiss botanist (Jean Louis Berlandier, 1828) and an Anglo captive (Frank Buckelew, 1866). Each provides startling and unanticipated insight into Lipan rituals, beliefs and practices.

By the time the first anthropologists and ethnologists began to gather data on the Lipan Apaches in the late nineteenth century (1884-1897), the tribe had been scattered to the four winds. In 1884, ethnologist Albert Samuel Gatschet was able to compile a Lipan vocabulary from several Lipans held at Ft. Griffin (Texas) before their transfer to an Oklahoma reservation. While the Lipans living at Ft. Griffin retained knowledge of the language, the Mexican Lipans were, after 1850, the primary repository of traditional culture. Since many members of that group ended up on the Mescalero Reservation in New Mexico, it was to that place that the anthropologists went, beginning with James Mooney in 1897, in order to seek the Lipan Apaches. However, it was not until 1934, when Morris Opler began a series of interviews with the Lipans in New Mexico, that a picture of the scope and complexity of Lipan history and culture began to emerge. Morris Opler's work was followed by that of Harry Hoijer and Andrée F. Sjoberg, but the cultural information collected was never analyzed in comparison to earlier Spanish or Anglo cultural observations. This book seeks to complete such a comparative analysis.

An ethno-history of the Lipan Apaches is long overdue because the stereotypical image of the Lipan as a "cruel thief," a notion which runs deeply and consistently through two centuries of non-tribal sources, cries out to be addressed. It is easy to see why they were stereotyped, but such a one-sided view fails to address the issues which help to explain why the Lipans acted as they did. While contemporaries resorted to the stereotypical image when viewing the tribe collectively, they were often surprised to find the Lipans to be "sagacious, shrewd and intelligent" when dealing with them individually (Irion, 1838: 44).

My interest in the Lipan Apaches began as I was told the story of *Chevato* (1852-1931), a Lipan shaman who was among a group of Lipan and Mescalero Apache raiders who kidnapped a young German boy named Herman Lehmann from his family's Texas homestead in 1870. The storyteller was *Chevato's* grandson, William Chebahtah. Together, we co-authored a book that preserved the remarkable oral history *Chevato* left to his children. Yet *Chevato's* tale recorded only the end of one chapter of Lipan history in northern Mexico. Like Augustina Zuazua, I was anxious to learn the beginning. As Tribal Historian of the Lipan Apache Tribe of Texas, I am privileged to see the larger context as the past and the present merge seamlessly into an on-going history of an indomitable people.

One reason a comprehensive ethno-history of the Lipan Apaches has never been written is because the majority of eighteenth century archival sources are in Spanish. All translations in this book are my own and I take full responsibility for their accuracy. However, I would also like to gratefully acknowledge the assistance of David McDonald, translator of the Béxar Archives in San Antonio. Grateful acknowledgment is also given to David Gohre, Tribal Linguist of the Lipan Apache Tribe of Texas, for his assistance in matters relating to the Lipan language and the problems presented by the Gatschet Lipan vocabulary.

I hold no pretensions to the credentials of an anthropologist, linguist or archeologist. I have been trained as an historian. However, I see the job of an historian as being similar to the work of scholars in these disciplines because we all work with bones. In the case of historians, the bones used are archival documents and, to a lesser extent, oral histories. The historian seeks to recreate, to rebuild the skeleton of the person, place or group by fitting together bone with bone, document with document, and then fitting the recreated form into the larger picture. Thus, in this book, when observations are made on topics within the general purview of other disciplines, such as anthropology or linguistics, they are made from a historian's perspective, seeking to frame the discussion within the scope of the larger historical perspective. However, there is still plenty of meat on the Lipan bone for profitable study by other disciplines, and I would particularly encourage archeo-astronomers to seek further meaning in Lipan eclipse rituals.

In general, the Lipan Apaches have always been seen by outsiders as the fleas on the dog—the dog being analogous to the general record of events which makes up the history of Texas and northern Mexico, and the fleas being a metaphor for the irritations and frustrations felt by those persons compiling the historical record. The Lipan Apaches can be found burrowed deep into the skin of the history of these borderlands. The life blood of one sustained the other, while the host scratched frantically to expel or exterminate the irritation. Heretofore, scholars (and the historical record) have generally viewed the Lipan Apaches from the perspective of the dog. We might know the dog, but the time is long overdue for a thorough examination of the fleas.

Nancy McGown Minor
Bergheim, Texas
August 2008

Part I

Lipan Apache Origins and Early History

Chapter 1

Translation and Meaning of the Tribal Name "Lipan"

The urge to name an unknown or newly-encountered object, animal or human group by its form, function or observable characteristics is a basic human impulse. And, in most cases, once an object, animal or group is given a name, an identifiable body of knowledge is built around that name over time so that, if one speaks the name "elephant," a picture of that animal, its physical characteristics and perhaps even its habitat comes to mind. So it is with many of the Apache tribes of the American Southwest. If the name "Chiricahua" is spoken, a picture of that tribe's nineteenth century leader Geronimo comes to mind, as well as the body of knowledge about that tribe contained in nineteenth century records. If the names "Mimbres" or "Navajo" are spoken, one can point to their weaving or pottery as an expression of their tribal identity. Traces of the Tonto (or Coyotero) Apaches and Gila Apaches can be found in their early settlements near Spanish presidios in Arizona and New Mexico. If the name "Mescalero" is spoken, one can point to their present-day location on a map of their reservation, as well as Spanish documents dating from 1725 which identify that tribe by the name "Mescalero."

None of this holds true for the Lipan Apaches. To speak the name "Lipan" brings forth no vision of the people. They left no buildings or pottery to be excavated. The baskets woven by Lipan hands have not survived and the beadwork on their clothing has turned to dust. In truth, Texas archeologists have had more success in identifying Archaic sites (3,000 years BC), than success in identifying sites occupied by the Lipan Apaches from 1600-1800 AD. There is no Lipan Reservation in Texas, nor is the reservation they share with the Mescaleros located within territories once claimed by the Lipans. The Lipan Apaches enter the historical record as indistinct shadows, poorly defined. Were they among the Apaches seen by Coronado on the southern Great Plains in 1541? Were they among the Apache groups first encountered in 1683 by Spanish explorers in Texas? To confuse matters even further, the first specific Texas reference to Lipan Apaches (1732) calls them *Ypandis*, not Lipans.

Early Spanish explorers generally recorded only the most cursory information regarding the Indian tribes they encountered, but from 1541 on, the Apache groups living on the southern Great Plains were tagged with such a bewildering series of names that it is virtually impossible to untie the knot and determine which Spanish observations relate to the early Lipan Apaches. Conversely, early Spanish expeditions to Texas referred to any and all Apache groups they encountered simply as "Apaches," without tribal distinctions. Thus, the body of knowledge surrounding the Lipans of the sixteenth and seventeenth centuries has been stunted by too much conflicting information about the Plains Apaches and too little information about the Texas Apaches.

Many scholars have adopted a "dump and jump" approach when dealing with Plains Apache-Lipan issue and a "lump and jump" approach when dealing with Texas Apache-Lipan issue. Many of the early Plains Apache groups are "dumped" into the Lipan tribe, as scholars have assumed such groups as the Ochos, Rio Colorados, or various groups of Cuartelejo Apaches were early versions of the later Lipans. However, there is no solid evidence to link any of these early Plains Apache groups to the later Lipan Apaches of Texas. Conversely, when dealing with early Texas Apaches, scholars have followed the Spanish example and lump all Texas Apache tribes into one generic "Apache" group. Then having muddied the waters, scholars "jump" into the historical record and take up the Lipan tribe in its fully-formed eighteenth century incarnation. None of these approaches have led to a greater understanding of the Lipan Apaches. Rather than rely on a "dump/lump and jump" approach to an examination of the early Lipans, a more profitable path is to look to the Lipan people and see what claims they made about their early tribal history.

Early Spanish records do not reveal any evidence which would provide clarity regarding the tribal name, so scholars have assumed that the name "Lipan" represented either the name of a chief or the name given to the tribe by their enemies (Hodge, 1912: 768). Although their language and culture were studied by some of the most eminent anthropologists and linguists of the twentieth century, only one man ever asked for a translation or definition of the tribal name. James Mooney was told that the tribal name "Lipan" was "a Spanish corruption of a name applied by some other Indian tribe" (Mooney, 1897a). Unfortunately, Mooney never probed beyond this explanation, nor did he probe the origin of the word he recorded as being the name by which the Lipan tribe called themselves—*Ná-izhán*—translated by Mooney as "Ours" or "Our kind of people" (Mooney, 1897a). [1] If Mooney had probed a bit deeper, he would have found that the name *Ná-izhán* probably derived from the *Natahe ("Mescal People")* or *Natagés (Nah-tah-hays)*, a Mescalero-affiliated Apache group who lived along the Pecos River (Dunn, 1911: 265-276). Rather than look at the tribal name "Lipan" as a name bestowed by others, such as the Spanish or enemies, a more fruitful approach is to look for a definition within the language of the Lipan people. Once this is done, solid evidence can be found which not only translates the tribal name, but goes to the very essence of the way in which the Lipan Apaches viewed themselves, their place in the world, and the very planet itself.

The Light Gray People

In order to fully understand the translation of the tribal name "Lipan," as well as the symbolic extrapolations that spin off from that translation, one must take a short trip through Lipan cosmology and look at the world through their eyes. I use the word cosmology not to describe a branch of astronomy, but in a more general sense to describe the Lipan view of the way in which their universe, consisting not only of the physical world around them but of the entire planet as well, was structured.

For the Lipan Apaches, all life existed within a circle. Just as the inside of a Lipan tepee was circular, with the frame anchored in place by four primary poles, so all tribal life existed within the circle of the camp. Myths were passed from generation to generation, religious rituals were conducted and war or raiding victories were celebrated as the people stood or sat in a circle. The entire tribe made seasonal migrations which corresponded to a rough circle as they moved from camp to camp hunting buffalo, or gathering and processing *agave*, wild fruits or cactus tunas. Indeed, the existence of the very earth on which they trod was envisioned as a circle in space, anchored at the four points of the compass. Out of this original vision grew a complex cosmology, as certain compass points, numbers or colors began to be viewed as more sacred than others. For the Lipan Apaches, the number four was sacred and items grouped in a set of four (such as the four points of a compass) were imbued with that sacredness (Opler, 1940: 31 note).

The Lipan view of the world was not unique, but was a view shared by all Apachean groups. However, what differentiated the Lipans from other Apache tribes was the particular color scheme they assigned to the four points of the compass, as well as the use of their cosmology to provide a link between tribal myths and the tribal name. The Lipans ordinarily associated the following colors with the four points of the compass: North/white, East/black, South/blue and West/yellow.

Figure 1.0   Lipan Apache World View (in English and Lipan)

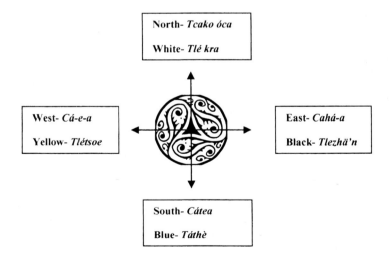

(Sources: Opler, 1940: 18; Gatschet, 1884: Schedules 7 and 14)

The Lipan emergence myth explained the tribe's origins, stating that the Lipans emerged upon the earth in the north and circled the globe in a clockwise fashion. While some Apache tribes settled in the west and others settled in the north, the Lipans continued their journey and settled in the east (Opler, 1940: 13-16). When the Lipans combined their emergence myth with their cosmology and added in the color-directional symbolism attached to their view of their universe, they produced a rich tapestry full of symbolic meaning. In their emergence myth, the Lipans were saying that in the ancient past they moved from the north, represented by the color white, toward the east, represented by the color black. If this migration is seen in terms of a color palette, as the Lipans moved to the east, they were adding the color black to the color white, resulting in the color gray.

The Lipan word for a light gray hue is *lépai (probably written orthographically as lépa-i and pronounced leh-pah-ee or even hleh-pah-ee)* (Gatschet, 1884). The word can be abbreviated in the form of *pai, páyi,* or seen in the prefix *pa-* (Gatschet, 1884). Mooney recorded the Lipan word for a light gray hue as *klipă,* based on the pronunciation he heard (Mooney, 1897b). The Lipan word designating the concept of the Tribe, or The People, is *ndé* or *indeh* (Mooney, 1897b). When the two words are combined, the result is *lépai-ndé* or *klipă-ndé.* The earliest Lipan vocabularies (Gatschet and Mooney) seem to indicate that the first syllable of the word *lépai* was to be pronounced in a guttural manner, possibly as *hleh-* or *klih-*. [2] When the second and third syllables *(pah-ee-indeh)* are elided together, they form *pandeh.* The result is *hleh-pandeh* or *klih-pandeh.* When pronounced as a single word, it becomes *hlehpan, klihpan* or *Lipan*— "The Light Gray People." Embodied within the tribal name was the color-directional code which directly linked the Lipan emergence myth, their ancient migration out of Canada and their eventual settlement in Texas.

The Lipan choice of a color to designate their tribal identity is interesting, providing much insight into the Lipan people and their view of themselves. When Gatschet recorded the first Lipan vocabulary in 1884, he stressed, through heavy underlining, that the Lipan word for gray referred only to a light hue and not to a dark or charcoal gray. This distinction receives added importance when viewed through the prism of Lipan color-directional belief. The east was sacred because it was the direction of the rising sun. Killer-of-Enemies, the primary spirit deity, lived in the sun. Yet, the Lipans never claimed that their journey after emergence took them as far eastward as it was possible for them to go in a geographic sense. In other words, the Lipans did not claim possession of the east, represented by the color black. They merely claimed that they journeyed toward the east and reached an eastward point. Thus, Lipan tribal identity embodied a continuous process of journeying, always moving from the white of the north toward the black of the sacred east. The Lipans would always remain in the gray area, not only because they had no fixed abode and preferred to follow ancient seasonal migratory paths, but because they were always in a process of journeying toward a better knowledge of the sacred. Of all the Apache tribes, the

Lipans believed that they alone were tinged with an extraordinary degree of sacredness, since their tribal name indicated that some of the sacred black power of the east resided among them. The sacred power made itself available to tribal members so that they could use that power to harness the world around them. And, of course, the Lipans believed that their sacred powers, the possession of which was revealed in the tribal name, always triumphed over the powers of their enemies, particularly the Comanches.

As the Lipans undertook their continuous, circular journeys of seasonal migration, they walked or rode across the limestone, caliche and alkali rising from the Balcones Escarpment above San Antonio and running west across the Edwards Plateau to New Mexico. As the tribe moved, their feet stirred up particles of white dust, coating the clothing and skin of the people and causing them to look as if they were covered in a fine layer of gray ashes. In addition to the dusty covering they received as they traveled, the Lipans "smeared themselves with and put white dirt in their hair" (Ximenez, 1761: 27). The coating of body and hair with a white paste acted as a sunscreen, but the act also had ritual significance since it represented a physical embodiment of the tribal name. Thus, the name Lipan, or "The Light Gray People," had a physical and ritual component, as well as a mythic, symbolic meaning.

When the Comanches first came into contact with the Lipan Apaches, they must have seen Lipan warriors whose skin and hair appeared whitish-gray in color due to a coating of alkali paste. [3] The Comanches incorporated this distinctive Lipan physical characteristic with a distain for their new enemies, christening the Lipans with the name *Esikwita ("gray buttocks")*, which not only described the color of the paste covering Lipan hair and skin, but described the posterior view the Comanches hoped to have in battle as the Lipans ran away in fear (Comanche Language Committee, 2003). The prefix *Esi- (the color gray)* in the Comanche term of derision was also an acknowledgment of the Lipan tribal name.

The Lipan Apaches first appear in Texas records in 1732, when Governor Bustillo y Zevallos led a military expedition against the *Ypandi (pronounced Yeh-pandee)* and three other tribes who were massing north of San Antonio in order to launch attacks on the settlement (Bustillo, 1733). This peculiar spelling was a Spanish attempt at a phonetic approximation of the Lipan syllables, but there was no exact Spanish equivalent to the *kli-* or *hleh-* sound, so the Spanish used an archaic "Y" form which, when pronounced, sounded like *Yeh*. In 1743, Fr. Benito de Santa Ana spelled the tribal name *Ypande*, a change which probably reflected an attempt to more accurately capture the elided second syllable (*pai-indeh* or *pan-deh*) (Santa Ana, 1743b: 90). Fr. Diego Ximenez was one of the first to spell the tribal name in its modern form as *Lipanes* (Ximenez, 1761a: 26-27). However, Fr. Ximenez merely modernized the older Spanish spelling rather than reaching back to the original Lipan words. In writing the tribal name using the letter "L," Ximenez was indicating the sound produced in modern Spanish by the *ll-* prefix (which is pronounced as *"yeh,"* equivalent to the older

"Y" form). Thus, Ximenez was indicating that the tribal name was to be pronounced as *Yeh-pan-nes*. This distinction was soon lost, however, and the pronunciation of the tribal name quickly evolved into *Lee-pahn-nes*. When the name was translated from Spanish into English, it became *Lipan (Lee-pahn)*.

Lines of Evidence and Methodology

The evidentiary problems inherent in a study of early Lipan Apache history center upon the scholarly value assigned to the few sixteenth and seventeenth century historical documents which mention Plains and Texas Apaches. Scholars following a "dump and jump" approach place a loose interpretive value on such documents, connecting some of these groups with the early Lipans on the basis of cultural similarities and geographic location (Tunnell and Newcomb, 1969: 141-151). This author strongly discourages such an approach, since the 1500's and early 1600's were times when all Apache tribes were in the process of developing tribal identities and many were still moving about in a migratory pattern as they sought "homeland" territories. When viewing early Lipan history from the perspective of historical documents alone, this author believes a strict interpretation must be used. The Mendoza expedition to Texas in 1683 found "Apaches" between the Colorado and Pecos Rivers, but such documents alone cannot lead to a conclusion that the Apaches were Lipans. They could just as easily have been Mescaleros or *Natagés*.

Oral history represents a second evidentiary category which can be used to offer perspective on early Lipan Apache history, but, as seen in the James Mooney mistake cited earlier, the use of oral history without verifying the pedigree of the transmitter presents dangerous pitfalls. When oral history claims are made in the absence of supporting historical documents, such statements must be considered simply as unverified claims. However, the Zuazua tribal history represents a weightier category of oral history than stories passed down within one family. The Zuazua history can be classified within the extensive Lipan oral literary tradition recorded by Morris Opler and, as such, represents a body of beliefs about the culture and history of the Lipan tribe. The claims made in the Zuazua history regarding early Lipan history in Texas prior to 1732 (the date of the first historical supporting document) are not offered by this author as conclusive evidence. Rather, they are presented as a Native perspective, or the sequence of events by which the Lipan people described their early experiences in Texas.

Chapter 2

The Origin of the Lipan Apaches

The old Lipan storyteller looked across the fire at the circle of young faces, each of whom was watching him eagerly and intently. It was the duty of the tribal elders to pass on to the children the myths and legends of the tribe, and tonight the old storyteller had chosen to tell the story of the origin of the Lipan Apaches. As with all myth, the story of the emergence of the Lipans onto the earth's surface would be the telling of their beliefs in the form of a tale, with bits of historical detail interspersed within the story to ground it in reality. The old man drew a deep breath, closed his eyes, and began his tale, his *kónä*:

> Down in the lower world, in the beginning, there was no light; there was only darkness. Down there, at the bottom, were some people. They knew of no other places; they lived there.
> They held a council down there. They discussed whether there was another world. They decided to send someone above to find out. They looked at each other and asked who should be sent out.
> One said, 'How about Wind?
> They asked him. Wind agreed to go.
> Wind went upward in the form of a whirlwind. Wind came to this earth and found nothing but water covering the earth. He blew the breath of life and rolled back the water like a curtain. After he had done this, land appeared and the water was all to one side. The ground was very level. There were no mountains on the earth. The earth was just like ashes or like the places where there is white alkali on the earth's surface now.
> Then the people in the lower world sent out Crow to look over the dry land. But Crow saw the dead fish that had been left once the water rolled away. He stayed to pick the eyes out of the fish and never returned to the lower world as he had promised to do.
> The people wondered what had happened to Crow. They wanted news, so they sent Beaver out. The water was getting low now, so instead of going back to his people, Beaver busied himself building dams.
> The people wondered what had happened to Beaver. They wanted news, so they sent Badger out. He was faithful to his fellows in the lower world. He came up and looked around and saw that all was dry up there. He went back and told the others and they were happy, for he was the only one who did faithful work.
> Then the people of the lower world sent out four men to look over the world above. These first four who came up on earth to prepare it were called by the word that means Indians. These four chose one from who were to be made the things of the earth as we know it now. They selected Mirage and put up Mirage in the form of a ball. They walked away from Mirage and looked and it looked very pretty. That ball of mirage became a part of this earth.
> Now they fixed the world. They made hills and mountains. They made a little lightning. They made little arroyos, and water came running to them. That

is the way the earth and the mountains, the hills and the water were made. At first it was all level, but of Mirage they made all the things of the earth.

Now all was ready on the earth. Springs and channels were made. All was prepared for the people of the lower world and they prepared to ascend. They came up to the upper world and they are here now as animals, birds, trees and bushes. The real humans were not here yet. But the animals, birds, trees and bushes were people at that time and could talk as humans do. They had one language and all understood each other. These were the first people. Even the rocks, plants and grasses that are on this earth now were among these people and each represented a different tribe.

Then the real people emerged from the lower world. The place where they came up was to the north and to the west of where we are now. After they came up, they moved around the edge of the earth. The sun and the moon took the lead; they were with the people. The sun is the man and we call him Killer-of-Enemies. The moon is the woman, and we call her Changing Woman. Killer-of-Enemies taught the Lipan how to live on this earth.

The real humans moved around the earth. The first to stop were the western people, the Chiricahua perhaps. As they went along clockwise, different peoples dropped off. As they stopped, they became different tribes and had different languages. After the western people dropped off, the next to stop were the northern tribes. All the northern tribes used the dog for a horse.

The very last people to stop their journey were the Lipan. When they reached the east, the Lipan stopped their journey and found a home. Now, all the people were fixed on the earth. [1]

The Lipan emergence myth told by the old storyteller was the same story that the elderly *Nàada-ìnìí* must have used as a preface to the Lipan history she passed on to Augustina Zuazua, for Augustina stated, "That one [i.e. *Nàada-ìnìí*]/ how the Lipan on the earth/ that when the earth was made/ that one/ then she would tell it to you" (Hoijer, 1939a: S108). The same emergence story also contained nuggets of data later confirmed by ethnologists, anthropologists and linguists, so that, if the story is stripped of its mythic flourishes and reduced to its bare bones, the long migration of the ancient people who would one day be known as the Lipan Apaches can be seen.

The Lipans always insisted that the site of their "emergence" was located to the north and west of their eventual destination of Texas and, in truth, their journey did begin in the great McKenzie Basin of Canada, cradle of so many of the Amerindian tribes who would later inhabit the Great Plains and the American Southwest. The ancient Lipans were one of six Athapascan-speaking, Apachean groups who began a slow migration south out of Canada at some point after 1300 (Hoxie, 1996: 25).

In Lipan mythology, this ancient parental Apachean group was called "The Spotted Wood People." After the creation of the physical world, the Lipans believed that beings emerged from below onto the earth's surface in a specific order, with the natural world of animals, plants and trees being the first to emerge. The second emerging group was "The Spotted Wood People" who had more human attributes than the animals, but who were not yet fully human. The Lipans described the sequence in this fashion: "The animals used to talk. After them came the Spotted Wood People, then the real people. The Spotted Wood People didn't have much sense. . . . They were the ancient people." (Opler, 1940: 205-212) In Lipan mythology, the Spotted Wood People were foolish because they had not yet learned the basic structure of Lipan tribal identity, such as the use of the horse, bison and deer hunting, recognizing enemies such as the Comanches, and harnessing shamanistic power. This myth accurately reflected the fact that the separation of the Athapascan groups into differing tribes and the development of a tribal identity did not occur until after the parental Apachean group arrived in the American Great Plains. The Jicarillas, Mescaleros and Chiricahuas all had comparable sets of stories about an ancient group of foolish people who were the progenitors of the later Apache tribes (Opler, 1940: 205).

Linguistic evidence has shown that these Athapascan-speakers migrated out of Canada in two large groups. The peoples who would later become the Chiricahua/Western Apaches, Navajos and Mescaleros migrated together as one "western" group, while a second "eastern" group was composed of the peoples who would later become the Jicarilla Apaches, Kiowa Apaches and Lipan Apaches (Hoijer, 1938: 75-86 and Opler, 1975a: 182-192). This general southward movement of Apachean peoples in several large groups was reflected in the Lipan emergence myth, which described this early migration as peoples moving clockwise around the edge of the earth. A helpful visual image is to picture these migrations in the form of a clock. The Apaches emerged in the north (i.e. 12 o'clock noon) and traveled around the edge of the clock until they reached 9:00 p.m. At that point, the western Athapascan-speakers ended their migration, but the Jicarillas, Kiowa Apaches and Lipans continued on. The Jicarillas and Kiowa Apaches ended their migration at 12 o'clock midnight while the Lipan Apaches continued on, moving toward the east and ending their journey at 3:00 a.m.

By 1500, the six Athapascan-speaking groups had completed their long migration out of Canada (Hoxie, 1996: 25). They reached the southern Great Plains and upper Southwest, started the process of separation into smaller groups and began to develop differing group identities and cultural characteristics which would eventually give rise to six Apache tribes. The peoples who would eventually be called the Lipan Apaches were still joined with the eastern group of Athapascan-speakers and would have been one of the many groups designated by the general term "Plains Apaches," although they cannot be definitively linked to any specific group encountered by Coronado (1541) and subsequent Spanish explorers of the southern Plains.

The two centuries after the arrival of the proto-Lipan parental group in the upper Southwest (ca. 1500) were crucial periods of development for all the Apachean groups, as each group searched for territory to claim as a homeland. The Chiricahuas and Western Apaches adapted to the mountainous regions they inhabited west of the Rio Grande as it flowed through New Mexico; the Navajos also moved westward and settled northwest of Santa Fe, adapting much from the older Pueblo cultures that they found there. The Jicarilla Apaches moved into a region "bordered by the Arkansas River in southeast Colorado, the northeastern plains drained by the tributaries of the Canadian River" and the Chama River of northwestern New Mexico (Tiller, 1992: 4). The Mescalero Apaches ranged along the mountains and plains of eastern and southern New Mexico west of the Pecos River. Both the Jicarillas and Mescaleros developed cultures that reflected mountain and plains adaptations combined with Pueblo influences. The Kiowa Apaches, who remained in the southern Plains, developed a Plains Indian culture. Each culture reflected the group's adaptation to the terrain in which they inhabited.

The Lipan Apaches, who moved into the vast land later to be known as Texas, were no exception to the rule of cultural adaptation to landscape and environment. As they developed a tribal identity amidst the grassy plains, vast oak forests and arid wastelands of Texas, their adaptations caused their culture to differ in some subtle, but interesting ways from the rest of their Apache kin. They retained many aspects of their earlier adaptation to the Plains, while preferring to hug the mountains and camp near the headwaters of rivers, which were adaptations typical of a mountain people. One primary area of interest is the Lipan adaptation to the vast Texas Gulf coastal plains. Hints of a Lipan coastal adaptation peek out from the myths collected by Opler, which contain stories of alligators and *javelinas (wild boars)*. In one legend, a hurricane and associated tidal surge is described, as well as a description of the Texas coastline and the sea (Opler, 1940: 6). Unlike any of their Apache kin, the Lipans of Texas ate fish and constructed cow-hide boats which they used to cross the Rio Grande in flood (Opler, 1940: 283-284 and Hoijer, 1939a: S263-270).

In searching for traces of ancient relationships between the Lipan Apaches and the five other Athapascan branches growing out of the Apache tree, anthropologist Morris Opler and linguist Harry Hoijer found a number of similarities in kinship systems, language and mythology between the Lipans and the Jicarilla Apaches (Opler, 1940: 2-5 and Hoijer, 1956: 310-324). These similarities stood in marked contrast to the language, mythologies and certain kinship aspects of the western group of Athapascans, such as the Mescaleros and the Chiricahuas. These findings confirmed the Lipan sequence of migration in their emergence myth, with the western group breaking away first, while the Lipans and other eastern Athapascan-speakers continued on. Opler concluded that there was a "high probability that the Lipan are an off-shoot of a Lipan-Jicarilla group, [whose] line of migration took them east to the plains and south to the gulf, [and who] . . . separated before the ancient parental group had been much influenced by Pueblo agriculture and ritual" (Opler, 1940: 5-6). Opler estimated that "the ancestors of the Lipan and Jicarilla lived together until the beginning of the 17th century" (Opler, 1940: 6).

Opler's conclusions about Lipan culture were rather surprising, since the Lipans themselves never claimed kinship with the Jicarillas. The only contact between the two tribes after 1600 was sporadic, if contact occurred at all, and the Lipans and Jicarillas were not reunited until 1883, when the Jicarillas joined the Mescalero and Lipan Apaches on the Mescalero Reservation in New Mexico (Tiller, 1992: 90-94). However, the historical record reveals an extensive and prolonged relationship between the Lipans and the Mescalero Apaches, cemented by raiding and trading activities and capped by a political alliance after 1770. Yet, an examination of the myths, language and culture of the Lipans and the Mescalero Apaches reveals striking differences in three primary areas which relate to the origins of both tribes. The Lipans had a myth of emergence, while the Mescaleros did not; Lipan social strictures did not contain a mother-in-law avoidance, while such a stricture was found among the Mescaleros (Opler, 1940: 4, 7). In addition, "the Lipan names for important concepts or supernaturals of the myths show marked departures from Mescalero usage" (Opler, 1940: 3). These facts, in particular, led Opler to conclude that the close connection of the Lipans with the Mescaleros occurred within the historical period, while the Lipans shared a much older connection with the Jicarillas (Opler, 1940: 2-3).

A search for ancient connections between the Lipans and the Kiowa Apaches does not produce clear results. These connections have long been debated by modern scholars, with some only linking the two tribes generally within the southern Athapascan family tree, while others speculate that "the Kiowa Apache split off early from an eastern Apachean prototype culture that included the Jicarilla and Lipan and migrated northward into the Plains" (Brant, 1949: 61). The dating and circumstances of the separation of the Lipans and Kiowa Apaches are not revealed in Lipan oral tradition. [2]

The circumstances surrounding the Lipan separation from the eastern Athapascan-speaking parental group and the date of the tribe's entrance into Texas are events which are only hinted at in the historical record and Native oral tradition. The Jicarilla tribe does not have an oral tradition describing a separation from the Lipans. The Zuazua history begins with events occurring after the Lipans entered Texas. Archeologist Thomas Hester places the Lipan entry only within a general time frame "from the 1600's to the 1700's" (Hester, 1991: 83). However, a member of an 1828 Mexican scientific expedition to Texas, Jean Louis Berlandier, did record information relating to the early origins of the Lipan tribe and provided the only evidence possibly relating to a Lipan-Jicarilla separation.

> Since the most ancient times, the Lipans have lived in central North America. According to a Bidais tradition, they came to the Texas borderlands before either the Tehuacanos or the Comanche, whom we know were there at the beginning of the 18th century. It is said that an internal feud which split the nation was the cause of their migration. Those we know lived on the banks of the Rio del Norte [Arkansas or Red Rivers] at first. But finding they could not live with the other peoples who inhabited Texas at that time, they continued southward until they found the deserts which separate Bexar [San Antonio] from the so-called villages of del Norte. [3]

Berlandier credited a Bidais tradition which recorded an internal feud (between the Lipans and the Jicarillas?) which resulted in a division of the two groups and the migration of the Lipans into Texas. A history of the Lipan Apaches written by Domingo Cabello, Spanish Governor of Texas (1776-1787), fixed the location and approximate dating of the Lipan entry into Texas. After a discussion of the 1690 de Leon expedition to establish an east Texas mission for the Tejas Indians and the establishment of an east Texas presidio in 1720, Cabello stated,

> At the time which all I have heretofore related to you [occurred], they found the Indians of the Nations *Lipana*, and Apaches [i.e. *Natagés*], situated at 300 leagues [801 miles] from them above [i.e. north of San Antonio], spread out on the plains of the banks of the River of Iron Pieces which meandered between the north northwest and the northwest (Cabello, 1784: 102-104).

The River of Iron Pieces was associated, in later Spanish documents, with the Pease or Wichita Rivers of north Texas (John, 1981: 256). Both the Pease and the Wichita flow into the Red River, modern-day boundary between Texas and Oklahoma.

Thus, combining Opler's estimate of a Lipan-Jicarilla separation date (after 1600), Berlandier's information regarding an internal feud being the cause of the Lipan entry into Texas and Cabello's chronology and location, it seems probable that the Lipan separation from the Jicarillas and the Lipan migration into north Texas occurred at some point in the mid-seventeenth century, possibly around 1650.

Chapter 3

The Zuazua History

The Lipan history memorized by Augustina Zuazua recorded information disclosed by eighty-year old *Nààdà-ìníí*, who had been told the history of the Lipan Apaches by her grandmother. Zuazua was careful to say *Nààdà-ìníí* "did not lie" (Hoijer, 1939a: S100) and in order to stress the veracity of her memorization, Zuazua stated that if *Nààdà-ìníí* were alive, "she would tell it to you" in the same way that Zuazua had memorized the story (Hoijer, 1939a: S108). The tale contained actual events, some of which may have been personally experienced by *Nààdà-ìníí's* grandmother after 1800. However, the scope of the history stretched much further back in time, with the bulk of the information pertaining to seventeenth and eighteenth century migrations and Lipan culture. The story began at a point in time after the Lipans had migrated into Texas (ca. 1650) and ended in the nineteenth century after the Lipans began to have contact with Anglo settlers. Augustina Zuazua's history offers details which challenge traditional scholarly assumptions, presenting a unique view of seventeenth and eighteenth century Lipan life in Texas and Mexico. It also describes important tribal migrations which shed light on an early period of Lipan history for which no Spanish commentary exists.

The story of the Lipan Apaches relayed by *Nààdà-ìníí* is told in the classical style of oral history. That is, the story is told in circular fashion and was memorized as blocks of information; each block is keyed to some identifying topic or theme. Locating information, or information that anchors the story in time and space, is given, followed by a discourse on a particular topic or theme such as Lipan migrations or cultural aspects. Within each discourse, events are recounted in a rough chronological fashion, and cultural aspects are taken up in a thematic fashion. However, instead of carrying on the chronology or expounding further on the theme, the story circles back and information is relayed about the storyteller, which acts as the preface for another block of information, or topical discourse. The effect of this circling back within the story is much like verses of a song, with each verse followed by the same or a similar refrain. This style is more suited to a listening audience, where the locators serve as memory prompts for the storyteller, helping the teller to remember the sequence of memorized blocks of data. Thus, it can be somewhat confusing when translated into the written word. In addition, the Lipans' strong sense of local identity resulted in their use of terrain-oriented camp names that are generally impossible to tie to any known location. Fortunately, Hoijer was able to obtain the modern place name for the primary locator used in the story. All migrational information is tied to one geographic reference point, or primary locator, called "Many Houses," which was identified by Zuazua as the area around San Antonio, Texas. Other sites can be identified through general clues given by Zuazua and through educated guesswork.

Table 3.0   **General Outline of the Zuazua History**

Discourse 1- Pre-horse migration out of San Antonio, Texas area
             An old woman *(Nàdà-inii)* began her story
Discourse 2- Pre-horse migration out of San Antonio area
             Crossing the Rio Grande & acquisition of the horse
             An old woman told the story, Zuazua wrote down the story
Discourse 3- Migrations & camps in Mexico and Texas
             Descriptions of material & economic culture
             Zuazua wrote down story; veracity of the story
             How *Nàdà-inii* acquired the story
Discourse 4- Pre-horse migrations out of San Antonio and post-horse
             migrations in Mexico (recap of Discourses #1 & #2)
             Descriptions of social, material & economic culture
             Veracity of Zuazua's memorization of *Nàdà-inii 's* story
Discourse 5- Crossing the Rio Grande in search of fruit
             Nàdà-inii told of ancient ways
             Migrations after Anglo settlement of Texas
             Decision by tribal elders to return to San Antonio area

The Zuazua history begins with the assertion of a Lipan tribal claim to a homeland called "Many Houses" in the area surrounding the present-day city of San Antonio, Texas (Hoijer, 1939a: note S1). This claim is reiterated throughout the history. Because Zuazua stated that *Nàdà-inii* prefaced her history with a recounting of the Lipan emergence myth (Hoijer, 1939a: S108), both the history and the homeland claim must be viewed as extensions of that myth. The Zuazua history is a tale recounting what happened after the Lipans "stopped their journey and found a home" and the homeland claim is the process by which the Lipans "fixed" themselves upon the earth (Opler, 1940: 16). The way in which the Lipans asserted their claim to a territorial homeland was similar to the method used by the Jicarillas, who also rooted their claim to lands in northeastern New Mexico in their mythology (Tiller, 1992: 2-3).

> Many Houses/ at that named/ right there [was] their country.
> The Lipan then/ long ago/ an old woman/ she told about them.
> Then [her story] had begun/ a long time/ there [was] their country
>   / the Lipan....
> Then/ Many Houses/ the Lipan/ before it/ very long ago/ no one there
>   / their country/ anyhow/ there they went.
> Being on foot/ horses there were none.
> And then right there/ a long time/ [was] their country.
> Being many/ years passed with them (Hoijer, 1939a: S4-6, S17-20).

The Lipan Apaches arrived in Texas at an early but unspecified date ("very long ago") and claimed their homeland of "Many Houses." Their socio-political organization was that of a single tribal unit ("being many" indicates the entire tribe). They journeyed to their new homeland on foot, as they did not yet possess the horse, and they lived in their new homeland for "a long time" or "years." By stating that the tribe moved into unoccupied territory ("no one there"), the Lipans were asserting that they claimed the land around San Antonio long be-fore the Spanish claimed the site in 1718 (Chipman, 1992: 117). The choice of the San Antonio area made perfect sense, in the Lipan view, because it offered easy access to the vast buffalo plains running the length of Texas, but it hugged the hilly central region, offering protection.

The Lipan tribal homeland claim presents three sets of problems. If the Lipans occupied the San Antonio area before the Spanish, why did they call their homeland "Many Houses," assuming "houses" referred to fixed dwellings rather than tepees? [1] Did the Lipans name their homeland only after sustained contact with the Spanish at San Antonio and then apply the name retroactively to an earlier period? Or was "Many Houses" symbolic of the many tents repre-senting the tribe as a whole? Secondly, the San Antonio area was not unoccu-pied prior to the arrival of the Lipans or Spanish, but was territory inhabited by the Payayas, a Coahuiltecan group of hunter-gatherers (Hester, 1992: 80-83). Finally, there is the problem of dates, historical evidence and the generic Texas Apache vs. Lipan issue. The earliest reports of Apaches in Texas (1690-1723), which can be linked to the Lipans through Cabello's history, place the tribe in north Texas, not in the San Antonio area. Regarding the early location and movements of the Lipan Apaches, William E. Dunn offered the following sce-nario based on the archival record.

> The Lipan, when first known to the Texans, lived far to the northwest of San Antonio, on the upper reaches of the Colorado, Brazos and Red Rivers, but gradually they moved south before the advancing Comanches, until by 1732 they made their home in the country of the San Sabá, Chanas (Llano), and Ped-ernales. About 1750 some of them established themselves on the Medina, and others pushed on to the Rio Grande. The Natagés and the Mescaleros lived far to the southwest, in the country of the Pecos and the Rio Grande (Dunn, 1911: (202-203).

The Zuazua history offers a different sequence of events: the Lipans came to Texas, claimed a homeland in the San Antonio area, lived there a number of years and then began a series of migrations, one of which took the tribe back to north Texas. No dates are given, but the Zuazua chronology seems to indicate that the Lipans were in the San Antonio area by the mid-seventeenth century. At first appearance, this sequence would seem to answer many questions about early Lipan history and explain Lipan tribal movements before they were first encountered (ca. 1690) in north Texas.

However, the 1675 *entrada* of Fernando del Bosque and Fr. Juan Larios to the upper Nueces region of Texas found no Apaches in an area just west of San Antonio. The explorers did find groups of Coahuiltecan Indians, which would argue that the Lipans had not yet moved into the area and displaced the native inhabitants. When the Coahuiltecans were interviewed, they did not mention any

Apache enemies or Apache contact (Wade, 2003: 24-54). The only seventeenth century reference to Apaches in the general vicinity of San Antonio were the words of Jumano chief Juan Sabatea, who reported in 1683 that "Apaches" had appeared on the Concho River about 200 miles north of the San Antonio area (Wade, 2003: 236). Yet, there is no conclusive evidence to connect Sabatea's Apaches with the Lipans.

So, what are we to make of the claims presented by Augustina Zuazua as they relate to early Lipan Apache history? Because the Lipan tribal homeland claim is rooted in mythology, much of the early history presented by Zuazua must also be understood in a mythological context. That is, these claims represent a body of Lipan beliefs. While they offer a Native perspective and a Lipan explanation of early tribal history, many of the claims are without evidentiary proof. It seems likely that the strong Lipan association with the *villa* of San Antonio after 1750 was, in the Zuazua history, projected back in time to form the basis of a homeland claim. There is no reason to doubt some of the tribal migrations outlined within the history, since they do reflect historical events (i.e. a Lipan-Jumano conflict, Comanche aggression). However, these migrations did not occur as the Lipans moved out from San Antonio, but occurred as the Lipans migrated from north Texas towards the south.

Early Migrations

After establishing the early Lipan tribal claim to the San Antonio area, Zuazua outlines a series of four major migrations made by the tribe or by smaller groups within the tribe. The number four held sacred significance, further evidence that the Zuazua history contains a mixture of historical facts and mythological claims.

The first tribal migration was a movement of people from the San Antonio area westward toward the mountains. Since Zuazua dictated her history at the Mescalero Reservation in New Mexico, the reference to the "east" is a reference to Texas, while the phrase "this way" indicates a westward movement. It is assumed at this early point that the Lipans were moving as one tribal unit, since the history is always careful to note tribal divisions by stating that the numbers of people were "few," if a migration was the result of a separation by a smaller group, or "many" if the reference was to the tribe as a whole.

> And then in that way/ that which she said about it/ so those Lipan
> /they/ Many Houses/ they said that their country it became.
> And then she/ that old woman [said]/ right there/ at Many Houses
> /right around it/ right there/ there was a movement of people. . . .
> Over there/ the east/ to it/ the Lipan/ their country Many Houses
> Right there/ the Lipan/ [was] their country.
> Then to this way/ they went across.
> Many Houses/ at that named/ right there [was] their country. . . .
> Then to this way/ to the mountains there was a moving of peoples.
> The Lipan then/ to Many Houses/ there was again a movement of people.

Right there [was] their country.
Then the Lipan/ in this way/ they went back and forth.
(Hoijer, 1939a: S1-10, S112-113).

Rather than viewing this migration as a literal re-telling of historical events, it must be viewed through a mythological prism. Zuazua places the tribe back into its proper late-seventeenth century historical context, far to the west of the San Antonio area, but she uses imagery which describes Lipan movements from San Antonio to the "mountains" (of west Texas or southern New Mexico?) which did not occur until the eighteenth century. However, the most valuable clue in the passage above is the reference to an early Lipan trade route in the statement explaining that the Lipans "went back and forth" between Texas and New Mexico. Zuazua followed this thread in the next block of information by introducing a second important place name, "White Houses."

> The Mescalero from their country/ nevertheless there / they were going
>   back again/ Lipan/ [to] their country.
> From then on/ it being good/ they lived.
> The Lipan then/at White Houses/ they liked it/ their country.
> Anyhow then [to] Many Houses they went.
> The Lipan they were few.
> The Lipan then/ this way/ Mescalero/ to their country/ the Lipan they came
>   among them/ that in their country/ even though they liked it [a group
>   of Lipans returned to Texas, even though they liked Mescalero
>   country]. (Hoijer, 1939a: S11-16)

According to Zuazua, the northwesterly migration of the Lipans out of Texas brought them into contact with the Mescalero Apaches at a site called "White Houses." In the seventeenth century, Spanish expeditions found the Mescalero Apaches on the plains east of Santa Fe, although the southern extent of their range during that century is unknown (Tunnell and Newcomb, 1969: 147-148). The *Natagés (Nah-tah-hays)* lived along the Pecos River and were culturally affiliated with the Mescaleros, although they had strong political ties to the Lipan Apaches in the early eighteenth century. "White Houses" was most likely the Pecos Pueblo, a Spanish trade center located on the Pecos River southeast of Santa Fe, New Mexico. Alfred V. Kidder, who excavated the Pecos Pueblo site for many years, concluded that eastern Plains Apaches were present from about 1550 and arrived in increasing numbers through 1650 (Kenner, 1969: 10). Some of the eastern Plains Apaches trading at the Pecos Pueblo in the late seventeenth century were probably Lipans, who brought hides and captives to trade for cornmeal, tobacco, and metal knives, although this fact cannot be definitively proven (Flores, 1723: 3). The captives were probably taken in wars with the Tejas and Jumanos fought along the upper Colorado, Brazos and Concho Rivers from 1680 to 1690 (Wade, 2003: 236-240).

A second important clue in this section relates to a Lipan tribal division. Zuazua notes that the Lipans "liked" the lands around "White Houses" and even

considered making the territory their "country" (i.e. homeland), but a "few"
Lipans decided to return to Texas. While it is possible that this reference per-
tains to the Lipan separation from the Jicarillas (ca. 1650), it is probably a reference to a division within the Lipan tribe itself. This conclusion is borne out by a
statement made at the end of Discourse #1:

> The Lipan / then / the Forest Lipan /and Plains Lipan
> /they/ people with them/ they were (Hoijer, 1939a: S24).

When Morris Opler interviewed the Lipans in 1935, he was told that the
Lipan name for their tribe was "People of the Forest" *(tcici or tcicihi)*. Opler
wondered why the Lipans would name themselves People of the Forest "in view
of the late Plains orientation of this tribe" (Opler, 1940: 2). The Zuazua history
answers Opler's question, stating that the Lipans separated at an early date into
two divisions. In 1745, Fr. Santa Ana discussed the territorial range of these two
large Lipan groups.

> The *Ypandes* [i.e. Plains Lipans] go in as far as the Rio Salado [Pecos River] in
> the months of June and July, and then in the autumn all go down together [with
> the *Natagés*] to the San Sabá, Xianas [Chanas, Llano], Almagre [Honey Creek],
> and Pedernales Rivers, from which they pass to the Colorado. . . since this
> country is the home of the buffalo with which they sustain themselves (Dunn,
> 1911: 266).

The Forest Lipans, whom the priest called *Ypandes alias Pelones*, lived the
farthest north from San Antonio along the Red River and were a numerically
smaller group (Dunn, 1911: 267-268).

The Lipans were under intense Comanche pressure from the beginning of
the eighteenth century, but were not dislodged from the territorial ranges described by Fr. Santa Ana until after 1750, so the priest's description can also be
generally applied to the situation outlined in the first section of the Zuazua history to produce the following scenario: By about 1650, the Lipans separated
from the Jicarilla Apaches and migrated into Texas (Opler, 1940: 6). In the last
decades of the seventeenth century, they could be found on the upper reaches of
the Colorado, Brazos and Red Rivers (Dunn, 1911: 202-203). By 1680, the
Lipans and other Texas Apaches began to invade territory inhabited by the
northern Jumanos along the upper Concho and San Saba Rivers. They also began to apply pressure to the "Tejas kingdom" along the upper Trinity River
(Wade, 203: 236-240). The Lipans and other Texas Apaches developed a trade
route on an east-west axis between north central Texas and the Pecos Pueblo of
New Mexico. A dispute within the Lipan tribe led to a tribal division in the late
seventeenth or early eighteenth century. The Forest Lipans chose to return to the
upper Trinity/Red River region. Zuazua noted that they were "few," which not
only indicated a break-away group but corroborated Fr. Santa Ana's observations on the numerical size of the *Ypandes alias Pelones*. The Plains Lipans

"liked the Mescalero country" (i.e. the upper Pecos region) and remained to the west of the Forest Lipans, migrating from the upper Colorado to the Pecos River and back.

After recounting the tribal division, the Zuazua history then moves to a description of a second Lipan migration. After reiterating the Lipan homeland claim to "Many Houses," a second migration is described to a campsite called "Pairs of Stones lie about," which Hoijer noted was "a town in Mexico near Many Houses" (Hoijer, 1939a: S22). A territorial claim ("their country") is also extended to cover the new location.

> Then Many Houses/ the Lipan/ before it/ very long ago/ no one there
> /their country/ anyhow there they went.
> Being on foot/ horses/ there were none.
> And then/ right there/ a long time/ [was] their country.
> Being many/ years passed with them.
> And then/ that one/ their country/ they made it so
> /'Pairs of stones lie about'/ right there/ [was] their country.
> The Lipan/ just there/ they traveled about.
> The Lipan then/ the Forest Lipan and Plains Lipan/ they
> /people with them/ they were (Hoijer, 1939a: S17-24).

Again, Zuazua has moved into a mythological realm. The two closest modern Mexican towns in proximity to San Antonio are Piedras Negras and Nuevo Laredo, both of which are situated at ancient low-river crossings of the Rio Grande. Since Piedras Negras is mentioned elsewhere in the Zuazua history with a direct translation from the Spanish as "Black Rock," there is a good possibility that "Pairs of stones lie about" can be identified with the Laredo, Texas area. The Lipans were certainly present there from the late eighteenth century onward, but there is no historical evidence that there were Lipan Apaches in the Laredo area or in Mexico before 1750. From 1720 to 1750, reports from Coahuila mention only generic "Apaches" and Spanish lists of native tribes inhabiting Nuevo Leon and Tamaulipas (location of Nuevo Laredo) state that the "Apaches" had not yet penetrated those provinces in the 1730's (Jauregui, 1736: 9-23 and Gerhard, 1920: 327). Again, it seems as if Zuazua has taken a scenario which existed after 1750 and projected it back in time.

If this section of the Zuazua history is read thematically, however, it becomes clear that the reiteration of a homeland claim and the southern expansion of a Lipan homeland (i.e. a migration from San Antonio south to the Rio Grande), is simply a thematic preface for the two blocks of migratory information which follow. Those migrations (# 3 and #4) can be tied to historical events occurring in the late seventeenth and early eighteenth centuries. Migration #3 focuses on Comanche aggression, which forced the Lipans out of the Texas high plains and to the south. Migration #4 involves the southern expansion of Lipan territory into Jumano lands along the upper Concho and San Saba Rivers. The theme—the southward extension of Lipan territorial claims, both forced and purposeful—is painted in large strokes in migration #2.

The third Lipan migration described in the Zuazua history is composed of only three terse lines, yet they contain the spark which ignited one of the most decisive events in Lipan tribal history—the tribe's century-long conflict with the Comanches.

> The Lipan then/ some of them/ to Comanche/ their country /some of them /they went about.
> The Lipan then/ they did not like it.
> And then/ back to their country they returned/ to Many Houses
> (Hoijer, 1939a: S25-27).

Interestingly, Zuazua does not claim that the Comanches invaded Lipan territory, but that a group of Lipans entered Comanche lands and "went about." The earliest archival references to the Comanches (1706) come from New Mexico and place the tribe in eastern Colorado, where they made repeated raids on Apache *rancherias*. The first Spanish report of Comanches in Texas was made in 1743, but "the extent of [Comanche] penetration below the Red River is unclear" in the late seventeenth and early eighteenth centuries (Kavanagh, 1996: 63, 79). There is no evidence that the Lipans were in eastern Colorado in 1706, so it is likely that the Lipans crossed the Red River and moved into the southern Great Plains. Why they would do so is unclear, but they were probably looking for horses and testing the boundaries of territory claimed by other tribes in such a quest. Whatever the reason for the journey to Comanche country, the Lipans got more than they bargained for. Domingo Cabello provided the following vivid description of a climactic running battle between the Lipans, *Natagés* and Comanches fought somewhere between north Texas and southwestern Oklahoma at some point between 1690 and 1723:

> [The Spanish] found the Indians of the Nations *Lipana*, and Apaches *[Natagés]*, situated at 300 leagues [801 miles] from them above, spread out on the plains of the banks of the River of Iron Pieces [possibly near Wichita Falls, Texas] which meandered between the north northwest and the northwest; however, they lived in a state of continuous warfare with the numerous and ferocious Nation of the Comanches, for whom incidents arose to give a battle; the fighting lasted nine days, [leaving] piles of skeletons, and came even to the slopes of the large mountain range of iron [Wichita Mountains of southwestern Oklahoma] where is born the river of that name; [the battle] brought about a loss for the *Lipanes* and Apaches, who were forced to abandon their homeland *[patrio]* and seek safe asylum where they would not be pursued by their enemies, by guiding themselves this way [southward into central Texas] to these territories, stopping before the Colorado River and the Brazos River, where we found them at 120 leagues [320 miles] to the northeast. [The enmity remained so great after the battle], if the Indians of these three Nations rose up on Judgment Day, their bones would fight one another (Cabello, 1784: 104).

The fourth migration described by Augustina Zuazua is a movement by the Lipans to a region or to a people called "the Crow."

> The Lipan in their country/ just that/Many Houses/ its vicinity
> /there was a movement here and there.
> Those Crow Indians/ there to/ the Lipan/ [was] their country
> (Hoijer, 1939a: S 28-29).

Although Hoijer showed the translation of the Lipan word *gài hìi* to be "Crow Indians" in this instance, when the migration is recapped in Discourse #4, the same word was noted by Hoijer as a reference to a place, rather than to a tribe of Indians:

> Then that/ to right there/ that [place]/ Crow/ that is named /there
> /there was moving about (Hoijer, 1939a: S116).

The identity of "the Crow" (either as a people or a region) is a mystery, as no further clues are given. There is no evidence of any linkage between Texas Apaches and the Shoshonean tribe of Crow Indians who inhabited the upper Great Plains in the area of present-day Montana. Given the context of the Zuazua history, the migration to "the Crow" is a migration made within Texas.

Spanish sources hinted at an epic struggle in late seventeenth century Texas between the "Apaches" and a number of Native groups, particularly the Tejas and the Jumanos, as the Apaches sought to expand their territory from north Texas southward into Jumano lands along the upper Concho and southeast into Tejas territory. Jumano chief Juan Sabatea characterized these struggles in 1683 as "wars" (Wade, 2003: 236). "In July 1688, Diego de León, an Ervipiame, informed Alonso de León that the Ervipiame, the Tejas, the French and possibly the Jumano had attacked the Apache" (Wade, 2003: 153). In 1690, Alonso de León stated that the Tejas were continually at war with the Apache, whose lands lay to the west of the Tejas. Alonso de León's information was confirmed in 1690 and 1691 by Frs. Massanet and Casañas (Wade, 2003: 161). By 1731, however, the Jumanos were fighting alongside the Lipans *(Pelones)* in an attack near the Béxar presidio at San Antonio. By 1732, the Tejas had joined a Lipan coalition (Bonilla, 1772: 19 and Dunn, 1911: 228).

Although the "Crow people" of the Zuazua history could be the Tejas, or a group within that confederation, it seems likely that Zuazua is probably referring to the Jumanos, who were called *rayado* by the Spanish because of their black-striped facial painting or tattooing (Hickerson, 1994: 116-117). This connection is strengthened when the known Lipan territories described by Fr. Santa Ana in 1745 (Pecos to San Saba to the Colorado River for the *Ypandes* and along the Red River for the *Ypandes alias Pelones)* are compared to Jumano lands of 1683 along the Concho and San Saba Rivers. The "moving about in the lands of the Crow people" and the establishment of a territorial claim ("their country") in Crow lands are most likely abbreviated references to the territorial expansion of the *Ypande* division south to the San Saba/Llano/Pedernales line. The Crow bird was the primary Lipan mythological figure associated with hunting, particularly the buffalo hunt (Opler, 1940: 123-124). Since the San Saba and Llano region contained large buffalo herds, this section of the Zuazua history could be read as a migration to "buffalo country" which was, of course, controlled by the Jumanos. While details regarding seventeenth century tattooing practices of Native Texas groups are unknown, and while Jumano chief Juan Sabatea's "Apache" enemies of 1683 cannot be definitively linked to the Lipans, a tentative link can be established between the "Crow" people of the Zuazua history, the Jumanos and a Lipan southward territorial expansion in the late seventeenth century.

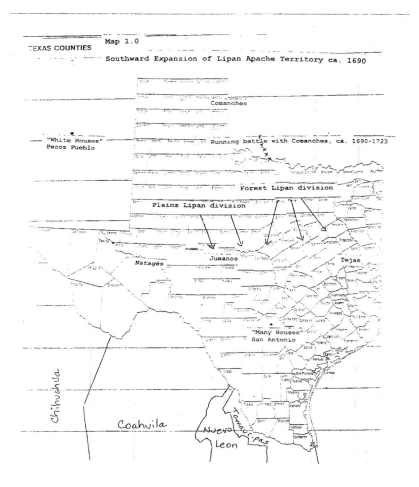

Migrations after 1750

In addition to recounting late seventeenth or early eighteenth century Lipan migrations, the Zuazua history also tells of two important migrations made after 1750. The first was the 1751 movement of a large group of Texas Lipans across the Rio Grande into northern Coahuila, where they formed a new band called the *Kû'ne tsa (Big Water People)*. This movement was reported by Texas Governor Domingo Cabello, who attributed the move to inter-tribal conflict, but confessed "we don't know why the Lipans remained below the Nueces and Rio Grande Rivers and made their dissentions" (Cabello, 1784: 115-116) In truth, Cabello reported an acrimonious split between Lipan accomodationalists, who wished to retain contact with the Spanish at San Antonio and even wished to enter Spanish missions, and a large traditionalist faction who sought to preserve traditional culture and only wished to make war and raid Spanish settlements.

This dispute had been simmering among the central Texas Lipan bands for almost half a century, but the tipping point, correctly identified by Augustina Zuazua in her history, was a smallpox epidemic that swept through the *rancherías* after Lipan prisoners were returned to their families upon the conclusion of a 1749 Lipan-Spanish peace celebration at San Antonio. The Lipans believed that the returning prisoners wore articles of mission-issued clothing which were infected with the smallpox virus. When others touched the clothing, particularly children who were reunited with their freed parents, the disease was transmitted, igniting an epidemic (Dolores, 1749b: 118-119, Santa Ana, 1750b: 140, Galván, 1753a: 13-15). A large group of Lipan traditionalists, who saw no profit in close contact with the Spanish if such contact resulted in epidemic, left the Lipan camps along the upper Nueces and moved permanently across the Rio Grande. Zuazua described this migration in the following manner:

> The Lipan/ their camps/ they were many.
> So then disease came to them; there being many/ they died.
> Therefore in this way/ they traveled.
> That country [was] Black Rock.
> To there they moved (Hoijer, 1939a: S41-45).

A direct translation of "Black Rock" into Spanish yields the border town of Piedras Negras, Coahuila, and indeed, this town marked the primary route of entry for Lipan bands traveling from central Texas into northern Coahuila. Once across the Rio Grande, the Big Water band set about establishing camps in the mountains bordering the valleys of San Fernando de Austria and Santa Rosa. They hunted buffalo from the herds that still existed in northwestern Coahuila as late as 1900 (Coopwood, 1900: 232).

> Then that country/ they made it so.
> Many Houses [San Antonio]/ and in another town also [in Coahuila].
> And then those mountains/ their country/ they made it so.

Wild Plum Trees/ the Lipan/ their country/ they made it so.
Stone Head Mountain/ Serrated Top/ White Banded Mountain/
    /Red Cedars/ at there/the Lipan/ [was] their country....
Those Lipan/ Serrated Rock/ Bitter Medicine/Mountain That Lies There
    /long ago/ buffalo/ they killed them.
Their meat/ they ate it/ and their hides/ they tanned them.
Those towns/ they customarily went with them
    / [and] they sold them to the Mexicans.
And then/ with those/ all that is lacking/ they bought with it
    /blankets/ and anything else (Hoijer, 1939a: S46-50, S54-57).

In time, the Mexican Lipans named their country in a manner reminiscent of
the name bestowed on their homeland near San Antonio, Texas. Their new Coahuilan homeland was known as "Circular House," a possible reference to the
round cupola over the sacristy of the mission church of San Bernardo (near present-day Guerrero, Coahuila) and the arched barrel-roofed tombs in the attached
cemetery (Hoijer, 1939a: S121-128). [2]
    The final migration outlined in the Zuazua history was a movement of peo-
ples in the nineteenth century. By 1821, two Texas Lipan bands had been drawn
toward the trade opportunities presented by the foundation of the Austin colony
in east Texas. These bands settled for a time with the Tonkawas along the lower
Colorado River and both tribes sought military alliances with the new Anglo
settlers. However, the two Lipan band chiefs (*Flacco* and *Cuelgas de Castro*)
became disenchanted with their Anglo allies by 1840 when the Indian policies of
the new Republic of Texas proved injurious to their interests (Schilz, 1987: 41-
50).

Then she spoke thus: 'The whites in their country/ there being many
    /the Lipan/ there were many.'
And that/ they did not like it/ and then they started to go back/ back home.
They spoke thus: 'For what reason/ in our country/ being far away
    /from it/ we are here?'
And then/ going back/ to their country/ they returned.
That only was their country/ at Many Houses.
And then/ right there/ [was] their country/ and then/ they being many
    /they died (Hoijer, 1939a: S274, S276, S283, S287, S290, S303).

The Lipan bands, who had previously migrated eastward, returned to the
San Antonio area and south Texas by 1844-1846 (Green, 1844: 150-151 and
Neighbors, 1846: 13-14). In 1849-1850, a smallpox epidemic swept through
Lipan *rancherías* in the San Antonio area, forcing survivors to flee either into
Mexico or toward the west to escape the epidemic (Ball, 1988: 267-270).

Chapter 4

Early Lipan-Spanish Contacts in Texas

> I have heard from my people how in the old times they used to go out in
> the flats and catch those wild horses. That's how they got their horses. There
> were many wild horses out in the plains. They got away from the Spaniards and
> then became wild. This story is about a Lipan fellow. This fellow liked to chase
> wild horses. He looked down from a hill once and saw the horses standing there
> as if they were in a corral. He watched and saw a tiny person come out from a
> hill and walk toward them. The horses . . . allowed this little person to approach
> them. Then the little man showed himself. The horses noticed it at once. [The
> man] jumped on a big stallion, one which had never been ridden before. The
> Lipan wanted to see what kind of a little fellow this was. The Lipan was now
> nearer and could see that the little person was dressed in something that shone
> and he wore a hat too. The hat had a little brim. (Opler, 1940: 76-77)

The Lipan legend cited above contains an interesting detail which indicates
the story might well contain an authentic memory of early contact between the
Lipan Apaches and the Spanish. The little man, "dressed in something that
shone" and wearing a short-brimmed hat, brings to mind a sixteenth century
Spanish explorer dressed in armor which covered the torso and wearing a short-
brimmed, peaked helmet. The Plains Apaches would have seen just such a sight
as the Coronado expedition set out from the Pecos Pueblo of New Mexico in
1541 to explore the vast southern Plains (Hoxie, 1996: 25). Although there is no
evidence to link the Lipans to any specific Plains Apache group encountered by
the Spanish in the sixteenth and seventeenth centuries, the legend did preserve
an ancient tribal memory of a connection between the Plains, the Spanish, and
the horse, as well as the curiosity and intense interest these animals must have
sparked in the minds of the early Lipan Apaches.

The acquisition of the horse was the single most significant technological
acquisition in the history of the Lipan tribe. To understand just what a profound
impact the horse had on the Lipan Apaches, one need only turn to the Zuazua
history and its description of Lipan life before the arrival of the horse.

> And the men/ [with] spears/ those also/ there/ anything/ they killed
>   them with it/ antelopes/ those like it/ and mountain sheep too.
> Just those/ they lived on them.
> And being on foot/ they hunted them/ anything that they got.
> In that way/ they packed it to wherever their camp was.
> To wherever it is/ they carried it back.
> That in such fashion/ they were made long ago
>   /their horses there were none.
> In that way on foot/ they went about.
> The Lipan in that way/ on foot/ they carried things about
>   /even the children/they went about carrying them.
>   (Hoijer, 1939a: S240-247)

Noteworthy in this description of pre-horse Lipan culture is its unique feminine perspective. The Lipan acquisition of the horse, while certainly crucial in the development of warfare and hunting practices, was also a development of immense practical importance in the lives of Lipan women. The horse not only allowed the tribe to migrate at a faster pace, it eased the burden of Lipan women, who no longer had to carry food, shelter and children on their backs. If the horse represented a quantum leap in technological improvement for Lipan men, who became expert horsemen, the horse also represented liberation for Lipan women.

Equally noteworthy is the absence of any mention of the use of dogs to transport the camp. This cultural feature had been observed among the Plains Apaches since Coronado's 1541 expedition. Morris Opler noted that "the Southern Athapaskan word for horse originally meant dog," an indication that the Apaches used dogs before they acquired the horse (Opler, 1940: 15). On the other hand, the Zuazua history neither mentions the use of dogs nor the eating of dog meat, leading to the assumption that either the Lipans had never used the dog for transport or had eschewed that practice at a very early date and retained no memory of their former practice. The Lipan emergence myth stated that the "northern" Apache tribes used dogs and the Lipans did not include themselves in this group. However, Francisco Ruíz noted in 1828 that a northern portion of the Lipan tribe "hunt game and prefer dog meat to other kinds of meat; they eat it with relish and even feed dog meat to their sick" (Ewers, 1972: 8). Although scholars have theorized that the Ruíz description was a reference to the Kiowa Apaches, such a connection cannot be definitively proven.

The Lipans and other Texas Apaches acquired the horse by the late 1600's (Chipman, 1992: 15-16). In 1691, Fr. Massanet and Terán de los Rios met a number of Native groups, among them the Jumano, near the Guadalupe River in central Texas. All the Indians were mounted on horses and rode on small riding saddles with stirrups. When Fr. Massanet asked where they had obtained these saddles, he was told that they had taken them from the Apaches in war (Wade, 2003: 153-154). If the Texas Apaches had saddles by 1691, then they had horses and had learned how to ride them.

The Lipans probably acquired their horses from a number of different sources in the late seventeenth and early eighteenth centuries. The first horses seem to have been wild Spanish mustangs which were caught on the Plains. The Lipan myth describing the creation of the horse by the primary spirit deity, Killer-of-Enemies, contained specific instructions for catching wild horses on flat prairie land where there were no physical barriers to assist in the catching process. Killer-of-Enemies called up a heavy rain, causing the horses to stand "hunched up, trying to protect themselves from the rain." They were then approached on foot and roped (Opler, 1940: 30). The inclusion of such factual knowledge of equine behavior in an important horse-creation myth, and the ingenious method used by the Lipans to exploit such behavior (i.e. wait for a heavy rainstorm to catch a wild horse), argues that it was an early practice.

Some horses might have been obtained through raids on Spanish settlements in New Mexico, particularly the Pecos Pueblo (Kidder, 2000: 16). However, such raids were sporadic and there is no evidence which would specifically include the Lipans in the groups of eastern Apache raiders. Horses might also have been obtained through raids on the Comanches, a tribe which placed great cultural importance on the possession of large numbers of horses. However, it is hard to see how the Lipans could have attempted more than a few raids on Comanche horse herds before drawing Comanche ire and setting off an all-out war, which is what occurred after 1700.

The early Lipans probably acquired most of their horses in their wars with the Jumanos and Tejas. In 1683, Jumano chief Juan Sabatea told the Spanish, "In the Kingdom of the texas [Tejas] so much food is produced that even the horses and mares are fed on corn;" Sabatea also noted that the Jumanos had "many herds of mares" (Wade, 2003: 239). Lipan raids on these herds probably accompanied the southward extension of Lipan territory into central Texas.

However, the Zuazua history presented another view of the source of the Lipan acquisition of the horse, locating that momentous development as occurring across the Rio Grande in Mexico.

> Then the Lipan/ to their country/ when they had moved/ Many Houses
> /to the place called/ there/ those that had moved/ the Rio Grande
> /then/ they traveled across.
> They were very poor.
> And then/ just there they traveled about.
> And then/ the Mexicans/ they were very good to them.
> And then/ in every way they helped them.
> And then/ their horses they had acquired.
> And then/ [with] those only they went about
> From there on/ because they liked it (Hoijer, 1939a: S30-37).

Zwazwa circled back later in the history to reiterate the information.

> Then Circular House/ there/ from each other/ the Lipan/ in their country
> Then/ just that/ they traveled about.
> Now these Lipan/ just those/ from each other/ their countries
> And then in that way/ that/ they liked it.
> That their camps/ houses/ around them/ and then
> /so their horses/ they became.
> The Lipan then/ burros/ just those/ they went about by means of them
> (Hoijer, 1939a: S126-131).

A literal reading of these blocks of information poses numerous problems. If Zuazua was speaking of the tribal acquisition of the horse and locating that acquisition in Coahuila—as she seemed to be when she stated that the Lipans were "very poor" (i.e. without the wealth represented by herds of horses) and tied the discussion to the Lipan Coahuilan homeland of Circular House—there is no archival data which supports this assertion. San Juan Bautista, the first mission and presidio complex established along the Rio Grande in Coahuila, was founded in 1698-1700, but testimony regarding the founding contains no mention of Apaches, although other Native tribes are named (Cuervo, 1699: 1-10). When the Lipans are first mentioned specifically by name in Texas Spanish records (1732), the tribe was already mounted and was found at least 100 miles north of San Juan Bautista. By 1734, there were "Apaches" in Coahuila who joined with the Tobosos to raid the San Juan Bautista horse herds (Ecay, 1734: 66-69). However, there is no evidence to link these generic "Apaches" to the Lipans and the horse thefts were hardly instances where the Mexicans were "very good" to the Apaches and "helped them in every way."

There is only one series of events in the historical record which seems to fit the situation outlined by Zuazua. After concluding a peace treaty with the Spanish at San Antonio in 1749, the Lipans moved to territories west of San Antonio between the Medina and the Rio Grande Rivers in April 1751. A tribal division caused one large group of Lipans to cross the Rio Grande and claim Coahuilan territories as their new homeland ("Circular House"). The Spanish settlers of Coahuila received the Lipans in peace, "an accomplishment that speaks well of our settlers, who gave safe conduct to transit to all parts" (Cabello, 1784: 115). In relaying information about the Lipan acquisition of the horse, Zuazua seems to have used events dating from 1750 and projected those events back in time. The same transposition is used to frame a discussion of early Lipan migrations (see Chapter 3). This transposition should alert us that Zuazua is speaking figuratively, not literally. The Lipan acquisition of the horse was part of the larger process of Lipan southward expansion into central Texas. Tribal herds were augmented by the Lipan displacement of the Jumanos from the upper Concho and their early wars with the Tejas Indians.

One area of early Lipan-Spanish contact in Texas provided an enduring legacy in Lipan daily life. The Zuazua history credits the Spanish at San Antonio with introducing food items which expanded the Lipan diet.

> That long ago/ Mexicans/ their food/ they did not know it.
> And then/ Many Houses/ when they went at that time
>   /they learned about it.
> That which the Mexicans eat: coffee, sugar, and wheat and pumpkins and
>   beans and corn and chili.
> Long ago the Lipan/ that sort/ not eating/ they did not know about it.
> And now everything/ they have learned about it.
> All of it they eat it/ it has become. . . .
> That Many Houses/ their country/ long ago/ nothing they knew.
> Only Indian customs/ and after a long time/ something
>   /they learned about it.
> And then/ that corn/ they customarily planted it.
> That at that place/ Many Houses/ there/ the Mexicans they showed it to
>   them.
> That the planting [of corn]/ then they learned about it.

Then wheat/ that its flour/ the Lipan/ how/ that they eat it
    /they did not know it
In that way they told about it to them.
Lipan women then/ those they showed it to them/ the Mexicans
    /how they eat it
(Hoijer, 1939a: S89-93, S133-140).

The Lipans were planting corn long before any European contact. Explorers of the southern Plains in the sixteenth and seventeenth centuries observed Apaches planting maize, and the Zuazua history makes clear that the ancestors of the Lipans also practiced this form of agriculture, crediting "Indian customs." Lipan captive Frank Buckelew explained the customary planting method, as he observed it in 1866. Lipan women found an area of fertile soil next to a stream, cleared off any brush and dug holes haphazardly with an axe, dropping seed corn into the holes (Dennis, 1925: 93). However, Zuazua also credits the Spanish in San Antonio with refining Lipan agricultural techniques, perhaps teaching them to plant in a row or teaching them to plant their corn inside enclosures so as to protect the plants. Such tutelage could have occurred no earlier than 1733, as the Bustillo campaign of 1732 brought a tenuous peace and the initiation of Lipan trade contacts at San Antonio, or 1749, when a Lipan band led by *Boca Comida* entered Mission San Antonio de Valero (Olivan, 1733: 214 and Dolores, 1749a: 114).

As contact between the Lipans and the Spanish at San Antonio increased after 1750, the Lipans began to enjoy many of the food items used by the Spanish, particularly sugar and chili peppers. The latter items were included annually as "gifts," intended as a means of pacification, bestowed on the Lipans and *Natagés* from 1749 to 1756. [1] Lipan women were also taught how to use flour to make tortillas. It was in this form that wheat was added to the Lipan diet, rather than in the form of bread.

The importance of the cultural and technological acquisitions gained by Spanish contact cannot be denied. For the Lipans, the Spanish were a rich feast, providing food items to be acquired through trade and gift. However, the price of admission to the banquet was pacification and missionization, a price generally deemed unacceptable by the tribe. On the other hand, once the chimera of Gran Quivera gold had been exposed and the Plains Apaches made it aggressively clear that they would never bow to Spanish servitude, the Apaches held nothing that the Spanish coveted. The Spanish in Texas didn't need the Lipan Apaches, but the Lipans grew to need the Spanish. This unequal relationship did not bode well for the Lipans, who were being forced to expand their territories ever southward in order to escape the aggressive Comanches. The southward expansion of Lipan territory set the tribe on a collision course with the northward extension of Spanish frontier settlement. With their enemies at their backs, and Spaniards on their horizons, the Lipan Apaches found themselves, at the dawn of the eighteenth century, the men in the middle.

Spanish Names for the Lipan Apaches

When the Spanish founded the presidio of San Antonio de Béxar and its ac-
companying mission, San Antonio de Valero, in 1718, they knew there were
Apaches in Texas, but correctly believed these Indians lived hundreds of miles
to the north. They were confident that they could deal with the Apaches because
Spanish policy was one of conciliation. The Viceroy, Marquis de Valero, instructed that the Apaches inhabiting the southern Great Plains and north Texas
be attracted "with tactful prudence to friendly intercourse with our people. Con-
sequently, an alliance with the Apaches would serve as a cordon of armed garri-
sons to protect these dominions along the northern line" (Valero, 1719: 64). An
alarming report made in April 1718 by Diego Ramon, Captain of the presidio at
San Juan Bautista, failed to check Spanish plans for a settlement at San Antonio,
which was officially founded in May of that year. Ramon reported that Texas
Apaches attacked a mule train between the Colorado and Guadalupe Rivers and
that two Apache captives, from the Ponico and Patahua tribes, told Ramon that
"the Apaches were declaring their intention of destroying the Presidio on the
river and the [presidio] in the [province of the] Tejas." (D. Ramon, 1718: 62-63)
The presidio near the Tejas Indians was located in east Texas, but the "presidio
on the river" was either San Juan Bautista, on the Rio Grande, or the new settlement at San Antonio. The Apache threat never materialized, but the words of
the Indian captives should have alerted the Spanish that their movements were
being closely watched throughout Texas.

What the Spanish could not have known was that the Comanches had entered north Texas by 1718, sparking a war with Texas Apaches. Domingo Cabello noted that the two primary Apache groups involved in the conflict were the
Lipans and the "Apaches" (Cabello, 1784: 104). The term "Apache" was used
by the Spanish of this era to refer to the *Natagés,* a Mescalero-affiliated group
(Dunn, 1911: 266). The infant settlement at San Antonio was spared hostilities
from 1718 to 1723, not only because the Texas Apaches inhabited lands at least
300 miles to the north, but also because their running battles with the Comanches kept the Apaches focused on their enemies. However, Lipan and *Natagés*
battle losses soon forced both tribes southward to the banks of the Colorado and
Brazos Rivers and, still fearful of the Comanches, "they determined to explore
the land to the south in order to move away from the many who were contrary to
them." (Cabello, 1784: 104)

In 1723, a group of Lipans came into contact with two Spanish woodcutters
at the Pass of *Elotes (green ears of corn),* about twenty miles northwest of San
Antonio. The Pass had been named by the Spanish for the corn they found growing there and had been named prior to any contact with the Apaches. However,
the name identifies the site as a Lipan seasonal agricultural camp and the tribe
maintained a presence in the Helotes area until at least 1856 (Long, 1996: 548).

As the San Antonio settlement grew from 1723 to 1732, with the founding
of new missions and an influx of settlers, Apache livestock raids began. The
identity of the raiders in each instance cannot be determined beyond the fact that

Cabello said they were both Lipan and *Apache/Natagés* (Cabello, 1784: 105). In 1723, presidio Captain Nicholas Flores, following the trail of Apache horse thieves, led a punitive expedition which attacked a *ranchería* near the Colorado River in the vicinity of present-day Brownwood, Texas. Flores never detailed the composition of the *ranchería* beyond the fact that it contained generic "Apaches." However, a female prisoner revealed that the *ranchería* was one of five large camps under the leadership and direction of a single *Capitan Grande* (Flores, 1723: 2 and Dunn, 1911: 207-208). This information, which dovetails with later data regarding known Lipan band and divisional structure, coupled with the location of the *ranchería* at the time of the attack, indicates a strong likelihood that the horse thieves Flores trailed from San Antonio were Lipan.

The first written document which specifically named the Lipan Apache tribe and connected them to the San Antonio area was a battle report written by Texas Governor Bustillo in 1732. Bustillo's report was summarized by later commentators, among them Domingo Cabello (1784). In September 1731, a small number of Apaches brazenly made off with fifty horses from the presidio's horse herd. A small number of soldiers gave chase, but a few miles from the presidio they were ambushed by over 500 warriors, each well-armed with bows, arrows and metal-tipped lances. When the soldiers thought their end was near, they dismounted at the foot of a tree, determined to fight to the death. However, just as suddenly as the ambush was sprung, the Apaches retreated, leaving the Spanish survivors convinced they had witnessed a miracle (Dunn, 1911: 227-228). Presidio commander Almazán deduced from the spent arrows that the attackers were "Apaches, *Pelones*, and *Jumanes* . . . all three of which are very numerous in Indians and very warlike" (Dunn, 1911: 228).

The Texas Provincial government was determined to avenge the attack. On December 9, 1732, Governor Bustillo attacked an Indian *ranchería* on the San Saba River with a force of 157 Spaniards, 60 mission Indian auxiliaries and one cannon (Dunn, 1911: 230). The *ranchería* was composed of 400 tents and contained 800 warriors from four "nations": Apaches, *Ypandi ("whom we call Pelones"), Yxandi* and *Chenti* (Bustillo, 1732 and Perez et al, 1732). The four nations represented a tribal alliance which had been created when the *Yxandi* and *Chenti* joined with the Apache and *Ypandi* to attack the Spanish at San Antonio (Almazán, 1733). The *Chenti* were probably the Tejas Indians, given the similarity to *Cenis*, the Tejas tribal name recorded by Joutel in 1687 (Foster, 1998: 297). The *Yxandi* were probably "one of several bands that later came to be spoken of collectively as Lipan Apache Indians" (Campbell, 1996: 1135). The Apaches were the Mescalero-affiliated *Natagés*, while the *Ypandis* were the Lipan Apaches. When Almazán's identification of the spent arrows is combined with Bustillo's battle report and Cabello's summary, an interesting picture emerges of Lipan Apache tribal alliances in the first decades of the eighteenth century. Almazán noted that the arrows littering the battle site near the Béxar presidio in 1731 were *Apache (Natagés), Pelones (Lipan)* and *Jumanes (Jumanos)*. The Jumanos had moved from a state of war with generic "Apaches" in 1683 to an alliance with the *Natagés* and Lipans by 1731. Bustillo's 1732 attack revealed that the Tejas, once former enemies of the generic "Apaches" of Texas, had joined in an alliance with the *Natagés* and Lipans against the Spanish.

The San Saba *ranchería* attacked by Bustillo was a war camp and Indian prisoners revealed the existence of an even larger *ranchería* about 360 miles further north, occupied by the *Ypandi (alias Pelones)*. The tents of this large *ranchería*, which were pitched close together, covered an area of about ten miles (Bustillo, 1733). The large *Ypandi (alias Pelones) ranchería* was composed of more than 1700 persons.

All were subjects of two chiefs, each of whom had one of the two divisions of Lipans and Apaches *[Natagés]*, all of whom composed one Royal dominion. All of this was told to the Viceroy, who approved the execution of a few of [the Apache prisoners who revealed this information] (Cabello, 1784: 107-108).

Cabello's note that the Lipans and *Natagés* were "all subjects of two chiefs, each of whom had one of two divisions" seems to be a slight error. If Campbell's identification of the *Yxandi* with the Lipan Apaches is correct, then the *Yxandi* were the Plains Lipan division spoken of in the Zuazua history, while the *Ypandi (alias Pelones)* were the Forest Lipan divison.

Further elucidation regarding the ties between the *Ypandi, Pelones* and *Natagés* was given in 1743-1745 by Fr. Santa Ana, who was able to provide a more detailed and specific picture of the Apaches encountered by Bustillo along the San Saba River in 1732. Fr. Santa Ana was also the first to note that the Lipan tribe was composed of two large divisions, information which allows us to connect the tribal divisions of the Zuazua history with the historical record.

Fr. Benito Fernández de Santa Ana was born in Berán, Spain. In 1731, the twenty-four year old Franciscan priest was sent to Texas to oversee the San Antonio de Valero Mission. His first Apache experience was not a pleasant one, occurring soon after he crossed the Rio Grande into Texas. A group of raiders attacked Fr. Santa Ana and a fellow priest on the road, "robbing them of their baggage and horses and killing two of the five soldiers who accompanied them" (Habig, 1996: 984). In spite of this inauspicious first contact, Santa Ana came to believe that a more effective means of ending Apache raids was through gentle inducement and persuasion, rather than through punitive military campaigns (Santa Ana, 1743b: 95). Toward this end, he sent a series of letters to the Viceroy in March 1743 advocating the establishment of an Apache mission. As part of his argument for such an establishment, Fr. Santa Ana outlined the information he had gathered on the Apache tribes of Texas. The priest began his series of letters with a general summary of the Apache problem along the northern Spanish frontier:

The entire sum [of Apaches] are bandits and pour out from many hideouts eating up the land; they have been recognized making entrances into Saltillo, Nuevo Leon, the Province of Texas, Louisiana, and all the provinces from

Nueva Viscaya to New Mexico. They have left these places in the west and be-
sieged more to the North searching for an expanded country and [a country]
populated by many people, ones that can give them very good horses and [the
Apaches are] armed with cutting lances and good *azeradas*, a kind of pointed
hatchet, bows of bone or animal horn and arrows feathered up to the flint
(Santa Ana, 1743a: 65).

In a second letter, Fr. Santa Ana narrowed the scope and addressed the
problem of the Texas Apaches encountered by the Spanish at San Antonio, noting that they were composed of three separate groups. The Texas Apaches
shared a common goal with other Southwestern Apache tribes in the early decades of the eighteenth century—a quest to obtain horses.

The Indians that wander around and occupy this country are divided into
three portions that the Spanish call *Ypandes*, Apaches and *Pelones*, and, in the
language of the . . . Indians of the North—*[the] Azain, Duttain, and Negain*.
The *Ypandes* and the Apaches have about 500 warriors [literally 'Indians of
bow and arrow'], and the *Pelones* have about 800; these latter ones live very
remote from this Presidio and from all the rest and are less bold and they live in
stillness because they have small numbers of horses. The *Ypandes*, who are
more immediate to this Presidio, almost always live united with the Apaches
who have numerous horses, but this does not slake their appetite to have many
more, for with robbery, these bandits steal things along the road that passes
from New Mexico to Texas; they take the lives of many fellow Indians and
Spaniards without forgiveness (Santa Ana, 1743b: 89-90).

Fr. Santa Ana was able to augment his information when he accompanied a
1745 military expedition to Apache country north of San Antonio. When the
Santa Ana material is examined in its totality, the three groups of Texas Apaches
come into focus.

I. "Apaches"

Fr. Santa Ana used the term "Apache" to refer singularly and specifically to
the Mescalero-affiliated *Natagés (Nah-tah-hays)*. This usage was later adopted
by Texas Governor Cabello. In a 1745 letter to the Viceroy, Santa Ana clarified,

The *Natagés* Indians, reputed among the Indians of the North as true Apaches,
lived on this occasion not far from and to the west of the *Ypandes* [i.e. west of
the Colorado River]. They are fewer in number, but prouder and more over-
bearing than the rest, and their chief man was captain of the *Ypandes* (Dunn,
1911: 266).

The Spanish found the *Natagés* living on the Pecos River in Texas as early
as 1729, when a map of northern Coahuila not only indicated the settlements of

the *Natagees*, but called the Pecos the *"rio Salado o del Natagee*," or the "Salty River of the Natagees" (Barreiro, 1729). Fr. Santa Ana also noted the Pecos River orientation of the *Natagés*, saying, "Their own country is on the said Rio Salado [Pecos River], where they enter into the jurisdiction of Conchos." (Dunn, 1911: 266)

The close relationship and aspects of shared leadership between the *Natagés* and the Lipans would lead one to logically assume that the *Natagés* were part of the Lipan tribe. However, Fr. Santa Ana believed the *Natagés* to be Mescalero Apaches, explaining to the Viceroy in 1745,

> The body of these *Natagés* comprises in itself the Mescaleros and Salineros Indians, or better, shall I say that they are one and the same Indians with different names which the Spaniards have given them in the various localities *[terreños]* in which they have seen them (Dunn, 1911: 266).

The grouping of the *Natagés* with the Mescalero Apaches, rather than with the Lipan tribe, was echoed by a second priestly observer in 1762. Fr. Diego Ximenez stated,

> The Indians robbing and murdering in Texas are those ones called *Natagés*, Mescaleros, *Pelones*, Faraones, and proper [true] Apaches, who [all] live separated from the *Lipanes* and [who live] to the northeast and west [of the Lipans]. We suspect some from those nations [*Natagés*, Mescaleros, etc.], their followers, and others comprised under the name Apache have intermarried with some *Lipanes* (a custom no longer practiced), [and] it is true that each has preserved some trading [with each other]." (Ximenez, 1763b, 168-169)

Phelipe de Rabago y Teran, the Spanish military commander who assisted Fr. Ximenez in establishing two missions for the Lipans on the upper Nueces River in Texas, also believed the *Natagés* to be part of the Mescalero Apache tribe (Rabago, 1761: 165-166).

The curious note in the Santa Ana letter stating that the *Natagés* "chief man was captain of the *Ypandes*," speaks to a shared leadership between the two tribes. In the same letter, the priest stated that the *Ypandes* were "intimate friends and relatives" of the *Natagés*, indicating unity through marriage and kinship (Dunn, 1911: 266). These unions were made to cement a political alliance but, as noted by Fr. Ximenez, the practice had begun to decline by the mid-eighteenth century. However, the early political alliance of *Natagés* and Lipan Apaches formed the basis for historic Lipan claims of kinship with the Mescalero Apaches, since the *Natagés* were a Mescalero-affiliated group.

II. *Ypandes*

These were Lipan Apaches who, according to Fr. Santa Ana, inhabited central Texas along the upper Colorado River. In the months of June and July, their seasonal migrations took them to the Pecos River. In autumn, they returned to the San Saba and Llano River region to hunt buffalo (Dunn, 1911: 266). Cabello stated that the *Lipanes/Ypandes* began to filter down into areas northwest of San Antonio as early as 1723 (Cabello, 1784: 104). They were accompanied by *Natagés*, with whom they "almost always live united," an indication of the ties between the two groups based on alliance marriages, kinship and shared goals such as robbery (Santa Ana, 1743b, 89-90). Fr. Santa Ana estimated the *Ypandes* and *Natagés* contained a total of 500 warriors, an estimate much too low given more precise population totals obtained two decades later. Given the *Ypande/Lipan* territorial range described by Santa Ana, and the physical landscape of that range, it seems certain that the *Ypandes* were the Plains Lipan division mentioned in the Zuazua history, particularly since their migratory route from the upper Colorado to the Pecos crossed the Edwards Plateau, a region classified as a section of the Great Plains Physiographic Province (Wade, 2003: xix).

III. *Pelones (Bald Ones)*

Fr. Santa Ana described this Apache group as living far from San Antonio, as well as living far from the *Ypandes* and *Natagés*. In 1745, Santa Ana specified the *Pelones* inhabited lands "irrigated" by the Red River, which placed them in north central Texas (Santa Ana, 1743b: 92). These statements were validated in 1763 by Fr. Diego Ximenez, who stated that the *Pelones* Apaches lived to the northeast of the Lipans (Ximenez, 1763b: 168). The location of the large *Pelones ranchería* disclosed by the prisoners taken in the Bustillo attack (1732) was said to be 364 miles from San Antonio, which would place the *ranchería* south of the Red River between Ft. Worth and Wichita Falls, possibly near Bowie, Texas (366 miles from San Antonio). Seven years after Santa Ana wrote his series of letter to the Viceroy, groups of Apaches began to attack the new missions of San Xavier (1746-1755) and San Ildefonso (1749-1755) located along the San Gabriel River in north central Texas (Urrutia, 1750: 2-4). Although the tribal affiliation of the attackers was never stated, it seems likely that the raiders were, or included *Pelones*.

Although able to field more warriors than the other two Apache groups, the *Pelones* were described as less warlike because they had fewer horses. The 800 warriors mentioned by Santa Ana in 1743 would yield a rough group population estimate of 1,600 to 2,400 persons (assuming one wife or one wife + child per warrior). This estimate is close to the *Pelones ranchería* population total given by the Bustillo prisoners (1700 persons in tents pitched in a 10-mile stretch).

The Bustillo evidence clearly equates the *Pelones* with the Lipan tribe. Given the *Pelones* territorial range described by Frs. Santa Ana and Ximenez, it is reasonable to assume that they were the Forest Lipan division mentioned in the Zuazua history, particularly since their habitation area included a unique natural feature of north central Texas called Cross Timbers, two long narrow strips of forest region which begin in the "eastern half of Cooke County [and] extend southward through the eastern parts of Denton, Tarrant and Johnson counties and the western parts of Grayson, Dallas, Ellis and Hill counties" (Cross Timbers, 1996: 421-422). When Morris Opler was told by his Lipan informants in 1935 that the name of their tribe was "People of the Forest," he was probably speaking to *Pelones* descendants of the Forest Lipan division, who inhabited areas of the Texas Cross Timbers in the early 1700's.

By 1760, the *Pelones* no longer appear in Spanish records as a separately named Texas Apache group, leading to the assumption that they had been pushed southward by the Comanches and other "Indians of the North." However, the *Pelones* never merged with the Plains Lipan divisional bands in the eighteenth century. Rather, *Pelones* remnants comprised the Green Mountain and Sun Otter bands who lived to the east and southeast of San Antonio by 1780. Some members of these bands fled the San Antonio area for New Mexico after 1850, under the leadership of Chief *Magoosh*, where they joined with the Mescalero Apaches (Ball, 1988: 267-270). The *Magoosh* group made up the original core of the Lipans living on the Mescalero Reservation by 1900. The pedigree of Opler's *Pelones*-descended informants was verified by James Mooney, who noted that the *Magoosh* group "came from beyond San Antonio— near ocean" (Mooney, 1897b).

A translation of the Spanish term *Pelones (baldheaded ones)* generally indicated a distinctive Indian cultural trait wherein part or all of the hair of the head was purposefully removed, but this application cannot be extended to the type of hairlessness practiced by the *Pelones*, or Forest Lipan division. Many nineteenth century observers noted that Lipan men never cut their hair and wore it over one shoulder in a long braid reaching to the ground. However, Frank Buckelew, a Lipan captive in 1866-1867, stated that Lipan men plucked the hair from their eyebrows and chins daily (Dennis, 1925: 56-57). Since Buckelew also noted that this was an "ancient custom," it seems probable that the appellation *Pelones*, when applied by the Spanish to the Forest Lipans, referred to a face devoid of facial hair.

However, there is one bit of tantalizing evidence which indicates the *Pelones* appellation might have also been applied to the Lipans because of a noticeable genetic trait. Chief *Magoosh*, leader of the core group of *Pelones*-descended Lipans living on the Mescalero Reservation, was bald. Another Lipan explained in an oral history, *Magoosh* "was a great and good leader—and the only bald Apache I ever saw. There were people who thought that he had been scalped, but that wasn't true. Why no hair grew on his head I don't know" (Ball, 1988: 267). A photo of *Magoosh* taken before 1940 shows the chief was bald on the crown of the head, with short, thin wisps of hair on the sides of the scalp (Ball, 1988: 268). This would seem to indicate alopaecia, or baldness of the scalp, and might provide another interpretation of the Spanish name *Pelones*.

Part II

Lipan Apache Culture and Cultural Adaptations, 1700-1900

Chapter 5

Physical Appearance and Manner of Dress

Physical Appearance

The Lipan man presented an imposing sight to outside observers. Maybe it was the way he held his head or narrowed his eyes as if sizing up an opponent, "daring even for the most minute advantages" (Ximenez, 1761a: 27). Or perhaps it was the confidence he projected, a confidence born of his independent spirit. Lipan men were generally "quite tall, between 5 feet 6 inches and 5 feet 9 inches in French measurement [i.e. between 5'10½" and 6'1½" in U.S. measurement]," while the average height of Lipan women was about 5 feet. [1] They were "erect, lithe, well proportioned, graceful in their movements," and in the opinion of Jean Louis Berlandier (1828), "by far the most agile natives in the country" (Ewers, 1969: 129). Their complexion was a dark copper, with their noses being "neither large nor flat" (Ewers, 1969: 129). Lipan women were "much smaller and less perfectly proportioned than the men," but were considered, nonetheless, to be quite pretty with good figures (Hollon and Butler, 1956: 277).

When Fr. Diego Ximenez observed the Lipan Apaches in 1761, he noted a particular custom relating to physical appearance that sprang directly from the meaning of the tribal name itself. The priest stated that Lipan adults "smeared themselves and put white dirt in their hair; instead of powders, the children are usually nude" (Ximenez, 1761a: 27). When the alkalai dirt or paste was applied to dark copper skin, the result was a ghostly, light gray appearance. Restricting the practice to adults would seem to indicate that the wearing of white paste as body adornment was a mark of one's entry into the tribal consensus, the *ndé* or the People. The practice can be seen in the names of some mid-eighteenth century Lipan chiefs. *Cabellos Blanco (White Hairs)* was a chief of the *Pelones Lipanes (Forest Lipan division)* in 1763 and *Pastellanos (The Baker, i.e. covered in flour)* was a Plains Lipan chief of a west Texas band in 1750.

The use of white paste was not universal among all Lipan bands in the eighteenth century. An alternate style can be seen in the name of *Cabellos Colorado (Red Hairs)*, a chief who led a band which inhabited areas southwest of San Antonio in 1738. By the nineteenth century, the use of red or vermillion face paint had become common place for all bands and the tribe generally obtained their face paint through trade or gifts. In 1800, the Spanish at San Antonio were providing almost eighteen pounds of vermillion per month as gifts to the two Lipan bands still inhabiting the area. [2]

It is difficult to discern exactly why white alkalai paste was discarded as body adornment, particularly since it was so closely tied to tribal identity. An evolution of stylistic preference seems to be too simplistic an explanation. However, the color red symbolized warfare and the 1738 appearance of *Cabellos*

Colorado and his red body adornment occurred at a time when the Lipans near San Antonio were growing increasingly hostile prior to an attack on the *villa* in 1745. Perhaps a combination of Spanish military and slaving expeditions in the 1740's, combined with intense pressure from the Comanches and other "Indians of the North" throughout the 1700's, led to a Lipan belief that the tribe existed in a constant state of warfare. Thus, white alkalai paste, which had marked the evolution of a tribal identity in the mid to late 1600's, was discarded for the symbolic red of warfare which characterized tribal experience in the 1700's.

The Lipan face itself was free of eyelashes and eyebrows, as these were removed with tweezers. Both men and women removed facial hair. Berlandier (1828) commented that the "vermillion paint" enhanced their dark copper skin, with the facial "features, otherwise not at all disagreeable . . . disfigured with sundry paintings. . . . I know that they pull out all their facial hair, being particularly careful to remove the eyebrows. Several men I saw had small mustaches, neither very thick nor very long." (Ewers, 1969: 129) Frederick Law Olmstead (1850) reported that "the faces of both sexes are hideously streaked with paint" (Olmstead, 1978: 293). In describing Texas Lipan chief *John Castro*, Olmstead called attention to the "heavy brass rings" hanging from his ears, while "across his face blazed a vermillion streak, including the edge of the eyelids, whose motion had a horrid effect. The eyelashes and eyebrows had, as usual, been pulled." (Olmstead, 1978: 293) Frank Buckelew, captured in 1866 by *Costalites'* band of Mexican Lipans, had his "face and body smeared with Indian paint" once he entered the Lipan camp after his capture (Dennis, 1925: 88). These references make it clear that face and body painting was a custom still practiced by both Texas and Mexican Lipans in the nineteenth century.

Both men and women wore numerous earrings, piercing both ears with long, sharp thorns. Lipan men "had from six to eight holes in [their] left ear and one or more in [their] right ear." (Dennis, 1925: 91) A Lipan warrior "always wore a pair of earrings, and on dress occasions he wore six or eight in his left ear." (Dennis, 1925: 91) Lipan women wore earrings of copper wire and beads in both ears (Dennis, 1925: 91).

Lipan Hair Style

There were two totemic or distinctly representational features used by outsiders to identify the Lipan Apaches: the long hair of the Lipan men and the tribal manner of dress. Although they generally removed all traces of facial hair (except, perhaps, a small mustache), the long hair of a Lipan man was considered his badge of identification to the outside world. It was one of the most readily identifiable physical characteristics differentiating the Lipans from other Texas Indian tribes. The Lipans called a man's plait of hair *ketsài 'rái* and differentiated it from a woman's braid. [3]

Lipan men wore their hair loose or fastened at the nape of the neck.

[S]ometimes [it was] braided and decorated with buckles or placques of silver, but they never cut it. . . . To the hair which nature gave them they add that of others, sometimes their wives', sometimes even horsehair, in order to make a braid that reaches to their knees (Ewers, 1969: 128-129).

Frank Buckelew (1866) also commented on the hair styling of Lipan men.

The Lipan warrior wore his hair cut off on the left side even with the top of his ear; the right side was long, almost reaching the ground when turned loose. They kept it folded up and tied with red strings. When done up in this manner it came to the shoulders. They often put little trinkets in their hair. (Dennis, 1925: 90-91)

The hair style of Lipan women was conditioned upon their age. Young women wore their "long hair loose upon their shoulders, but the old ones are obliged to cut their hair and give it to the warriors" (Ewers, 1969: 129). Buckelew specified that young Lipan women wore their hair in one long braid that hung down their backs, "but on dress occasions it was worn loose" (Dennis, 1925: 91).

Manner of Dress

The second totemic feature used by outsiders to identify the Lipan Apaches was their manner of dress. The basic items of a Lipan man's attire consisted of buckskin pants and shirt, or breech-clout and leggings, worn with knee-high moccasins. Women wore a buckskin blouse, skirt and high moccasins. Both men's and women's attire contained a profusion of fringe, or *hótsa*, and it was this buckskin fringe adornment that outsiders used to differentiate the Lipans from other Texas Indians, as well as from other Apache tribes (Gatschet, 1884: 17). The Lipan passion for fringe even extended to making fringed covers for the barrels of their muskets.

The Zuazua history dated the Lipan adaptation of buckskin for use as clothing as occurring only after the tribe migrated into Texas, tying it to the establishment of a Lipan trade route to New Mexico.

> And first/ Many Houses [San Antonio, TX]/ when they arrived
>   /these/ their clothing/ not/ it was good.
> Not/ they were dressed well/ they said.
> Then right there/ Many Houses/ to there they went about/ it happening so
>   /and then to the mountains [of west Texas or eastern New Mex-
>   ico] /they started back/ it happened.
> And then/ those deer/ they killed them.
> Then those buckskins/ they went back to town with them.
> It even became so/ their clothing/ much they have.
> And then/ very happy they became.
> (Hoijer, 1939a: S54-55, 58-63, 250-256).

Augustina Zuazua also described the fringed buckskin clothing and the process used by Lipan women to make that clothing:

> Long ago/ buffalo/ they killed them.
> Their meat/ they ate it and their hides they tanned them....
> Then deer also/ just those/ the Lipan/ they lived by means of them.
> Then those buckskins/ just those/ the Lipan their clothing [was]
> Then their shoes/ buffalo/ its hide
> They sew with it/ buckskin their shoes.
> The Lipan clothing/ it was fringed.
> Then Lipan men/ just that/ they too/ it being so
>   /their clothing [was] buckskin as were their shoes. . . .
> And then they/ the Lipan women/ deer/ their hides/ they scraped them.
> That stick on which the scraping is done/ they chopping it off/ horse's ribs
>   /they scraped with it.
> Then when they had finished/ brains/ they did so with it [i.e. they smeared
>   the hide with brains to cure it].
> Buckskin/ then/ they pegged it out with it.
> And then when it got dry/ then they scraped/ that they smoothed with it.
> Buckskin then/ they hung it up/ and now they tanned it.
> Then/ they tanning it/ it being finished/ buckskin shirts
>   /they customarily made them so.
> And then now/ fringed/ they customarily made it so.
> In that way/ the Lipan women/ they worked.
> And the men too/ their leggings/ they made them for them
>   (Hoijer, 1939a: S230-239).

The fringed buckskin feature of Lipan clothing was an item of adornment readily noted by Fr. Diego Ximenez (1761), who believed that the fringe was an attractive addition. He also noted the thorough, well-executed tanning process used by Lipan women to produce clean-looking buckskin, supple and buttery to the touch. In fact, the priest described Lipan buckskin using the Spanish word meaning "suede" to indicate the high quality of the tanning process.

> Their dress [costume] is a suede jacket. The sleeves go all the way up to the wrists. At the place where they join the shoulders some have little strands of the same suede hanging, which is very attractive. The pants are made of the same thing; they are joined to the stockings and the sandals, a type of shoe [i.e. moccasins]. All are made of suede. The women wear the jackets loosely. They are sleeveless. They wear suede skirts to the shinbone; some wear them shorter, to the knee. The skirts are decorated with some deer hooves or pieces of deer leather. Their sandals are also made of suede. . . . They dress in suede and they are honestly clean as much as can be expected considering their barbarity. (Ximenez, 1761a: 26-27).

The names of several Lipan bands indicated variation in clothing style within the tribe. The High-beaked Moccasin band and the Little Breech-clout band represented two Lipan groups whose clothing style relative to moccasins and breech-clouts differed from those items worn by other bands. Yet, the late eighteenth century leaders of both bands also bore names reflective of these stylistic differences, so it is possible that the band derived its name from that of the leader. The chief of the High-Beaked Moccasin band was *Zapato Sas (Shoe cut on a bias)* and the leader of the Little Breech-clout band was *Poca Ropa (Few or scant clothes)*.

Descriptions of the Lipan manner of dress in the nineteenth century showed few changes from the previous century. Berlandier commented in 1828,

> Their clothing is generally clean and well made. . . .[E]xtremely well-worked deerskin serves to make all their clothing. The Lipan wear a belt from which he hangs a bit of cloth in front and behind to hide his nakedness. Often a dagger hangs at his belt. A buffalo hide, tanned and decorated with painting, often hieroglyphic, serves him as a cloak. When it is cold the fur side of the mantle is turned inside, while in milder weather it is worn outside.... Lipan women, as far as their clothing is concerned, are the most decent of the natives. A sort of jacket of deerskin, covered with intricate decorations of glass beads, hides the upper part of their bodies. A deerskin skirt falls to the knee. Very long stockings of softly tanned deerskin serve for slippers, as well. The men generally wear only sandals. (Ewers, 1969: 128-129)

The buckskin clothing of Lipan women and children was described by captive Frank Buckelew (1866):

> The squaws took a fully grown doe skin, dressed it until it was as pliant as cloth, while the hair was left on the tail and the dewclaws on the legs. A hole was cut in the center of the hide, the head was put through this and the tail hung down the back. A short skirt made of deer skin came to the knees. Their leggings were fastened to a belt around the waist, and fit the limbs snugly from the hip to the ankle. Their moccasins were made with very high tops and doubled from the knee to the ankle three times; these stayed in place like men's boots. The young squaws were more careful about their dress, and beaded them elaborately. The bottom of their skirt was fringed with beads and on the bottom of this fringe were little tin jingles. On dress occasions they wore a piece of deer skin draped from the waist and reaching to the ankle. This was beaded and had fringe with the little jingles on it, and when they walked there was quite a tinkling noise. The children wore little shirts made of buckskin. There was very little difference in the way the boys and girls dressed until they were nearly grown, when he began to put on the garb of a warrior and she was dressed like a young squaw (Dennis, 1925: 91).

The adornment of clothing and moccasins with beading, called *yó*, was described in the Zuazua history as a gender-specific task (Gatschet, 1884: 17).

> Then these Lipan women/ their own clothes/ beads they sew on them
> /and on their shoes too (Hoijer, 1939a: S218).

Men's shirts could also be adorned with beads. In 1850, Olmstead encountered Chief *John Castro* and noted that the chief wore "a buckskin shirt, decorated profusely with beadwork" (Olmstead, 1978: 293).

In 1761, Fr. Ximenez commented that the Lipans "generally wear some of our clothes which they acquire or steal" (Ximenez, 1761a: 27). Clothing was acquired in order to augment the Lipan wardrobe. Captive Frank Buckelew stated that when a raiding party returned to the Lipan camp after a raid into Bandera County (1867), the "clothing taken in the raid was spread out for distribution among the families of the returning warriors" (Dennis, 1925: 111).

However, the theft of clothing also had a defined purpose in Lipan raiding and warfare. Certain articles of clothing, particularly shirts, were stolen during raids in order that the raiders would have a wardrobe to draw upon when conducting future reconnaissance missions. The oral history of Mexican Lipan *Philemon Venego* (b. 1885) specified that when the Lipans "killed an enemy they used none of the victim's clothing except the ammunition belt (for which they sometimes killed) and the shirt" (Ball, 1988: 269). Lipan raiding and warfare was successful for such a long period of time not only because of their refined ambush techniques, but because they took such pains in the gathering of intelligence before making an ambush, raid, or declaring war. Lipan warriors, dressed as mission Indians, would infiltrate missions and presidios, seeking Spanish military weaknesses. Dressed as Mexican peasants, they would enter small Mexican towns in order to trade stolen horses, or buy guns and ammunition (Schuhardt, 1878a). Dressed as Mexican bandits, they would steal livestock from Anglo ranchers in south Texas. Just as they often changed the appearance of stolen horses by adding "mane extensions" or covering white markings with black paint, they also disguised themselves when stealing the horses (Schuhardt, 1878a). The theft of clothing was an integral part of Lipan economic culture, allowing them to pass unseen through areas where the wearing of buckskin or breech-clout would have drawn unwanted attention, in order that a successful livestock raid could be conducted.

The Lipan acquisition of Spanish shirts was also believed to have been the cause of two terrible smallpox epidemics occurring exactly a century apart. In 1749, Lipan prisoners held at Mission San Antonio de Valero were released as part of the celebration of a Lipan-Spanish peace treaty. When the prisoners returned to their *rancherías*, they wore clothing given to them at the mission. The Lipans believed the clothes, and particularly the shirts, bore traces of disease which spread quickly among the Lipan families as parents were reunited with their children. The majority of the Lipan smallpox victims in 1749 were children (Dolores, 1749b: 118-119). In 1849, another smallpox epidemic raged among the Texas Lipan bands. *Philemon Venego* related,

> Some years after the Alamo the Lipans suffered an epidemic of smallpox. How they got it his people did not know, but they were sure it was from the Mexicans. . . . They suspected that the illness might have been occasioned by their wearing these shirts (Ball, 1988: 269).

Some of the first official Spanish gifts of clothing to the Lipans were made in 1761 by Don Phelipe de Rabago y Teran, who later complained that he had paid out of his own purse for "corn, tobacco, sugar, clothes and hats" given to several Lipan chiefs (Rabago, 1761: 169). These gifts were only the beginning of an outpouring of Spanish clothing largesse, as they sought to cajole the Lipans into entering missions or into signing peace treaties. By 1799, the Lipans developed a ritual that they insisted be performed when they received a gift of clothing as a gesture toward cementing a peace treaty. When three Texas Lipan chiefs rode into Laredo, Texas in June 1799 to sign a peace treaty, they were presented with rich gifts of red cloth trimmed in gold, red hats trimmed in silver ribbons, canes with silver handles, red silk handkerchiefs, and entire wardrobes of shirts, shoes and pants. The Spanish military commander at Laredo, Conde de Sierragorda, informed the Viceroy,

> We should, as well, give [the Lipan chiefs] the *cuenta* (bill, count or tally) according to the custom of these same Lipans and to the three Captains of their nation and those with them. This action [giving the Lipans the gift tally and the acceptance of this action by the Lipan chiefs] is supposed to alert the Viceroy that, with great brevity, they [the Lipans] intend to turn themselves around, preparing to dwell in the clothes [wear the clothes]. As I informed you previously, taking the exact count to them will justify to all that they will be presented with such a count when they walk with us and that they will advise me without danger from the time after being presented with the clothes. (Sierragorda, 1799b: 12-14)

By 1800, a gift of clothing to Lipan chiefs had become a ritualized ceremony, with promises of good behavior conditioned on the formal exchange of the gift tally. The Lipan manner of dress, originally a tribal distinction differentiating the Lipan Apaches from other tribes, did not show much evolution in style over time. Rather, the Lipan use of clothing evolved over time, becoming ritualized in matters of raiding, warfare and peace.

Chapter 6

Lipan Apache Material Culture

Habitation

The Lipans were a people at one with their physical environment and when they viewed the world around them, they saw it in terms of terrain and physical features of the landscape. They migrated from one camp to another throughout the year as they searched for food. "Those Lipan/ their custom/ and in that way they often stopped. Then several days having passed/ to another place they will be moving again. Not long/ camps in one place" (Hoijer, 1939a: S152-159).

Lipan camps were not generally named by the type of food source hunted or gathered at that location, such as "buffalo camp" or "mescal camp." Rather, the Lipans, with their focus on terrain, gave their camp locations names such as "Stone Head Mountain," "Covered Springs" and "Black Rocks that Lie There" (Hoijer, 1939a: 50-56). After accessibility to food source, terrain was a major consideration in the Lipan choice of camp location, as well as playing a role in their choice of dwellings. In fact, one strong argument against grouping the Lipans solely within a Plains Indian culture is their focus on terrain and their use of a dual system of habitation—tepees and *jacales (brush huts)*—which combined elements of a Plains culture with elements of Apache culture more prevalent among the western Apache tribes (John, 1991: 151).

Lipan camps could generally be found on "leafy plains and rivers" (Ugalde, 1781c: 120). They preferred to camp along flowing water sources and in the foothills of mountainous regions. In winter, "they sought the southern slopes of hills. In times of danger, they either camped on high bluffs overlooking a river—strategic spots for observing the movements of the enemy— or fled to hilly country where they could more easily be concealed" (Sjoberg: 1953: 87). The Lipan choice of camp location differed from sites chosen by the Mescaleros. The latter tribe preferred inaccessible mountain regions, where they camped along "ridges and crests, and [where] waters trickle out" (Ugalde, 1781c: 120).

Where terrain made it possible, the Lipans chose to dwell in tepees. The tepees varied in size, with smaller tepees "occupied by only three or four persons; the larger ones, which were usually more numerous, housed ten to twelve individuals" (Sjoberg, 1953: 87). The tepees were "always pitched with the doorway facing east," since east was a sacred direction of the sunrise. Even after exposure to Christianity, the Lipans continued to perform rituals associated with the sun (Ewers, 1969: 134). When the camp was moved, the tepees were dismantled, with the tent hides and tepee poles packed on the backs of horses or mules.

In addition to tepees, the Lipans also constructed or erected brush huts, called *jacales* by the Spanish. [1] These brush huts were erected when the Lipans wished to set up a temporary camp, either because they feared an enemy attack or because they wanted to camp alongside a water source only long enough to plant and grow corn. A Spanish report from a 1778 military campaign against the Lipans along the Pecos River mentioned encountering Lipan *"jacales* and seeds from *milpas (small irrigated plots of land)* which we knew enabled them to live in this spot" (Ugarte, 1775: 264-265). Lipan *jacales* were constructed by cutting a number of small branches or slender poles. The poles were arched over to make a rough frame, which was then held in place with buffalo, cow or horse hides thrown over the top (John: 1991: 151). Fr. Ximenez described the *jacales* as "tents [made from] branches in the form of a dome" (Ximenez, 1761a: 27).

Lipan camps were called *rancherías* by the Spanish and this term was adopted by later Texas settlers. A *ranchería* could contain as few as three or four tepees or as many as several hundred. In many cases, a combination of te-pees and *jacales* were observed in one *ranchería*. In 1788, Juan de Ugalde de-scribed Lipan *rancherías* as being "opulent" (Ugalde, 1788a: 326). A sense of that "opulence" can be gained from the observations of Samuel Henry Starr, serving in the U.S. Army at the Texas frontier post of Ft. Mason. In an 1853 letter to his wife, Starr described a Lipan *ranchería* on the upper Nueces River.

> The property the wealthy tribe of Lipan Indians had . . . was of a very valuable description of Indian goods amounting to more than 80 wagon loads of robes, deer, otter and other fur skins, tents, kitchen and household articles, blankets, billing and pack saddles, women's dresses and trinkets, large stores of corn and provisions, tools, weapons, etc. The Lipan were a very wealthy tribe, half civilized, living in a large village at the head and between the forks of the Nueces River. $10.00 or $12.00 is nearer the mark of the amount destroyed, which latter sum you seem to doubt (Starr, 1853).

Physical environment dictated the way in which the Lipans constructed their tepees, since the areas they inhabited did not contain trees whose limbs could provide long, straight poles capable of producing a sturdy frame that was also easily portable. The Lipans chose to use long poles of yucca or sotol in or-der to produce a strong, yet light-weight frame that was easy to assemble and disassemble. Over this frame of yucca or sotol poles, the Lipan draped and wrapped buffalo, horse or cow hides. Augustina Zuazua described the Lipan process of making a tepee:

> And now then/ those yucca stalks/ their tipis were made by means of them.
> Then those buffalo/ their hides/ having been tanned/ they are tied together.
> Those poles/ having been tied together for it/ their tipis are made by means of it
> The Lipan/ those smoke flaps/ their tipis are so made with them.
> Now the tipi/ it having been made so/ inside/ beds they made them so.
> Branches/ they took them inside.
> In that way/ the Lipan/ their tipis [were made] (Hoijer, 1939a: S79-85).

The interior of the Lipan tepee contained bedding and rugs as well as personal items, clothing and food, which were packed into leather containers (Hoijer, 1939a: S86-88). The Lipan word for bed *(ndé)* was the same word used to indicate the tribal people as a whole (Gatschet, 1884: 15). This bit of symbolic word play indicated that the Lipans were a foundational people (in the sense of the English word "bedrock") who arose to the earth and emerged upon it much as one would arise from a bed (i.e. a point within the circle of the tepee) and emerge into the circle of the camp through the open door of the tepee. Buckelew (1866) described a Lipan bed as being made of "grass or small cedar twigs, piled up two or three inches thick, and over this they spread a hide dressed with the hair on it, allowing the hair to be next to them." (Dennis, 1925: 92-93) An individual would roll up in a blanket and sleep on the dressed hide.

Since the Lipans believed that all life existed within a circle, and a tepee or *jacal* symbolized the circle of life of individual families within the circle of the whole band or tribe, Lipan habitations were viewed as symbols as well as homes. By erecting a tepee with the doorway facing to the east, the Lipans were allowing the sacred to enter the circle of their home, as well as providing a way for sunrise rituals to be performed. The Lipans also performed shamanistic rituals associated with new habitations and erected tepees and *jacales* to be used solely in a ritual context. Fr. Diego Ximenez stated that any new Lipan tepee or *jacal* had to be blessed by a shaman before it could be occupied.

> All of the Indians come together whenever new houses or tents are blessed. The sorcerer [shaman] disguises himself as a bison; he predicts good or bad events that will occur in each of new house or tent. No Christians are permitted near the area where the ceremonies are taking place (Ximenez, 1764: 177).

Tepees and large *jacales* were also erected in order that specific rituals might be conducted in them (Ugalde, 1788a: 323). Buckelew (1866) reported that, in order to celebrate a peace agreement between the Lipans and the Kickapoos, the two tribes jointly constructed a "large brush tabernacle about thirty feet wide and fifty feet long. It was left open at each end, the sides being walled up with brush and twigs." (Dennis: 1925: 105-106) The structure was used for nightly dances to celebrate the peace between the two tribes.

The Lipan tepee changed little in appearance or construction from the eighteenth to the nineteenth centuries. However, as the buffalo herds dwindled, and it became more difficult for the Lipans to obtain buffalo hide to be used as tepee coverings, they increasingly substituted cow, deer or antelope hides when constructing their tepees. After the Civil War, as Lipan contacts with the U.S. Army in Texas increased, they also began to use sail-cloth tenting material, stolen or received from the military, as coverings for their tepee frames.

There is also an interesting change from the eighteenth to the nineteenth centuries in the vocabulary used to describe Lipan dwellings. The vast majority of eighteenth century Spanish sources use the word *tienda (tent)* when describing a Lipan dwelling. There are only two or three instances in which the Spanish used the word *jacal (brush hut)* to describe a Lipan dwelling. This usage would seem to indicate that *jacals* were not commonly observed. By the nineteenth century, while there were still many Lipan tepees observed, more observers began to comment on the Lipan use of the *jacal*, leading to the conclusion that the Lipans reverted to a more general use of the *jacal* as the tribe was pushed into marginal areas by advancing Hispanic and Anglo settlement.

By the end of the nineteenth century, the *jacal* had come to symbolize not only the poverty and reduced state of the Lipan Apaches, but its contents illustrated the adaptation of the Lipans to the material culture of their surroundings. Ethnologist Albert S. Gatschet, who observed these brush hut dwellings at Ft. Griffin, Texas in 1884, recorded his impressions. He noted,

> One half of the Lipan and Tonkawa lodges are of brushwood, mesquite trees bent over forming the framework, the others [dwellings] are of sail cloth tents, or a combination of the two. They are oblong, exposed to wind and rain-floods; the objects seen in them are beds, coppersmith [i.e. copper items], chickens, dogs, turkeys, barrels, bags, saddles, water casks (or pilgrim bottles of tin), metlatls (grinding stones), trunks, women nursing babies, guns, pans, saucer-cups, blankets—nothing aboriginal except the Indians themselves (Gatschet,1884:19).

There had been pressure on the Lipans, since the beginning of Spanish missionary efforts in 1750, to forsake their tepees and *jacales* and move into fixed settlements. The priests had some initial success in converting a few Lipans to Christianity, but they failed to convince them to live permanently in pueblos associated with the missions. In 1764, Fr. Diego Ximenez reported there were over "four hundred Lipan Indians" in camps around the two Lipan missions Ximenez founded along the upper Nueces River of Texas. Ximenez described them as being "restless and seditious. . . . [They] live in the mission part of the time. When they leave the missions it is either to escape from the enemy or to search for food."(Ximenez, 1764: 175). An 1805 census of Indians living at Mission San José (San Antonio) showed only one Lipan resident, an eighty-year widow named *Maria de Jesus* (Mission San José, 1805: 120-123).

The Spanish were somewhat more successful in getting the Lipans to remain camped in one location for a prolonged period of time. A 1784 report stated that the Lipans left their *rancherías* near the mission of San Juan Bautista (Coahuila) on the Rio Grande in order to move forty leagues downriver to a location near Laredo, Texas known as *Piquete*, where they "took shelter for some years . . . with an official subaltern and 25 men endowed by the Colony" (Cabello, 1784: 332). However, the only Spanish attempt at creating a military "reservation" for the Lipans proved to be too expensive and the effort was soon abandoned. Juan Antonio Padilla noted in 1820, "it has not been possible to induce [the Lipans] to live in fixed habitations" (Hatcher, 1919: 56). Berlandier reported in 1828 that Texas Lipan chief *Cuelgas de Castro* said that "he has several times tried to get the scattered *rancherías* to join into villages but that most of the Lipans are unalterably opposed to such a move" (Ewers, 1969: 134). The final attempt to induce the Lipans to abandon their seasonal migrations was made around 1850, when the Governor of Coahuila set aside a Lipan settlement area at Hacienda Patiño, located near the town of Zaragosa, in an "attempt to pacify them and teach them agriculture" (Latorre, 1976: 217). The settlement was temporarily abandoned in 1869 after a Mexican Army attack, although Lipans continued to inhabit the area and returned to the settlement by 1900.

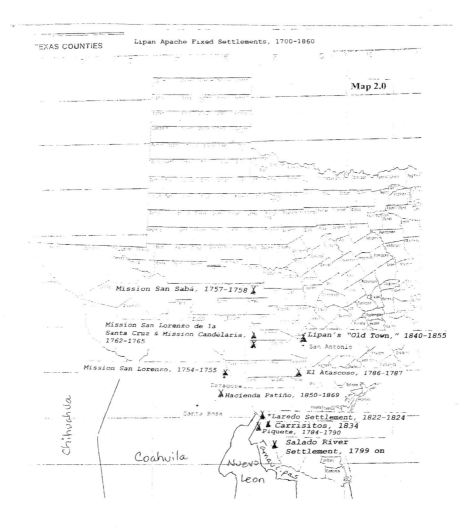

TEXAS COUNTIES   Lipan Apache Fixed Settlements, 1700-1860

Map 2.0

Mission San Sabá, 1757-1758

Mission San Lorenzo de la
Santa Cruz & Mission Candelaria,   Lipan's "Old Town," 1840-1855
1762-1765
                                    San Antonio

Mission San Lorenzo, 1754-1755   El Atascoso, 1786-1787

                         Zaragosa
                         Hacienda Patiño, 1850-1869

Chihuahua   Santa Rosa   *Laredo Settlement, 1822-1824
                                     Carrisitos, 1834
                                    Piquete, 1784-1790
            Coahuila   Salado River
                                     Settlement, 1799 on
                         Nuevo
                         Leon

Horse Trappings

The Lipan Apaches traditionally made their own saddles and stirrups (Hoijer, 1939a: S203-204). Frank Buckelew observed the process in 1866.

> The Indian saddle was . . . made by fitting two forks of hackberry timber to a horse's back, and cutting two flat pieces of the same wood about an inch thick and two inches wide and about two and one half feet long, these were cut to fit on the forks and formed the seat of the saddle. These four pieces were carefully placed together; two pieces of green rawhide, with the hair left on, were cut to fit snugly over it all and securely sewed with buckskin. (Dennis, 1925: 74)

The Lipan Apaches whittled a saddle horn on the front fork, as well as constructing and attaching stirrups "to fit the whole foot" (Dennis, 1925: 74). In addition to rawhide stirrups, the Lipans also used iron stirrups if they could be obtained through trade or theft (Flores, 1723: 3). Saddle blankets were made from soft antelope hide, while bridles, reins and lariat ropes were made of rawhide (Dennis, 1925: 74). Iron horse bits were preferred, but hackamore bridles were used if iron bits were not available.

Offensive Weapons- Bow and arrow

The primary Lipan offensive weapon was the bow and arrow. The construction of these items was a gender-specific task.

> Then right here/ the Lipan men/ arrows/ they made them.
> Feathers/ they feathered arrows with them.
> Bows also/ cow/ its sinews/ bowstrings they made them.
> And then they tightened them/ cow/ its sinews.
> Then now flint/ they ground it/ and then arrow flints/ they made them.
> And then any animals they shot them with it (Hoijer, 1939a: 192-197).

Lipan bows were made of "cedar wood or winter savory sticks" (Ximenez, 1761: 26).

> To strengthen [the bow wood] they cover them with nerves which they remove from the back of the knee of the cattle they kill. With an awl they beat them severely or crack them removing the transversal fibers and leaving those that follow a straight line alone until they are like loose silk. They wet it in their mouths. They begin to arrange them according to the longitude of the bow once they have been moistened with saliva. Afterwards they bind the bow transversally with another [nerve] or leave it attached with a coating of glue which they put on the top. They make the glue with pieces of cattle hides that they cook with deer horns. They test it on their fingers until they judge it strong enough. They make the strings from the same nerves which are twisted and stretched. It must be from a horse or mule because cattle nerves have little resistance (Ximenez, 1761a: 26).

By the nineteenth century, Buckelew noted that the Lipans were using mulberry wood, in lieu of cedar or winter savory. The bows were usually about four feet long. "Some of the bows were made stiff in the middle and had their string near each end, and the ends curved back slightly. Others were made with a uniform curve and spring throughout." (Dennis, 1925: 118) [2]

Lipan arrows were made of cimarron wood (Ximenez, 1761a 26). If cimarron could not be obtained, the Lipan used any "hard, firm wood, which was well-seasoned and always kept in a dry place" (Dennis, 1925: 118). The style of feathering on the arrow shaft showed some change from the eighteenth to the nineteenth centuries, as did the type of projectile point. In 1743, generic "Apache" arrows were described as being feathered "up to the flint" (Santa Ana, 1743a: 65). By 1866, however, the feathering pattern on Lipan arrows had been reduced to "three feathers tied on one end with sinew" and flint projectile points had been replaced with a "spike made of iron, generally barrel hoop iron, cut in the shape of the Indian flint arrow heads, and tied to the arrow with sinew" (Dennis, 1925: 118). Opler reported that Lipan arrows used by adults "for hunting or warfare always bore three feathers. . . . Arrows with one or two feathers were made for children. . . . The Lipan never used an arrow with four feathers." (Opler, 1940: 25)

The Lipan warrior carried his bow and arrows in a quiver made of calf or deerskin which hung by a strap from the left shoulder (Dennis, 1925: 118). It was necessary for the warrior to periodically check the arrows in his quiver to determine whether or not they remained straight. Warriors would take each arrow, "passing them between their teeth biting them at intervals," in order to straighten them "in case they were bent" (Dennis, 1925: 34-35).

The Lipan vocabulary contained a number of nouns and verbs relating to the bow and arrow, indicating the importance of this weapon, so it is not surprising that the arrow itself became a ritualized item. Buckelew commented in 1866 that after the Lipan slaughtered a steer, whose meat they intended to dry and store, "they took their arrows one at a time and carefully passed them through the clotted blood, being very careful that every part was covered." (Dennis, 1925: 57) Buckelew also reported that the Lipans "sometimes poisoned the arrows they used in battle, which if they did not kill a person instantly, the poison would kill the victim in a few days." (Dennis, 1925: 118-119)

Lance and War Club

A second offensive weapon used by the Lipans was the lance. Although eighteenth century Spanish sources mention the Lipans possessing and using the lance from 1743 on, the only descriptions of the weapon come from Buckelew.

[The lance was] a long dangerous looking weapon, made of fine steel, the blade being fastened to a wooden handle with a nice brass ferrule. The lance showed considerable skill and workmanship, but I was never able to learn where or how they got them (Dennis, 1925: 119).

Berlandier (1828) stated that the lance was "usually tipped with the straight blade of a Spanish saber, 2½ feet or so in length, with a shaft 8 or 9 feet long. They adorn it with feathers and various gaudy ornaments." (Ewers, 1969: 130)

There are only three references in early eighteenth century sources to the possible Lipan use of war clubs. In 1743, Fr. Santa Ana noted that generic "Apaches" carried "a kind of pointed hatchet" which must be a reference to a war club (Santa Ana, 1743a: 65). In 1749, Lipan and *Natagés* chiefs in San Antonio used a war club in a peace treaty ritual (Cabello, 1784: 111-112). In 1769, the priests in San Antonio informed the Viceroy, "Those named Apache are considered without a doubt to be the most war-like, using offensive weapons such as arrows, pikes [lances] and 'pounders' [war clubs]" (Béxar, 1769: 89). However, none of these references specifically mentioned the Lipan use of war clubs. No later Lipan chronicler ever mentioned their use and war clubs were not found among the spoils of Lipan camps after military attacks. Early references to Texas Apache war clubs were probably references to *Natagés* weapons.

Firearms

The Spanish provided weapons to many Texas Indian tribes, but they consistently refused to arm the Lipan Apaches because that tribe posed a large threat to the Texas settlements. However, once the French began to arm the Comanches and their Wichita allies in the 1740's, the Lipans began to seek technological parity, eventually developing an elaborate network of alliances with east Texas tribes, who had access to weapons through French traders in Louisiana. In 1749, the Lipans at San Antonio were believed to be ignorant of guns and their use (Cabello, 1784: 113). However, within a decade the situation radically changed, for Fr. Ximenez noted in 1761, "Although the Lipans use arrows, they are skillful with muskets which they acquire from the nations to the north as well as those which they steal from us" (Ximenez, 1761a 26).

The Spanish did provide gifts of firearms to Lipan chiefs who signed peace treaties. (Ramirez, 1778: 13, 34). Yet the guns given as gifts to Lipan chiefs represented only a small fraction of the total number of firearms possessed by the tribe. The Spanish probably would have been shocked had they known the true number.

From 1750 to 1830, the Spanish consistently underestimated the number of Lipan firearms, assuming that the measures they had taken to deprive the tribe of weapons had been successful. Manuel Merino (1804) voiced the general Spanish consensus in 1804.

> Among the Mezcaleros [sic], *Lipiyanes* and *Lipanes* there are some firearms, but because of a lack of ammunition as well as a means of repairing them when necessary, they value them little. They often end up putting them to new uses, making them into lances, knives, arrowheads, and other instruments which they value highly" (John, 1991: 154).

Berlandier (1828) agreed with Merino's assessment, stating that the Lipans "use guns only in special circumstances, but the bow they use continually in hunting and warfare, both offensive and defensive. In their hands, the bow is undoubtedly the most fearfully deadly of weapons." (Ewers, 1969: 130)

As early as 1786, only two decades after the Lipans first began to acquire firearms, the Governor of Texas complained that the Lipans were so well supplied with "powder, bullets and muskets... [that] rare is the Indian among them who does not have two muskets with sufficient powder and bullets." (Cabello, 1786a: 35-36). The lack of ammunition did not deter the Lipans. There is some evidence that the Lipans had learned how to manufacture gunpowder by 1778 (Sjoberg, 1953: 89). In the event that gunpowder was not readily available, the Lipans were not averse to attacking powder stores in towns in order to obtain ammunition. On March 7, 1790, over 200 Lipan warriors attacked Laredo, Texas. Their first act upon entering the town plaza was to "seize [and empty] the warehouse of gunpowder." (Menchaca, 1790: 401-404). The Lipan possession of firearms was much more widespread than the Spanish ever believed and the use of those guns occurred on a more regular basis than the shots fired in "special circumstances" cited by Berlandier.

The Spanish tendency to underestimate the number of guns and ammunition possessed by the Lipan Apaches was a case of purposeful ignorance. In 1775, Pedro Joseph Leal and Carlos Rioja of San Antonio were brought to trial for their "unlawful trade of gunpowder, bullets and French tobacco [selling them] to the Lipan Indians." (Rodriguez, 1775: 26-45). However, the case was eventually dropped for lack of evidence. Unfortunately, the Spanish paid dearly for their assumptions regarding the Lipan possession of firearms.

The wars and revolutions which swirled around the Rio Grande in the early nineteenth century only increased the number of firearms and ammunition available to the Lipan Apaches. Two years after the fall of the Alamo, the new Republic of Texas was giving, as a gift to Lipan chiefs, "3 fine Rifle Guns @$40.00 [each] . . . [and] 19 Cannisters [sic] Rifle Powder @ $2.00 [each]" (Republic of Texas, 1838: 35, 37). The government of Texas might have changed, but a government policy of giving firearms to Lipan chiefs who signed peace treaties had not changed in sixty years. The Lipans always sought to take advantage of political instability and use it to benefit the tribe.

Defensive Weapons- Shield and Armor

The Lipan warrior defended himself with a shield. The only description of the construction of a Lipan shield comes from Lipan captive Frank Buckelew. Shields were made from thick, un-tanned bull hide which was cut in an oval shape, soaked in water and shaped by placing it in a shallow hole to dry. When the hide had dried, it was ready to be made into a shield. Two slits were cut in each side. A loop of buckskin was placed in the slits and drawn together. "Small holes were punched in the edge and a drawstring run through these [which was] drawn up and evenly tied." (Dennis, 1925: 116-117)

Buckelew also described the manner in which the warrior carried his shield.

> When in battle they would run the left arm through the two loops of buck-
> skin inside the shield and hold it between them and their enemy to keep from
> getting shot. When they shot the bow and arrow the whole body was exposed,
> but only for an instant, as they were very quick with this deadly weapon. I have
> seen these shields hung up and men take a rifle and shoot at them, and the bul-
> let would glance off almost every time. The ball had to hit the shield dead cen-
> ter if it went through. (Dennis, 1925: 117)

The shield was large enough for a warrior to crouch behind and generally
remain safe from gunfire during a battle (Dennis, 1925: 117). There are reports
of the Lipans using shields in raids through 1870 (Opler, 1940: 232, 234).

The Lipan warrior did not wear metal body armor. However, Spaniards attacking a *rancheria* (possibly Lipan) along the Colorado River near present-day
Brownwood, Texas in 1723 found horses wearing "buffalo hide armor with
many spots the colors of blue, green, red and white" (Flores, 1723: 3). In 1749,
the Lipans were known to place on their horses "an encumbrance of buffalo hide
which they use as a defense against arrows." (Cabello, 1784: 113) Leather horse
armor does not appear in Lipan mythology, so the style was probably adapted
from the Comanches, whose horses are depicted wearing leather armor in petro-
glyphs dating from 1650-1750 (Mitchell, 2004: 115-126).

While other tribes discarded their horse armor over time, the Lipans continued to use hide skirting on their horses throughout the eighteenth century. In
1788, Juan de Ugalde met with three Texas Lipan chiefs south of San Antonio.
All the chiefs were "armed with muskets and with bows and arrows with plumes
[or tufts of feathers], hides and defensive skirts of hide on their horses giving
them the form of warrior spirits." (Ugalde, 1788b: 349). In view of the thorny
brush of south Texas, the continued Lipan use of leather horse armor made perfect sense.

By the end of the eighteenth century, Spanish cavalry troops along the
northern frontier adapted Lipan horse armor for their own use. In 1772, Spanish
Provincial commanders mandated that frontier cavalrymen use leather leg
guards with vaquero-style saddles (Jackson, 1986: 82-83). However, when the
regulations were enforced, Commander Hugo O'Conor noted that instead of
leather leg guards, the cavalrymen were using "leather side skirts to protect the
legs from thorny brush" (Jackson, 1986: 83). The skirts were tied to the pommel
of the saddle and stretched back to the stirrups on each side of the horse, protect-
ing the horse and the rider's legs. This particular form of saddle and leg guard
adapted by Spanish frontier cavalrymen owed much to their intimate knowledge
of the utility and practicality of Lipan Apache leather horse armor.

Chapter 7

Lipan Apache Economic Culture: Hunting and Gathering

Hunting

The Lipan Apaches were specialized hunters and gatherers who used complex skills and organizational patterns in their collection of meat and plant food items. The Lipan "economy was based on hunting and gathering techniques which required a large and varied territory for the maintenance of the population" and the tribe certainly found a land rich in animals and plant foods once they migrated into Texas (Opler, 1975b: 15).

The primary food source for the Lipans, from their entry into the southern Great Plains until about 1850, was the bison. It was the seasonal migration of the buffalo, as well as locations where buffalo could be found year-round, that defined Lipan habitation patterns. Faint echoes of old Lipan buffalo camps remain in the geography of modern Texas: the town of Lipan near the upper Brazos, Lipan Spring and Lipan Flat along the upper Colorado River, and Lipan Creek between the Brazos and the Colorado. [1] The buffalo inhabiting these areas of Texas migrated seasonally, moving north in April and May and returning south in October "sometimes as far as the neighborhood of Béxar. Large herds of them, it is said, stay the year round on the banks of the Rio Colorado de Texas, as well as along the Rio Guadalupe." (Ohlendorf, 1980: 372-373)

In 1743, Fr. Santa Ana reported that the Lipan Apaches undertook two annual migrations. In the months of June and July, the Plains Lipans or *Ypandes* moved from the upper Colorado to the Pecos. Santa Ana did not specifically state that the Lipans hunted buffalo as they moved west every spring, but he did note that the Lipans hunted buffalo in the fall along the Pedernales, Llano and San Saba Rivers (Dunn, 1911: 266). However, Spanish military commander Pedro de Nava reported a slightly different hunting pattern. De Nava explained that Lipan buffalo hunts were conducted in two seasons of the year.

> From spring through June, the [Lipan] Apaches commit themselves to the north seeking the males.... In November and December is the second hunt for the buffalo that have fled the cold as far as the Rio de San Pedro [Devil's River in southwest Texas] (De Nava, 1791b: 541).

In addition to the buffalo herds found in Texas, buffalo could also be found across the Rio Grande in the northern Mexican provinces of Nuevo Leon and Coahuila. Buffalo herds were noted as early as 1560 in areas that later saw the founding of the provincial capitals of Saltillo and Monterrey, and these herds may have seasonally migrated from the interior toward the Gulf coast and then returned in the fall (Coopwood, 1900: 229-232). Before 1625, Spaniards from Nuevo Leon went into the "department of Coahuila to trade with the Indians, exchanging cotton and woolen textures for skins of *sibolos*, deer and other animals." (Coopwood, 1900: 231) In 1750, soldiers in Coahuila and Nuevo Leon were ordered to take "kettles, load their pack animals with salt, and go out to kill the [buffalo] cows, try out their tallow, dry their meat and dress their skins." (Coopwood, 1900: 232) Because the soldiers were hunting buffalo, they were charged with failure to properly protect the Spanish settlers from Indian attack.

As late as 1830, the Lipans were still able to hunt buffalo along the San Marcos, Guadalupe and Colorado Rivers of central Texas (Ewers, 1969: 131). However, as the buffalo herds in Texas diminished, the Lipans began to cross the Rio Grande to hunt buffalo in northern Mexico. Coahuila, Nuevo Leon and Tamaulipas still contained buffalo in relative abundance as late as 1858 and one "wild" herd of about forty animals still existed in Coahuila as late as 1900 (Coopwood, 1900: 232). The Texas band led by Chief *Cuelgas de Castro* had their primary buffalo camp at *Estacas* (Tamaulipas) where they hunted buffalo until at least 1840. Hispanic settlers in the area reported seeing "a pet buffalo cow [which] Chief *Castro* had trained to follow his saddle animal."(Coopwood, 1900: 231) In Coahuila, as late as 1847, buffalo could be found in abundance in the plains "along the foot of Sierra del Carmen" as well as in the Santa Rosa valley near the town of Melchor Musquiz (Coopwood, 1900: 232).

As the buffalo migrated in spring and fall, so the Lipan hunts were restricted to these seasons in order to entrap the buffalo by taking advantage of the natural movements of the herd. One buffalo trap or fall utilized by the Lipans from at least 1750 on were the cliffs along the banks of Cibolo (Buffalo) Creek near the present-day San Antonio suburb of Selma, where the buffalo were herded over the cliffs in order to kill them. The Lipans were still using the same process as late as 1854, when lawyer William Davenport, who bought land on Cibolo Creek next to a Lipan camp, wrote home to his sister in Virginia,

> Just yesterday I went with Mr. Castro [i.e. Lipan chief *Castro*] and some other apache [sic] gentlemen to hunt.... The cliffs here are white with caves in them. I watched in surprise as the apache [sic] men ran the buffaloe [sic] over the side of the cliff to fall on the rocks below. I went with them and they gave me and Nancy a half bull to smoke for the winter (Castro Romero, 1996).

Where the geography of the region did not contain natural features that could be used to trap the buffalo, the Lipans conducted a mounted buffalo hunt known as a *carneada*. Fr. Diego Ximenez described these mounted hunts in his notes and letters written from 1761 to 1764. Preparations for the hunt began with shamanic consultation. The shaman would invoke, through "incense" and tobacco smoke, the power of an effigy representing a spirit deity. The Crow was the primary Lipan mythological figure associated with the buffalo hunt (Opler, 1940: 123-124). Once power was invoked, the effigy would "speak" to the shaman, informing him as to "where the bison can be found" (Ximenez, 1764: 176-177). Once this information was given, word was spread among several different bands via a crier, or *tatolero* (Ewers, 1969: 134). Several bands would then gather together and move to the propitious location. The men would prepare for the hunt, "taking their leave well armed and well mounted, leaving their families [at the main camp] entrusted to the old men" (Ximenez, 1761a 26-27). As the men approached the bison herd, the hunt leader (a man specially chosen for the occasion) would order the men to split up into smaller groups, each with its own leader. The smaller groups would surround the herd and advance simultaneously from all sides, shooting at the buffalo with bows, arrows, and muskets, or throwing lances. The hunters were usually mounted on horses, and those Lipans not mounted were assisted by those on horseback (Ximenez, 1761a 26-27). Manuel Merino (1804) noted that a Lipan *carneada* took "time and defensive measures, because they will carry it out in lands adjacent to enemy nations," so, added to the excitement of the hunt was an element of risk and tribal vulnerability that raised the stakes each time the Lipans gathered together in large numbers to procure their main food source (John, 1991: 153).

By the end of the eighteenth century, as the buffalo herds in Texas and northern Mexico dwindled, the Spanish made several efforts to teach the Lipans how to conserve their primary meat supply. In 1781, Juan de Ugalde wrote, "the Lipan eat buffalo, and as a consequence we have succeeded with some of them in getting them to conserve more and the breed has grown in those spots where they have been assisted." (Ugalde, 1781c: 120).

Although the Lipan process of hunting buffalo changed little from the eighteenth to the nineteenth centuries, the shamanistic ritual attached to the hunt did change over time. As exposure to Christian missionaries increased after 1760, the Lipan use of an effigy to invoke spiritual power prior to the hunt was discarded, although the use of tobacco smoke to invoke supernatural power and the process of shamanistic prediction attached to the buffalo hunt continued. However, the ritualistic symbolism of the Lipan buffalo hunt was extended and applied to other areas of shamanistic practice. In January 1799, Lipan chief *Chiquito*, during peace negotiations with Conde de Sierragorda, remarked, "because all the Lipan *rancherias* suffered from smallpox, they found it very necessary that they be precise when hunting buffalo" (Sierragorda, 1799a: 199). The Lipans continued to believe that a strict adherence to rituals associated with the buffalo hunt could invoke strong supernatural Power.

After the bison, the deer ranked second as a Lipan source for meat and hides. Deer were generally hunted by small groups of men or lone individuals who tracked the animals on horseback. Once a herd of deer was sighted, the men dismounted and silently approached the animals. Although deer hunting was generally a small group endeavor, one 1779 Spanish source reported over 1,000 Lipans from several bands hunting deer on the Texas coastal plains (Cabello, 1779b: 528-529). Lipan ritual attached to the deer hunt mirrored rituals used by other Apache tribes. The Lipan hunter was always careful to "leave the eye and something from between the ribs for Crow," the mythic guardian of the hunt (Opler, 1940: 125).

The third most common Lipan source of meat and hide was the antelope. These animals were "sought, especially for their skins" (Sjoberg, 1953: 82). The hunting technique employed to kill large numbers of antelope was to surround the herd. Buckelew participated in such a hunt in 1866. After surrounding the herd, riders would "slowly close in on them, riding in a circle and each time making the circle smaller, firing a volley of arrows" (Dennis, 1925: 99).

The Lipan meat diet also included a variety of animals and birds inhabiting Texas and northern Mexico and differed in several important respects from the diet of other Apache tribes. The Zuazua history mentions the tribe eating wild pig *(javelina)*, turtles, mountain sheep, quail, rabbits, turkey, wild pigeons and even rats (Hoijer, 1939a: S76-77, 198, 240). Buckelew (1866) observed that the Mexican Lipans did not like to eat duck, but the Zuazua history stated that the Lipans did eat duck meat, so it seems there was variation in meat preferences among different Lipan bands (Dennis, 1925: 95 and Hoijer, 1939a: S100). Other Apache tribes did not eat fish, but the Lipans, although they did not catch fish, were not averse to eating fish that had washed up on shore of the Texas Gulf coast after a storm (Opler, 1940: 283).

Perhaps the most striking dietary difference between the Lipans and other Apache tribes was the Lipan consumption of bear meat (Hoijer, 1939a: S74-75). Lipan chief *Xavier* boasted to Juan de Ugalde in 1781 that the region of Coahuila in which he located his band's *ranchería* "was spacious enough to enclose buffalo, much deer and bear to eat" (Ugalde, 1781e: 144). Other Apache tribes, particularly the Chiricahuas and the Mescaleros, considered bear meat to be taboo since they had a supernatural fear of the animal (Opler, 1940: 70). On the other hand, the Lipans had no supernatural fear of the bear and attached no strictures to the eating of bear meat or the use of bear pelts (Opler, 1940: 70).

Gathering

The Lipans gathered and processed many of the same plant foods gathered by other Apache tribes, particularly the Chiricahuas and the Mescalero Apaches. Gathering was a gender-specific task, where Lipan women searched for plant foods whose perennial nature ensured their continuing availability year after year. To state the precept with a Lipan turn of phrase, "On the mountains, everything, that which grows again and again, that they eat it." (Hoijer 1939a: S159). The Zuazua history listed a wide variety of cactus species *(Opuntia)*, cactus fruit or tuna, yucca *(Y. aloifolia and Y. gloriosa)*, mescal *(Agave)*, tule, palm and mesquite beans *(G. Prosopis)* which supplemented the meat in the Lipan diet (Hoijer 1939a: S65-70, 72).

Flavoring and seasoning of food was provided by mountain chilies, as well as by wild onions, which were collected and thrown into the cooking pot with boiled meat in order to add flavor. Wild grapes were gathered in the Texas Hill Country (Hoijer 1939a: S71). Honey was procured from wild bee hives and boiled to use as a sweetener, although the risks attendant in gathering the honey were sometimes great, as the hives were generally found in high caves or tall trees (Dennis, 1925: 72). After the Lipans began trading with the Spanish, one favored trade item was raw, unrefined sugar, or *piloncillo*, which was mounded into a cone and was similar in texture and color to the brown sugar of today.

Once the flavorings and seasonings were gathered, they were added to meat which was boiled in metal cooking pots over a fire *(kó)* (Gatschet, 1884: 50). As early as 1743, Fr. Santa Ana noted that the Lipans had "iron pots, frying pans and other vessels of different metals" that he assumed had been "traded for with other Europeans." (Santa Ana 1743a: 68) The Lipans generally ate only twice a day since "noon is too hot for them to cook" (Gatschet 1884: 69). Cooking fires were started with a fire stick, described by Buckelew as a stick similar to a broom handle about three feet in length.

> It had a small hole about the center of its length with a notch cut in the side of the hole. Placing this on the ground, holding it in place with [the] feet, [the Lipan man] took another stick about the size and length of an arrow, placed the end of it in the hole in the large stick, and began turning the small upright stick rapidly between his hands, gradually lowering his hands and bearing down on the stick. This produced a fine wood dust, which worked out of the hole and down the little groove or notch onto a dry leaf. This dust, which became more and more heated as the turning was continued, was soon smoking and readily fanned into a flame (Dennis, 1925: 34).

Lipan women used basket-weaving and carving skills in order to make containers for the collection of the many plant food items eaten by the tribe. The Zuazua history described the process used by these women to create food containers, emphasizing the creativity necessary to produce a pleasing basket.

> And/ baskets/ they wove them.
> They/ their minds/ they work with them/ and then they search for
>   [food] with them.
> Anything that grows/ then these flat baskets that are sewn
> That yucca that has just ripened/ with its leaves [they gathered]
> And wooden bowls [they also used] (Hoijer, 1939a: S214-217).

Food was also collected and stored in cowhide containers—"a little pack they called it. It was decorated" (Hoijer 1939a: 87-88).

Water was carried or stored in two different types of containers. Buckelew mentioned seeing Lipan warriors wearing a water bag made of beef stomach. "This was closed at the top by means of a draw-string of buckskin and was usually fastened to the belt, so as to hang on the left hip. The water oozing from this sack, kept this hip always wet." (Dennis, 1925: 43) Women also made a larger water container by weaving small limbs together into the shape of a jug and coating the entire jug with resin or pitch so as to waterproof it.

The mouth of this jug was large enough to admit a squaw's hand. After woven [sic] and shaping it to their liking, it was pitched inside and out with rosin. A rawhide strap was run through a loop on one side, under the bottom and up through a loop on the other side. The straps were drawn over the shoulders and held tightly in each hand, the weight resting on the back and hips. This jug held five or six gallons of water and was quite heavy. The old squaws were often swaybacked from carrying such heavy loads (Dennis, 1925: 116).

Although the Lipans migrated through areas containing clay that could be used to make pottery, the Lipan Apaches were not pottery-makers. A 1962 archeological excavation of the Lipan missions along the upper Nueces River yielded only one nonwheel-made earthenware pot that the excavators felt might have been made or used by the Lipans in the 1760's (Tunnell and Newcomb, 1969: 79).

The Lipans used a specialized process to prepare many plant food items for consumption. Although the Apache method of processing mescal *(Agave)* has been well documented, the Zuazua history also detailed the specialized methods used by the Lipans for processing cactus, yucca and mesquite stems and beans.

> The Lipan then/ a cactus species/ they often baked it.
> One day having passed with it [after baking for one day]/ they take it out.
> And then they pounded it.
> And then it being molded into cakes/ that hard/ it having been dried/ they
>   eat it.
> Yucca also/dried into cakes/ it being so then that winter having come they
>   eat it
> Then from here on/ mesquite/ they usually pounded it into a powder.
> Then its fruit also/ they boiled it.
> And then/ just coffee/ it is like it.
> No sugar there was/ put in it/ but very/ it is good.
> Then its stalk/ just flour it was like.
> Its stalk/ they pounded it/ they squeezed [water] out of it and then just
>   flour/ it was like.
> And then fat/ they fried it with it/ and very/ it is good
>   (Hoijer, 1939a: S160-164, 174-185).

The Lipan method of processing mescal *(Agave)* was the same method used by many other Apache tribes, particularly the Mescalero Apaches, whose use of the *Agave* plant gave that tribe its name. When the mescal ripened in the late spring or early summer, the Lipan would dig out the bulbs of the plants, chopping off the leaves and stalks. They would then build a fire pit ten to twelve feet in diameter, line it with stones and prepare the mescal for baking. The baking process took two days, after which the baked mescal was removed from the pit, pounded and dried. "Then good it becoming/ [into] bundles they tied it/ with them." (Hoijer, 1939a: S173).

Frank Buckelew described the Lipans using the same oven-baked process to cook sotol bulbs *(Dasylirion wheeleri)*, which were then pounded into a thin sheet and dried. The dried sotol paste was then worked in a wooden bowl until it reached the consistency of flour; the sotol flour was then mixed with water and made into cakes which were cooked in the ashes of the fire. He pronounced the sotol cakes a "very good substitute for bread" (Dennis, 1925: 97-98).

The Lipan gathering of plant foods required the entire band to migrate in the early spring and summer to areas containing abundant quantities of cactus, mescal, mesquite and fruits. While these gathering activities were generally carried out by the women of a single band, the cactus tuna and mesquite bean "harvest" in June and July could also become a communal activity involving several bands (Rabago, 1761: 166). The harvest was accompanied by ritual dances done prior to leaving the camp (Lasaga, 1784: 272-273).

Plant food source areas within Texas were generally confined to west, southwest and south Texas, although wild grapes, mulberries, juniper berries, cedar berries and wild plums could also be found in central Texas. Plant food source areas could also be found throughout Coahuila and Nuevo Leon, and the migratory route of many bands took them back and forth across the Rio Grande River. However, many of the plant foods gathered and eaten by the Lipans ripened in the spring and early summer. At precisely the same time, the same areas of south Texas and northern Mexico generally received heavy rainfall, causing the Rio Grande River to flood. The most striking adaptation to this seasonal problem, and the unusual tool developed by the Lipans in order to facilitate the gathering of plant foods on either side of the Rio Grande, was the construction and use of a boat in order to cross the Rio Grande when in flood.

> Then [the Lipan] spoke so/ the Rio Grande Valley/ that water
> /there being much/ there is a flood.
> Cow/ its hide/ boats/ it having been made/ that cow hide/ its edge
> /they strung it/ with a rope.
> And the boat/ inside it/ sticks/ they laid them parallel.
> And now to the water/ the Rio Grande/ to the other side/ the boat
> /they took it out
> That over there/ some fruit/ therefore/ they now/ that fruit/ baskets
> /they picked it into them/ the fruit.
> And then the boat/ they put it into it/ and then
> /they usually put it into the water with it/ the boat.
> Then now they swam with it/ the rope/ it being stretched with it.
> The rope/ he holding it in his mouth/ he swam with it to where his camp
> was.
> Those Lipan/ in this way/ they worked.
> In that way they lived by means of it (Hoijer, 1939a: S263-272).

The Lipans were the only Apache tribe known to construct and use boats, although hides stretched over a bowl-like frame were used as boats by other Plains Indians. However, the Lipan boat of drawn-up cowhide and a slatted bottom was more sophisticated than the primitive Plains coracles. While Lipan boat-building might have been a Plains adaptation, the skill was more probably learned from observing the Spanish. Regardless of source, however, the Lipan utilization of boat-building skills in order to expand their food-gathering territory was a practical solution to an economic problem.

Mesteños and Domesticated Animals

The presence of herds of wild horses and cattle (*mesteño* herds) in Texas and northern Mexico presented the Lipans with a challenge and an opportunity to develop new skills and management techniques in order to utilize these resources. The Spanish word *mesteño* indicated an animal which was "stray, unbranded and ownerless," and could refer to either horses or cattle or both. (Jackson, 1986: 10) The sheer numbers of these animals, particularly wild horses or mustangs, was commented upon by many early Texas observers (Jackson, 1986: 595-596). From 1740 to 1778, the Spanish did not object if the Lipans butchered wild cattle or caught wild horses, as the animals were ownerless, living in a wild state, and therefore could technically be claimed by anyone brave enough to sling a rope around the neck of a wild mustang or attempt to pen wild cattle. If the Lipans had wished to supplement their food supply in a manner tacitly sanctioned by the Spanish, they could have hunted and captured animals from the *mesteño* herds. However, whether the capture of wild horses and the hunting of wild cattle was an easily accomplished task was another matter entirely.

The south Texas missions had been conducting annual cattle hunts since their foundation, but "the cattle fled hunting parties and turned even wilder, becoming more widely scattered than before. The more slaughters, the smarter the herds became at evading them." (Jackson, 1986: 44) As the cattle scattered into the south Texas brush country, even hunters as accomplished as the Lipans found it difficult to find them. The Lipans could not use the round-up techniques used on antelope and buffalo, as the feral cattle stubbornly remained inside the dense brush and could not be driven out onto the plains where they could be surrounded.

The techniques used by the Lipans to hunt wild cattle were probably an adaptation of Lipan deer-hunting techniques coupled with techniques learned from watching Spanish hide-and-tallow expeditions. The cattle would be rousted from dense brush by beaters on foot and on horseback, who would attempt to run the cattle out into an open area where they could be killed. But as anyone who has worked cattle in dense brush can tell you, trying to get large numbers of cattle out of the brush is very difficult. Only a few head at a time could be driven out of the brush and killed. The carcasses were then butchered on the spot and the hides, meat and tallow were packed into containers to be carried back to camp.

This forced the Lipans to hunt cattle much as they hunted deer, either singly or in small groups, but this approach lessened the number of animals that could be killed on each hunting trip. It was much easier to steal domesticated cattle, risking discovery and retaliation, than it was to pry a stubborn cow and calf from inside the black brush of south Texas. Once domesticated cattle were stolen, if they were not immediately slaughtered for meat, the Lipans would occasionally pasture them near their camps where the cattle were kept in a common herd and considered the property of the band as a whole (Dennis, 1925: 89).

The Lipans were more successful in capturing wild horses, but once caught, the animals still had to be tamed before they could be ridden and that process took time. Since the Lipans did not camp at one location for extended periods of time in many cases, enabling them to both catch wild mustangs and break them to a saddle, the tribe did not fully utilize this resource to supply all the horses needed by each band, finding it much easier to steal domesticated horses. Nonetheless, contemporary accounts indicate that the Lipans were well-known for their ability to catch and tame wild horses from the vast *mesteño* herds. Berlandier (1828) acknowledged, "[The Lipans] are excellent horsemen, and with great talent for breaking and training wild horses. They hunt wild horses, which Nature gives them in abundance." (Ewers, 1969: 156 and Ohlendorf, 1980: 542)

Although the Lipans viewed possession of large numbers of horses as a sign of wealth, they tended to value quality over quantity. Lipan mythology contains hints that the tribe bred horses, although probably not to the extent practiced by other tribes such as the Comanches (Opler, 1940: 77-78). A Lipan horse myth outlined the typical thought process involved in their decision to hunt wild mustangs. "One time they saw a bunch of [wild] horses out on the plain. They had been having a hard time getting horses lately. They came together and said, 'Let's try to get those wild horses in that big herd.'" (Opler, 1940: 75) In other words, the Lipans turned to the *mesteño* herds only when they were unable to steal enough domesticated horses. This same myth also outlined the typical Lipan preference for quality over quantity. "The Lipan wanted to get that particular bunch, although there were plenty of horses around, because there were many good ones in it." (Opler, 1940: 75) Once the wild mustangs were roped and captured, they were taken back to camp. During the day, Lipan horse herds were allowed to mingle together, where they were generally tended by young boys, often white or Hispanic captives. Both Frank Buckelew and Jeff Smith were assigned this task during the period of their captivity (Dennis, 1925: 94; Smith and Hunter, 2005:188). At night, "each warrior's personal herd of horses and mules was separated." (Sjoberg, 1953: 83-84)

The Lipans were somewhat successful in depleting *mesteño* cattle herds through slaughter by the end of the eighteenth century, although blame (or credit) for the round-up of the largest numbers of wild cattle must be laid at the feet of small Hispanic ranchers, who began their ranching venture with a few head and increased their herds by capturing and penning *mesteño* cattle, resulting in a burgeoning cattle industry in Texas and northern Mexico. However, it was easier to blame the Lipans for the declining numbers of *mesteño* cattle, since a Proclamation of 1778 claimed *mesteño* animals as property of the King of Spain and used their capture as a means of taxation (Jackson, 1986: 156). If a small rancher wanted to round up *mesteño* cattle over and above the number of head already claimed by 1778, a license was required as well as payment of a fee for each wild cow or horse taken. The fees collected were allotted to a *Mesteñas* or Mustang Fund, which was earmarked for use in buying the freedom of captives and the pacification of the Indians (Jackson, 1986: 157).

The 1778 Regulation did not specifically address the Indian capture and use of *mesteño* animals, but later bureaucrats interpreted the Regulations as extending a right to the use of *mesteño* animals by tribes who were willing to sign peace treaties. The 1822 treaty negotiated by Anastacio Bustamante with Texas Lipan chiefs *Cuelgas de Castro* and *Poca Ropa* contained language typical of the later Spanish interpretation of the *Mesteño* law as it applied to the Lipan Apaches. Article 6 of the treaty stated, "There will be no impediment to the hunting and chasing of wild cattle and horses that are collected, returning the lost ones [i.e. branded stock] to their owners, who will pay for them." (Bustamante, 1822) The Bustamante treaty also stated that "the government will give land and water so they [the Lipans] can plant and raise horses," but that promise was never fulfilled (Bustamante, 1822). A 1791 peace treaty negotiated by Pedro de Nava with Lipan chiefs *José Antonio, Malave, el Valazo* and *Ayatinde* is of interest because of the Lipan response to the Spanish extension of the right of capture of *mesteño* animals, along with the Spanish stipulations placed on that right of capture. Article 10 of the treaty stated,

> [T]hat when chasing *Mesteñas* [in this instance, the word referred to wild cattle], the Lipans will return the beasts that limp from a known brand belonging to Spanish troops, settlers or mission Indians, to the satisfaction of Sgt. Joaquin Gutierrez, or to another who, on our part, we designate (De Nava, 1791a: 527).

The Lipan response to this article was the following statement:

> Ten of the branded beasts in the corrals have been handed over to their owners, however, those [cattle] that are in the field, we will rope and keep them, to satisfy ourselves for the work involved [in catching them], which causes maltreatment to our horses (De Nava, 1791a: 527).

The capture or slaughter of wild *mesteños* made up a segment of the Lipan trade economy, but it was the theft and trade of domesticated animals, particularly horses, that composed the bulk of the illicit or secondary Lipan economy. The methods of theft and concealment of stolen horses were varied and ingenious, providing the Lipans with highly valued trade items such as horses and mules which could be traded for guns and ammunition; in early Spanish Texas, a mule was worth more than a horse. The Lipan shadow trade of horses for guns had been noted by the Spanish in Texas as early as 1749, and later commentators from the nineteenth century noted that the Lipan illicit trade continued. Juan Antonio Padilla stated in 1820 that the Lipans "sell horses and mules which they take in their round-ups," indicating the Lipan use of the *mesteño* herds (Hatcher, 1919: 56). However, Berlandier noted in 1828 that the Lipan horse trade went far beyond those wild animals they were able to rope or pen. He described the Lipan method of horse theft, passing off tamed horses as *mesteño* animals through alteration of the brand:

> The warlike and ferocious Lipan tribe, then at peace, was found encamped [between the lower Nueces River and Matamoros, Mexico].... They were there in search of wild horses, which were not lacking, and which travelers and the inhabitants of the ranchos of that region go to buy from them. In these wilderness regions a large number of domestic horses frequently run away from the dwellings or leave travelers afoot on the road. When the Lipans encounter animals with a known brand, they efface it and put on the one which the authorities have given them for their use. That pernicious custom, which is tolerated, leads them to commit a large number of thefts for which it is impossible to punish them, even upon encountering the *corpus delicti* in their hands. When they lack horses they steal from the herds of the inhabitants of the countryside. After the brands have been replaced by Lipan markings, these animals pass as having been caught as wild horses. Despite the just demands of the plaintiff, he cannot obtain his property, nor is the guilty one ever punished (Ohlendorf, 1980: 544).

After 1778, Spanish authorities issued a livestock brand to the Lipan Apaches, as well as to three other Texas Indian tribes who hunted wild *mesteño* horses. Quick to seize a golden opportunity, the Lipans were soon altering the brands of stolen animals by "burning the owner's brand with gunpowder or [the] use of a branding iron," changing the original brand to one resembling the Lipan "Arrow P" (Ewers, 1972: 6).

**Figure 7.0   Livestock Brands issued to the Lipans, Comanches,
Tancagues (Tonkawas) and Tahuacanos (Wichitas), ca. 1788-1828**

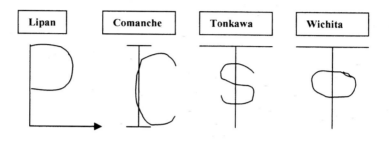

| Lipan | Comanche | Tonkawa | Wichita |

(Source: Livestock Brands, 1788-1828)

If Texans decried the Lipan theft of horses, they also utilized Lipan talent with horses. In 1810, four young Lipan men were employed on ranches near the old mission of Espiritu Santo (near present-day Goliad, Texas). Their job was to break horses, both *mesteño* animals and colts from domesticated herds (la Bahía, 1810). The techniques used by men such as these were adopted by later Mexican *vaqueros*, who then exhibited their skills as "bronc-busters" in a *charreada*, precursor to a modern-day rodeo. Thus, the actions of the Lipan wild horse tamers became immortalized in American culture.

Chapter 8

Lipan Apache Economic Culture: The Shadow Trade Economy

A strong argument can be made that without the constant, defining trauma of Comanche aggression after 1700, the Lipans would have, over time, followed the same pattern of economic system development seen with the Ollero band of Jicarilla Apaches, who moved away from a system of hunting and gathering toward a more intensive use of agriculture (Tiller, 1992: 26-27). Certainly, the environment found in Texas and northern Mexico would have allowed the Lipans such an adaptation. While still on the Great Plains, the Lipans practiced limited agriculture, using the produce of haphazard planting as a supplement to their hunting and gathering. As they moved into Texas, the Lipans found an environment rich in plants and animals, although these resources were widely dispersed. Lipan contacts with the Spanish at San Antonio after 1732 brought them increased knowledge of corn-growing techniques necessary to increase the tribal use of agriculture, allowing for an evolution from a supplementary use toward a primary basis of subsistence. Their early organization into two large, rather loosely organized divisions meant there was a high population density within each group. By 1750, all the elements were present for a slow transition of the Lipan economy from a primary pattern of migratory hunting and gathering toward a more settled agricultural pattern.

The Lipan propensity for agriculture was noted by a number of observers. José Francisco Ruíz (1828) noted,

> The Lipan do seem to have a disposition toward cultivating the soil. Between 1816 and 1823, while at peace with the Comanches, I observed that the Lipans grew corn, watermelon and squash along the Llanos, Cavereras, Guadalupe and other rivers (Ewers, 1972: 7).

Berlandier (1828) echoed Ruíz' assessment, stating that the Lipans had a "bent for agriculture" which was particularly visible at "the principal farm, known as the *Labor de los Lipanes*, the Lipan's Field," located near the headwaters of the Guadalupe River (Ewers, 1969: 132). Both Ruíz and Berlandier recommended that the Lipans be given farm implements and protected lands set aside for their agricultural use as a means of curbing Lipan raiding.

The defining moment with the greatest historical impact on Lipan economic culture was the arrival of the Comanches in Texas around 1700. Within fifty years, these aggressive newcomers pushed the Lipans out of the Red River basin, circumscribed Lipan territory and forced them out of the high Plains. The two large Lipan divisions splintered into at least ten smaller bands and the Lipan population was widely dispersed. In 1732, Lipan Apaches could be found on the Brazos and upper Colorado Rivers. By 1800, Lipan territory had been restricted to areas south and west of San Antonio.

In essence, the Comanche threat froze the slow trend of Lipan economic adaptation toward a more intensive use of agriculture. The Lipans soon found that camping at one location long enough to plant and harvest a crop made them dangerously vulnerable to Comanche attack. The Lipan propensity toward agriculture was a liability in their war with the Comanches, since many of their camp locations were conditioned on agricultural use and were near fertile river bottoms, rather than inaccessible locations necessary for tribal security (Stogner, 1998: 26-27). As the Comanches continued to aggressively push the Lipans ever southward over a half century from 1700 to 1780, the Lipan Apaches were rapidly forced to adapt to new circumstances and the economic adaptations already in progress, such as the increased use of agriculture to supplement food sources, were sidetracked.

Throughout the eighteenth century, as the Lipans were pushed into ever more marginal areas by continued Comanche threat and expanded Spanish presence in Texas and northern Mexico, the herds of buffalo which provided the primary Lipan food source were dwindling. As attacks and epidemics took their toll on Lipan population numbers, it became increasingly difficult for the Lipans to mount a sufficient number of warriors to hunt buffalo as well as provide security to the women and children remaining in camp. The rapid loss of territory to the Comanches after 1700 forced the Lipan economy to remain an economy of hunters and gatherers, as well as forcing them, in their reduced territories, to redirect their search for supplemental food supplies away from a trend toward an increased use of agriculture.

The arrival of the Spanish in central Texas by 1720 initially seemed to provide an answer to the problems facing the Lipan Apaches, providing a powerful protector who possessed greater technology than the Comanches as well as a local trading partner who possessed many desirable items. The Lipans were probably among the generic "Apaches" trading at the Pecos Pueblo of New Mexico in the late seventeenth century, obtaining sugar, cornmeal, *frijole* beans, knives, horse bits and iron stirrups (Flores, 1723: 3). However, a new Spanish trading partner located in south central Texas was welcomed by the Lipans, since they would not have to risk exposure to Comanche attacks as they crossed the plains to New Mexico. The first recorded trade contact between the Lipans and the Spanish at San Antonio occurred in 1733, as small groups of Lipans began to bring buffalo meat, deer skins and salt to the presidio to trade for tobacco (Basterra, 1738: 17-18). The salt was likely obtained from other Texas Indian tribes or from saline deposits along the Pecos River (Wade, 2003: 97).

Yet even as the Lipans were trading hides for tobacco, they were also stealing horses from the Spanish at San Antonio. The first thefts were probably born out of simple greed, as the Lipans merely extended their raiding culture, honed by a decade of attacks on Jumano and Tejas horse herds, to the new Spanish settlement. But military reprisals, slaving expeditions and the Spanish refusal to release Lipan hostages in a timely manner hardened Lipan attitudes. The level of theft grew and what had begun as an extension of ancient raiding culture grew into an organized enterprise. Successful raids brought the Lipans more animals than they needed to fill their immediate needs, while other Texas and Mexican Indian tribes possessed desirable trade items. A thriving trade economy based on the use of force was soon born.

Lipan raids on Texas presidios and missions might have remained at a constant low level of irritation but for one crucial development. As soon as the Comanches established an alliance with the Wichitas of northeast Texas (1740-1750), and as soon as French traders along the Red River began to supply the Comanches and Wichitas with muskets and gunpowder, the Lipan Apaches were forced to devise a strategy which would bring them the weapons they needed to answer their enemies in equal measure on the battlefield. The threat represented by the Comanche presence in Texas was the seed of the Lipan shadow trade economy. That seed was germinated when the first Comanche received a musket from a French trader. The Lipans needed guns but the Spanish were unwilling to supply them, so the Lipans developed a trade economy with east Texas tribes who were also being supplied with guns by French traders in Louisiana (Dolores, 1749a: 117). The east Texas tribes wanted horses and beef; the Spanish had horses and beef. The Lipan shadow economy of theft was born.

By 1762, Lipan livestock thefts in Texas and northern Mexico had risen far above the level characterized by the thefts undertaken as part of a "normal" Apache raid. The la Bahía presidio in south Texas reported,

> These Lipans inhabit the surrounding settlements and we do not have the strength or facilities for withstanding them. . . . From the cattle which supply the troops under my care, they have killed over one thousand head, and if no check is put to the arrogance and mischief of these [Indians], we shall witness the total disintegration of these missions. [1]

The town council of San Antonio complained in 1762,

> The Lipans, who being relentlessly harassed and pursued by their enemies and driven from their own lands, are very forward about settling in ours . . . where they subsist upon our bulls, cows and oxen, and help themselves to our horses (San Fernando de Béxar, 1762: 192-193).

Thirty years later, a single Lipan attack in Nuevo Leon resulted in twenty-one settlers killed, nineteen taken captive, 2,400 head of cattle slaughtered and 1,084 stolen horses (Nuevo Leon, 1791: 155-156).

The Lipan theft economy operated on the currency of horses, cattle and, to a lesser extent, captives. Stealing horses was the primary mainstay, since horses could be stolen and driven away quickly and were always in demand as trade items. The Lipans butchered large numbers of stolen cattle, taking away only the choicest cuts of meat and bones containing juicy marrow (Dennis, 1925: 47-49). Once the Lipans fed themselves the excess beef was traded away, leaving the cattle owners to rage over the mounds of carcasses that had once represented their livelihood. The taking of human captives to be used as slaves or adopted into the tribe had always been a component of Apache raiding culture.

In terms of the Lipan trade economy, the sheer volume of livestock thefts cannot be characterized as simply filling an economic need for food supplementation. Nor can they be characterized merely as part of the raiding culture common to all Apache tribes. Only the Mescaleros ever approximated the Lipan use of theft as an economic tool and even then, the Mescalero use of theft to fuel a trade economy only reached its zenith after 1865 whereas the Lipans had been using the same economic pattern for at least a century prior to that date. The sheer numbers of stolen livestock elevated the Lipan theft economy far above the level seen in the raiding cultures of other Apache tribes and can best be characterized as an organized shadow enterprise.

The Lipan shadow economy involved a large organizational structure encompassing men from all tribal bands, was secretive in nature, showed a surprising degree of coordination and was the foundational basis which fueled the conduct of "legitimate" Lipan trade. Each band generally chose to prey upon targets within its territorial range, but in many cases, rather than seek targets of opportunity, Lipan livestock raids exhibited an organized pattern. For example, in the spring of 1772, in the space of two hours, Lipan raiders from several bands made simultaneous coordinated attacks on Coahuilan haciendas and ranches located over two hundred miles apart (Moorhead, 1968: 34). Chiefs of adjoining bands worked together in a single interlocking shadow enterprise spanning hundreds of miles, funneling horses stolen as far away as Coahuila, Mexico to the Texas Gulf plains, where up to 3,000 horses would be traded at one time to east Texas tribes for guns and ammunition (Cabello, 1785: 141). The guns would be passed back down the line to the raiders who had stolen the horses in the first place. A horse stolen from a *barraca (stall)* in San Antonio could well end up on a French ship leaving New Orleans bound for Santo Domingo in the Caribbean (John: 1981: 338). Such was the long reach of the Lipan shadow economy.

The Lipans also used their ill-gotten gains to fuel a "legitimate" horse trade in animals that were passed off as captured wild mustangs. Berlandier revealed,

> The Lipans are constantly stealing horses, livestock and any herds left unguarded. . . . They alter the brands on the horses they steal, then sell them back to their original owners. With the profits from this and the sale of a few hides they manage to scrape together enough to buy the powder and shot they need. (Ewers, 1969: 132)

Lipan thefts of the nineteenth century also corrupted political entities in Mexico, as entire Mexican towns "adopted" the Lipans and acted as "receivers of stolen property," selling horses and cattle stolen by the Lipans to legitimate (but probably not unsuspecting) buyers (Brown, 1868, Schuhardt, 1878b).

The Lipan trade economy existed on two levels and trade at both levels was carried on simultaneously. On the "legitimate" level, the Lipans were hunters and gatherers who practiced a limited and haphazard form of agriculture and who traded hides and pelts in exchange for sugar and chilies. However, they also used their trading visits to the settlements to conduct reconnaissance for their next raids. In the words of the Spanish, "They give the appearance and simulation of peace while they tyrannically observe us and our weaknesses." (Rabago, 1755: 44) The Lipans were frequent visitors to the Coahuilan mission of Vizarron, where they traded for the high quality *Oka* tobacco cultivated by the mission's Indians, finding this particular tobacco variety "unspeakably pleasing." (Cabello, 1784: 142; Lizarraras, 1770: 27) However, many of the Vizarron Indians were enticed to join the Lipans on their raids in Coahuila. The Lipans also exchanged promises of peaceful conduct with various governments in exchange for food, clothing and the ability to conduct legitimate trade with the settlements. However, almost every Lipan peace offer was motivated by the need to seek protection against their true enemies—the Comanches—and under the cover of a peace treaty, the Lipan shadow economy galloped on, funneling stolen horses to the Bidais, Caddos, Oroquisas, Mayeyes and Cocos (Cabello, 1785: 140). In 1791, Spanish commander Ramon de Castro summarized,

> They attract our devotion for a time with their sweetness, concealing certain defects which arise from their ignorance, wild character and bad customs; they do this to enable possible trade or commerce and because of their obsequiousness, we bring opportune gifts, while they pledge our destruction at the same time (De Castro, 1791c: 104-105).

The historical record clearly indicates that if the Lipan Apaches had relied on "legitimate" trade alone, they would have never been able to survive Comanche aggression and Spanish expansion. They would have followed in the footsteps of the many other Texas Indian tribes who had to turn to the Spanish for protection out of weakness and necessity, only to enter the Spanish missions where they were decimated by disease. The Lipan shadow economy was certainly in place after 1750 and was probably the key to Lipan survival through the eighteenth and nineteenth centuries. Although the Lipans remained hunters and gatherers, they adapted a specialization through theft which allowed for the growth of a strong trade economy and the maintenance of their population.

The Lipan dual economic system of "legitimate" and "shadow" continued through the nineteenth century. As "legitimate" government gifts and the gun trade with other Indian tribes dried up after 1800, the Lipans adapted to changing circumstances and entered a cash economy, where they passed off stolen horses as *mesteños* in order to obtain money to buy ammunition. By 1830, the Lipans had been well-armed for half a century but were always in need of powder and gunshot. The independence of Texas (1836) and the signing of the treaty of Guadalupe Hidalgo (1848), which created an international boundary along the Rio Grande, were political events quickly seized upon by the Lipans and turned to their advantage. Border towns were now willing to provide a safe haven for

Lipan raiders riding hard out of Texas, and a Mexican government, resentful of its new neighbor to the north, was willing to turn a blind eye to the thriving trade in stolen horses and cattle. The Lipan shadow economy boomed after 1836 as horses and cattle stolen in Texas were driven across the river and sold in the marketplaces of northern Mexico.

By the mid-nineteenth century, Lipan trade networks had adapted to the changing political situations in Texas and Mexico. Gone was the trade alliance with east Texas tribes. The remnants of those tribes now lived on reservations. The Lipan shadow trade network relocated across the border to the small Mexican towns of northern Coahuila, particularly the town of Zaragosa which formally "adopted" the Lipan Apaches around 1850 (Brown, 1868). As the political situation in Mexico deteriorated after 1860, culminating in a French intervention, the Lipans continued to ply their shadow trade. Since there were no functional Mexican civil governments to tacitly sanction their illicit trade, the Lipans forged trading partnerships with the bandits and warlords who now controlled the Rio Grande (Schuhardt, 1878b). But by 1870, the Lipans were greatly weakened and reduced in numbers by the forces of outside events. However, they still sought to replicate traditional economic patterns and joined with the Mescaleros and even with Comanche raiding parties in order to steal livestock and sell the animals to Hispanic traders.

The Lipan gun and horse trade continued until 1881, corrupting political institutions in Mexico and border communities in Texas, as settlers found it cheaper to buy stolen horses and pretend they didn't see an altered brand. The Lipans could not relinquish their gun and horse trade, for they saw it as essential to tribal survival, as essential as the buffalo that once roamed the plains. It took sustained and coordinated campaigns by the U.S. and Mexican Armies from 1869 to 1881 to severely weaken the Lipan shadow economy. However, it was the regime of Porfirio Diaz (1877-1880, 1884-1911) which finally forced the Lipan Apaches to relinquish their shadow enterprise. Diaz asserted Mexican Federal control in the border regions, co-opted the bandits and warlords by turning them into government bureaucrats and eliminated the role played by many Mexican towns as receivers of property stolen by the Lipan Apaches.

Chapter 9

Lipan Apache Social Culture: Family, Kinship and Society

Cultural Observations- The Life Cycle

Lipan Apache family life followed the general Apachean pattern of family relationships. The basic social organizational unit was the matrilocal extended family composed of parents, their unmarried sons and daughters with their husbands and children. Mothers and daughters provided the axis around which family life revolved.

> As one might expect in a nonagricultural, mobile society, there were no calendrical rites, or ceremonies that had to occur at a specific time each year. Rather, the established or required rituals were associated with the individual life cycle and constituted a series of observances designed to guide a child through life's hazards from birth to maturity. (Opler, 2002: 23)

In 1761, Fr. Diego Ximenez observed that Lipan "mothers give birth in the natural manner," by which he meant that the expectant mother "assumed a kneeling position while an assistant held her firmly by the shoulders." Ximenez continued, "If there is some difficulty the old women bathe the mother with pots of cold water" (Ximenez, 1761a 26).

> After the child was born, the umbilical cord was severed four inches from the body, first having been tied off at about an inch and a half. The placenta was thrown where no animals would find it. After giving birth, the mother bathed herself and washed the infant with warm water carried in a bison horn. [The child] was then held up in turn to 'the four points of the compass' and was also 'shown to the sun.' (Sjoberg, 1953: 91)

"The mother was not supposed to nurse the child until it was at least two days old. Only after four days could she leave the house. A cradle-board was specially made for the infant when it was four days old" (Sjoberg, 1953: 91). The Lipan cradle-board, or "baby rawhide," was an adaptation taken from the Mescaleros and was not traditional to Lipan culture (Opler, 1940; 138). Before placing the infant in the cradleboard, the mother wrapped him in a piece of cloth and placed him on a skin covered with "certain weeds called *tlo-til-spai*" (Sjoberg, 1953: 91). The infant was kept in the cradle-board all day, "the Indian mother giving very little attention to her baby except to nurse him. At night he was taken out and slept with the mother" (Dennis, 1925: 92).

The naming of the child was done by the father a few days after birth (Ximenez, 1761a: 26). Fr. Ximenez noted that, "Newborn children are given the names of sticks *(palos)* or animals," trivializing a process and custom that carried a fair amount of ritual significance (Ximenez, 1764: 177). It was not uncommon for a Lipan man to be known by several names during his lifetime, with a name change effected at each major life transition or crisis. If a man committed a breach of social mores, he would change his name as a means of saving face since "to accuse someone else of one's actions when it turns out badly is a way of exempting oneself from the penalties attached" (Opler, 1940: 34, 183). When blame could not be shifted to another individual, a name change would allow the old persona to take the blame. The custom of name-changing to mark major life events can be seen in the life of *Dinero*, a Mexican Lipan who was orphaned at the age of eight. He was named *Enriques* by his father, received the name *Dinero* after being orphaned and changed his name to *Penaro* after he was accused of murder in 1891 and fled from the Mescalero Reservation to Oklahoma (Chebahtah and Minor, 2007: 47, 56-57, 148-149 and 158).

After observances associated with the birth and naming of a child, the next transition point for a Lipan child came at adolescence, where a young girls' attainment of puberty was ritually celebrated. Augustina Zuazua described the ceremony.

> Then sometimes/ these Lipan/ a ceremony they held for the adolescent
>   girls.
> And then they are happy/ they taking part in the ceremony.
> Masked Dancers/ they dance and the Lipan also/ they gambled.
> Then/ that they eat/ very much/ they liked it.
> The adolescent girls they danced/ and with them songs/ they go with it.
> A cowhide they carry it (Hoijer, 1939a: S146-151).

The girl's adolescent ceremony was a public event, rather than a private ceremony, involving complex rituals of dance and song. The Masked Dancers were "impersonators of the Mountain Spirits who, from their stations in sacred mountains, protected [the tribe]" (Opler, 2002: 24). The Dancers wore tall masks and bells attached to their breechclouts and waist sashes (Farrer, 1991: 112). The Lipan Masked Dancer cult was a late acquisition, adapted from the Mescaleros (Opler, 1940: 51). [1] The function of the cowhide, carried by the young girls as they danced, was not explained by Zuazua but its symbolism is not hard to detect. The puberty ritual was a celebration of fecundity and the hope for future children, where the "song cycle of the rite pictured a long and successful career for the girl and blessed in advance every substance and experience she might encounter on her life journey" (Opler, 2002: 24).

The next transition point in the life of an individual was marriage. "Marriage among the Lipan [was] an understanding between families rather than between individuals and particularly entail[ed] obligations between the married person and the relatives of his mate." (Opler, 1945: 135) A marriage union "was less the founding of a new social unit than it was the absorption of the couple into an on-going extended family." (Opler, 2002: 25) The Lipans did not traditionally mark a marriage with formal ritual. Rather, "marriage is performed by the suitor buying the one who is to become his wife from her father or principal relative, giving some horses, skins, or weapons for her." (John, 1991: 150) Fr. Ximenez observed,

> In order to marry, the suitor *(novio)* asks the father, brother or relative for the bride. He [the father] consults it with his wife and if it is convenient, they give her away without any ceremonies. To accomplish it, the suitor gives the parents hides, horses, horse-whips or something else (Ximenez, 1761a: 26).

By the nineteenth century, Lipan marriage practices had been widely influenced by the tribe's exposure to Christianity. Frank Buckelew described a curious "marriage ceremony" that had overtones of a baptismal rite.

> Perhaps the marriage ceremony was the most unique service of these uncivilized beings. A large beef hide was spread out on the ground and caused to cup up, basin fashion, by throwing heated rocks on the flesh side. This was taken to a secluded place some distance from the village, where it was partially filled with water.
>
> I visited the place selected and arranged by the contracting parties for a marriage ceremony. We dared not approach too near the place, so we concealed ourselves so we could easily witness their actions. The first persons to appear on the scene were the bride and groom. They marched up to the hide hand in hand, and stepping into the water they joined both hands and marched around in the water for some time. When this part of the ceremony was about completed, the parents of both bride and groom marched up to the scene very solemnly. After a few other formal ceremonies the whole party marched back to the village. There followed the usual dance and other gayeties of these simple folk. (Dennis, 1925: 113-114)

As was true of other Apache tribes, the Lipans practiced matrilocal residence and affiliation. When a man and a woman married, the husband left his family and local group and joined the wife's family and local group. Upon marriage, the new son-in-law took up his responsibilities and tasks within the circle of his wife's extended family. Out of respect and deference, the new son-in-law was expected to address his wife's family using "polite" speech, a special form of address that indicated his subordination and reinforced the fact that the son-in-law's loyalties now lay with his new family.

> The married man was expected to enter fully into the work of the encampment which he had joined, and he owed special courtesy and consideration to his relatives-in-law. Though he maintained a separate household, he and his wife lived in the extended family house cluster, and he cooperated in economic tasks with his father-in-law, his wife's unmarried brothers, and the husbands of his wife's sisters. If he had come from a different local group at marriage, he had to get acquainted as rapidly as possible with the characteristics and resources of the new setting. His wife underwent much less of a transition at marriage; she continued to participate with her mother and sisters in the gathering of the wild food harvests and in the many household tasks for which the women were responsible. (Opler 1975: 15-16)

The one area in which the Lipans differed from many other Apache tribes, particularly the Mescaleros, was in the social norms of behavior demanded of a son-in-law toward his wife's female relatives. A Mescalero son-in-law, for example, had to "avoid coming face to face with his mother-in-law and his wife's maternal and paternal grandmothers. Still other female relatives of his wife might, as a compliment to his wife and him, also request 'avoidance.'" (Opler, 2002: 14-15). On the other hand, the Lipans did not practice mother-in-law avoidance, although deference, respect and "polite" language were still required. Augustina Zuazua noted this difference in Lipan culture.

> And these Lipan/ those who are in-laws/ those/ they go about to them
> [i.e. they do not avoid them].
> The Lipan they were so (Hoijer, 1939a: S201-202).

Anthropologist Morris Opler did not believe the Lipan Apaches practiced polygamy (Opler, 1940: 43). However, three separate eighteenth and early nineteenth century sources contradict Opler, although the sources disagreed on the extent to which polygamy was practiced. Fr. Diego Ximenez noted in 1761, as he discussed aspects of Lipan leadership, "The valiant practice polygamy; the others are not permitted to do so." (Ximenez, 1761a: 26). This comment would indicate that the ability to take and support multiple wives was a benefit flowing from leadership or battlefield prowess. However, in 1764, Fr. Ximenez reported that, "Most of the [Lipans] have more than one woman. Women are easily discarded. The men are jealous of those with many women." (Ximenez, 1764: 177). The latter statement would indicate that Lipan polygamy was a generally accepted practice. Spanish historian Fr. Juan Agustín Morfi, who visited Texas in 1776, agreed with Ximenez' original assessment, stating that, "one or another of the [Lipan] captains has a multitude of wives, [but] this is not frequently the case, and ordinarily they content themselves with only one wife." (Chabot, 1932: 17) In 1820, Juan Antonio Padilla echoed Ximenez, observing that the Lipans "have many wives like the Comanches." (Hatcher, 1919: 56) Although Padilla did not expound further on Lipan polygamy, when discussing the Comanches, he noted, "They have many wives, as many as each Indian can support. Some of them have as many as eight." (Hatcher, 1919: 54)

Once married, the relationship between husband and wife could sometimes become difficult and strained because of the husband's jealousy or, occasionally, the adultery of the wife. In the case of a wife's adultery, the marriage bond could be broken for cause and with the acquiescence of the wife's parents, freeing the husband to find another wife. Fr. Ximenez commented in 1761,

> There are loose women whom they despise, although among many this is not an obstacle in finding a husband. If she is unfaithful after marriage, the husband punishes her by beating her with sticks and leaving her while he goes on to another *ranchería*. There are many modest women. The mothers have to beat them in order to take them away on occasion [from a bad husband]. Some

of the marriages may be difficult because the men are lazy, jealous or no good (Ximenez, 1761a: 27).

Fr. Morfi (1776) expounded on the "loose women" described by Ximenez.

[The Lipans] are zealous of the honor of their wives and daughters; they have not a high opinion of prostitutes whom they call *Ortiana Cortela*, and whom accompany them on their military routes and on hunting parties; the wives remaining in charge of the family and household at the *rancheria* (Chabot, 1932: 17).

Manuel Merino (1804) provided additional details about how the marriage was dissolved.

Often the [marriage] contract is dissolved by mutual consent of the spouses, and when the woman returns to her father, the latter gives back whatever [bride price] he received. Others end with the woman running away because of the bad treatment which she experiences. In such instances, she takes refuge under the protection of some Indian with a reputation for valor, and one who thinks himself weaker would not dare to dispute him (John, 1991: 150-151).

Just as the Lipan Apaches generally had no formal rites associated with marriage (at least until the 1860's) but marked that life transition with traditional customary practice, so also was their treatment of death. Gatschet summarized Lipan burial customs in 1884 by stating, "Dead Lipans are left on the ground and the family moves away." (Gatschet, 1884: 56) However, because death could provoke and draw forth the presence of ghosts *(bac'oc, vac'oc)*, or spirits of the dead, Lipan custom entailed specific practices which were rigidly observed upon the death of an individual (Opler, 1945: 134). It was necessary for the bereaved family to make arrangements for the burial of the body as soon as possible after death, even the very day that death occurred. An elderly relative or shaman, whose advanced age or ceremonial power offered protection against ghost sickness or any disorder arising from contact with the dead body, was approached, offered tobacco and asked to take charge of the preparation of the body for burial. A second person was often paid by the family to assist in the process, but finding such a person proved difficult at times, since many were fearful of handling a dead body (Opler, 1945: 123-124). The deceased's body was washed, dressed in its best clothes and jewelry and the hair carefully combed.

All the deceased's possessions were gathered, for everything he owned or frequently handled must be destroyed. These objects and the body are tied to the horse of the deceased, and the animal is led to the place of interment. Any person who meets the burial procession turns away, bows his head, and remains silent until the body has been carried past. Whenever possible, the body is buried in the mountains (Opler, 1945: 124).

At the grave site, a shallow trench was dug and the body and possessions placed in it. The body was laid in the trench with the head toward the east and sage was placed in the form of a cross at the head and feet.

> The elder or shaman spoke to the body of the deceased, telling him that he must go away peacefully and alone and must not look back or 'bother the relatives in any way.' These admonitions are particularly important when the body is that of a person who died while in the prime of life; it is expected that the very young and the very old will proceed to the afterworld without causing trouble for the living (Opler, 1945: 124-125).

The grave was filled with earth and stones and the horse of the deceased was shot at the gravesite, traditionally by shooting an arrow into its throat. If the deceased had owned many horses, it was only necessary to kill his favorite, which had borne its owner's body to the grave (Opler, 1945: 125). It was always necessary for the burial party to return to camp by a different route in order to avoid opening a path for the ghost of the deceased to visit his old haunts. Immediately after the burial, the entire camp was moved, generally in the opposite direction from the fresh grave (Opler, 1945: 126).

While the body of the deceased was being buried, the bereaved relatives began the mourning process. The burial, characterized by quick removal of the body and swift interment presided over by only one or two witnesses, stood in contrast to the mourning process, which was marked by an outpouring of familial and community emotion, with the women of the camp weeping and mourning the loss throughout the night (Dennis, 1925: 115). The relatives of the deceased would remove their good clothes as a sign of grief. Anyone who had touched the corpse was required to bathe and all would don old clothes and cut their hair. A bereaved widow often "shaved her head and went to a lonely spot and wept and mourned the loss of her brave for days." (Dennis, 1925: 115) The immediate family destroyed the possessions of the deceased and removed themselves from the larger community for a period of from four to eight days.

The Mexican Lipans, repositors of traditional culture, scrupulously observed the taboo against speaking the name of a deceased person (Opler, 1945: 126). On the other hand, the Texas Lipans, as observed by Albert Gatschet at Ft. Griffin in 1884, were "not afraid of giving the names of the dead relatives or other deceased persons." (Gatschet, 1884: 56)

The Lipans also practiced a sororate-levirate arrangement upon the death of a spouse. "If there were two sisters, one married and one unmarried, and the married sister dies, the sister left alive can marry that man if she wants to. She can take her dead sister's place. It's according to how the family feels about it." (Opler 1945: 137) The same arrangement held true in the case of two brothers, with the surviving brother marrying his brother's widow in order to keep the woman within the care of the extended family.

The Lipan Apaches believed in an afterlife. Fr. Ximenez commented,

> They believe the soul is immortal. All their possessions go with the dead. They believe that they will live with other countrymen nearby after death. . . . After death they are to live among their people reunited, they are to reunite with the separated (Ximenez, 1764: 177-178).

The Lipans also had a specific picture of the landscape of the afterworld, which was divided into two regions along a north-south axis. When a person died, the Lipans believed that their death was a result of a summons by their long-dead relatives, who wished the person to join them in the underworld. Once there, the deceased inhabited either the northern or the southern area, with the criteria for their place of habitation being the actions of the deceased while still alive. The northern part of the underworld was dark.

> A mist and faint fire arose from there and forms could be seen walking around as if they were in a heavy fog. A hill [separated the north from the south]. Those who were on one side would not go to the other side. . . . Over there, on the north side, where it is always dark, those who shoot things into others, those who are witches, live. They have a hard time there. Their food is nothing but lizards, snakes, horned toads, and those things that people on earth do not like. (Opler, 1940: 98)

In contrast, the southern area was "a beautiful country. Everything was green. A grove of cottonwood trees stood there beside a fine stream of water." (Opler, 1940: 97) The southern area was "a good place [where] only those who have been good when on earth belong." (Opler, 1940: 98)

Language and Literacy

In 1884, ethnologist Albert Gatschet compiled a partial Lipan vocabulary for the newly-formed Smithsonian Bureau of Ethnology (Gatschet, 1884). Sadly, he did not probe for nuances nor did he seek to explore how the Lipan language furnished categories which enabled the speakers to cope with social reality and with the wider world around them. If Gatschet had probed further, he probably would have found what Morris Opler discovered about Lipan myths in 1935— that Lipan language and myth opened up a window into a much richer world of Lipan thought and expression than had been previously known or appreciated.

An inquiry into the level of bilingualism and literacy among the Lipan Apaches of the eighteenth and nineteenth centuries reveals that the tribe used the Spanish language and written word not only to convey their thoughts, but also as tools to influence their interactions with outsiders. All early contacts between the Spanish and the Lipans were conducted through the medium of translators. In some cases, the translators were Spaniards who had been held as Lipan captives, but the Spanish also discovered early on that some Lipans spoke passable

Castilian Spanish. By 1820, Juan Antonio Padilla reported that, "Many of [the Lipans] have learned to speak Castilian, although with a poor pronunciation, but they understand it very well." (Hatcher, 1919: 56) The Lipan use of the word *buhala* for the Spanish word *bufalo*, as reported by Frank Buckelew in 1866, was probably typical (Dennis, 1925: 62). By the early nineteenth century, most Lipans were fluent Spanish-speakers who had become well integrated into Hispanic life. Berlandier (1828) commented that Lipan chief *Cuelgas de Castro* was "quite civilized. Castro, as he is called, speaks good Spanish and has a feeling for justice and equity." (Ewers, 1969: 134)

There are also a handful of letters in existence which illustrate the Lipan and *Lipiyan* use of the written word. [2] They consist of pleas or reports written to more powerful personages, seeking favor or assistance. The best and most instructive example comes from *Lipiyan* chief *Picax-andé Yns-tinsle*, who wrote to Juan de Ugalde one month after ratifying a peace treaty in March 1788 and after Ugalde had bestowed upon *Picax* the honor of bearing the Ugalde surname.

> My dear Sir and esteemed Father:
> On the 3rd [of April 1788] and regarding the matter to which I address my case, Lt. Casimiro Valdés with twenty men and the Interpreter Pablo Hernandez, who at my request [writes this] letter to Your Lordship, brought me news of a robbery near Agua Verde of six beasts and news that two of the beasts [horses] and an Indian belonging to my band had stopped at my house to eat, according to the aforementioned Lieutenant; that when they [the owners of the stolen animals at Agua Verde] went to go care for the beasts, they found them missing and determined that the two beasts [at the home of *Picax*] were known to them and then they realized someone had stolen them away and they were not able to catch up to them and recover the two beasts before they stopped at my place; the Lieutenant told me he had questioned all of the people of the *Lipanes* as to whether they knew the brands of these beasts that had been carried off, and told me that they had made their way to my *villa*, which upset me very much, and said he ordered all of my Captains and *Lipanes* to each tell him where the beasts had gone with care taken to ascertain if they had encountered them, and that the Lieutenant ordered them to bring them to me if they encountered them whether the animals were alive or dead; and that I will be liable for the [*mesteño*] tax, the said Lieutenant told me.
> The Interpreter assures me on the life of the Sacred Victory [Jesus] that I have been given a good gift in all the words that Jesus spoke to such as me, and these will guard me while I live. . . . I remain thankful for the Lieutenant and his soldiers since they said that they will be able to go out with me to look diligently at the horse herd to see if we have introduced any *mesteñas* and he told me that the group would include himself and his twenty men plus men that I sent and commanded. . . . .
>
> Rio San Diego [Coahuila], April 5, 1788
>
> Your son who reveres you,
> *Manuel Picax-andé Yns-tinsle de Ugalde*
> (Picax-andé, 1788: 372-374)

The letter dictated by *Picax* is a fascinating document on a number of levels, revealing much about the true relationship between the *Lipiyans*, Lipans and non-tribal outsiders, even professed "friends" such as Juan de Ugalde, and revealing just how infuriatingly difficult it was for the Spanish to deal with the Apaches. On the surface, the letter is cordial and deferential. It said all the right things, including profuse Christian references, as *Picax* assumed the role of "son" in deference to his "father," Juan de Ugalde. *Picax* displayed an attitude of openness and frankness, laying his problem at Ugalde's feet, informing his friend of a situation that *Picax* found distressing. It would be easy to believe that this letter was merely a warm reassurance from *Picax* to his beloved mentor, Ugalde, assuring him of his devotion to Spanish interests and his compliance with the pledge to return any stolen animals discovered in *Lipiyan* herds.

However, there was much more going behind the flowery words of the *Lipiyan* chief. Why did *Picax* choose to dictate a letter instead of orally relaying his message through the Interpreter Pablo Hernandez? *Picax* wanted to bypass any influence held by Lt. Casimiro Valdés. In other words, *Picax* wanted to complain directly about Valdés' conduct to Valdes' superior, Juan de Ugalde. What *Picax* found most upsetting about Valdés' accusation that *Picax* had harbored two stolen horses at his *ranchería* was not that the Spanish arrived in order to check his horse herd for stolen animals. Spanish troops arrived regularly at Hispanic *ranchos* and Indian camps to check the brands on animals to determine whether they had been stolen or captured from *mesteño* herds and illegally branded, always taking the view that the owners were guilty until inspection had proven them innocent. What galled *Picax,* and where Valdés had crossed the line, was by informing the *Lipiyan* chief that if the stolen animals were found (either dead or alive), he, *Picax*, would be liable for the *mesteño* tax. Valdés must have known, as *Picax* knew, that the *Lipiyans* and Lipans were exempt from the *mesteño* tax, since this tax money was supposed to benefit the Indians and bring them to civilization. What caused *Picax* great alarm, if Valdés' interpretation of the *mesteño* law was allowed to stand, was the possibility that the *Lipiyans* would not only be forced to begin paying taxes on the *mesteño* animals they captured, but that they would also be charged for every dead animal in the Province. In addition to his alarming threat, Valdés also crossed the line in directly questioning *Picax's Lipiyan* captains and his Lipan adherents. This was a direct affront to *Picax's* authority. So, *Picax* chose to dictate a letter to Juan de Ugalde adopting the tone of a sycophant, pleading for Ugalde to hear his case, in an attempt to curry favor with a man who had the authority to punish Casimiro Valdés. The *Lipiyan* chief chose to use a very Spanish vehicle—the writing of a flowery letter of appeal to a powerful *padrón (patron)*—in order to deflect a disastrous interpretation of the *mesteño* law, as well as to seek revenge for an affront. Lost somewhere in the verbiage of this letter and subsequent Spanish reports is the fact that the owners of the stolen horses never recovered them. Casimiro Valdés, while never officially reprimanded for his treatment of the chief, fell out of favor for a time. The letter from *Picax* accomplished its goal.

Chapter 10

Political Organization: The Lipan Band

Characteristics of Lipan Bands

If the extended family was the building block of Lipan society, the next most functionally important social unit was the Lipan band, composed of up to four or five large clusters of extended families. The Lipan band provided the structure for the most efficient use of resources, as they were "large enough for defense and the necessary group tasks, yet they were not cumbersome and vulnerable on that score, and within them individual initiative and sturdy personal characteristics were valued." (Opler, 1975: 16-17) Each cluster of extended families, or *ranchería,* was led by a headman and each headman acknowledged the leadership of a band chief, a leader with few formal status distinctions. The populations of the extended family clusters within each band "accepted [the band chief's] recognized leadership and [were] associated with definite territory of some extent." (Opler, 1975: 7)

In a 1975 study of nineteenth century Lipan and Mescalero Apache social structure prepared for the Indian Claims Commission, anthropologist Morris Opler termed the large Lipan socio-political organizational unit, composed of extended family clusters, a "local group" rather than a band, arguing,

> [while] a tribal consciousness was present . . . the tribal bond was loose; concentrated leadership and direction were lacking; and there was no mechanism for uniting the entire tribe for a common venture or to face a common danger. There are hints that a band organization may have been present at one time [but] there were few organizational consequences of this (Opler, 1975: 6). [1]

While the term "local group" is an apt description of nineteenth century Mescalero organization (and even Lipan societal organization of the late nineteenth century), this author respectfully disagrees with Opler's assessment regarding Lipan socio-political organization, particularly as it relates to the eighteenth and early nineteenth centuries. This author is convinced that there is sufficient evidence in the historical record to believe that the Lipans possessed a more highly structured socio-political organization than did the Mescaleros, since Lipan territories stretched over a much wider area containing a greater variety of resources and a greater potential for enemy threat, thus presenting a greater challenge in utilization and defense. The Lipan eighteenth century shadow trade economy alone provided a strong basis for chiefs from different bands to work together toward a common goal. If horses stolen from herds in Coahuila were to be traded to tribes in east Texas for guns, the chiefs of two or possibly three Lipan bands had to coordinate the smuggling activity in order to bring the horses to a common trading ground and then disperse the guns among different bands. The historical record is replete with such examples, all of which argue for a highly structured and organized Lipan political organization and thus argue for the terminology employed by this author to describe Lipan socio-political organization. What Opler described as a Lipan "local group," this author believes was of such a structured nature that it should more properly be called a Lipan "band," particularly if one is referring to eighteenth century Lipan political organization. Although Lipan tribal fragmentation at the end of the nineteenth century resulted in a political devolution into "local groups," this was a late development in tribal history. The Lipan Apaches were organized into two tribal divisions (Plains and Forest Lipans) for most of the first century of their residence in Texas (1650-1750). Comanche aggression after 1700 splintered the Plains and Forest Lipan divisions into from ten to fourteen bands and the Lipans retained this form political organization for at least a century (1750-1850) until Texas Indian Removal policies forced the tribe into Mexico after 1850.

Perhaps the best evidence in support of the argument in favor of a Lipan band structure comes from the pen of Spanish military commander Pedro de Nava. In 1791, de Nava described the ties binding the Lipan tribe together.

> The Lipan nation is composed of distinct groups connected progressively by narrow links of kinship relationships, alliances and patriotism *(patriotismo)*, assuring all those interests are preserved through robbery and the hunting of buffalo. (De Nava, 1791c: 530).

De Nava's comment lays bare the tiers of Lipan socio-political structure. First, he acknowledged the progression from the individual kinship ties binding extended family groups together within a *ranchería*, to the kinship ties binding several *rancherías* together in one band, to the kinship ties between bands formed through marriage. Each Lipan band was also linked by alliances based on marriage preferences, shared interests or territorial proximity. Finally, the tribe was united by a sense of patriotism, a concept which unified the Lipan people through an acknowledgement of shared culture.

De Nava's comment implied that the nature of Lipan leadership was structured to such a degree that it was able to mandate alliances between two or more bands. This is in contrast to Opler's observation that the Lipans did not possess leadership capable of such direction; both de Nava and the historical record indicate otherwise. Finally, de Nava noted the two primary communal activities that brought together a number of different bands—the shadow economy of theft and the buffalo hunt. Such large communal endeavors, particularly the coordination among bands necessary to conduct robberies and then trade the stolen goods, are the strongest argument that the Lipans were organized into a number of bands each under the leadership of a chief, rather than a looser group organization indicated by Morris Opler.

Upper and Lower Lipans; *Llaneros* and *Lipiyans*

Spanish records from 1732 to about 1780 consistently viewed the Texas Apaches as being principally composed of two groups—the Lipans and the *Natagés*. However, with the appointment of Juan de Ugalde to the governorship of Coahuila (1777-1783) and as military commander of Texas, Coahuila, Nuevo Leon and Nuevo Santander (1786-1790), the tribal nomenclature dramatically changed. This change in terminology had its genesis in Spanish attempts to splinter Lipan alliances and deal with the tribe on a band level, making war on some Lipan groups and peace with others. From 1780 to 1804, the Texas Apaches began to be referred to as Upper and Lower Lipans *(Lipanes de arriba y Lipanes de abajo)*, *Llaneros*, *Lipiyanes*, *Natagés* and Mescaleros. Who were these groups and what was their relationship to the Lipan tribe?

In 1796, Antonio Cordero offered information regarding the Texas Apaches, taken from the reports of Ugalde and other military commanders, as part of his report on the Apaches living along Spain's northern frontier. Cordero's information was reiterated by José Cortés in 1799 and Manuel Merino in 1804. The Lipans, "probably the most populous of all the Apache tribes," were divided into two branches (John, 1991: 163). The Lower Lipans *(Lipanes de abajo)* were those bands who inhabited the lower end of the Rio Grande-from San Antonio to Laredo and the coastal plains from Goliad County south throughout the Rio Grande Valley. The Upper Lipans *(Lipanes de arriba)* were those bands who inhabited an area from the upper Nueces River (west of San Antonio), across the Rio Grande into northern Coahuila and up the Rio Grande to the Pecos confluence (Moorhead, 1968: 203). Both Upper and Lower Lipans had "kinship and other ties with the Mezcaleros and *Llaneros*." (John, 1991: 164) The Mescalero tribe inhabited the Big Bend region of Texas, with their territory extending south across the Rio Grande to the *Bolsón de Mapimí* of northwestern Coahuila (John, 1989: 52).

The *Llaneros*, or *Cuelcajen-ne*, were "quite numerous with many warriors." (John, 1989: 52) Cordero specified,

> They occupy the plains and deserts lying between the Pecos River and the Colorado. . . . It is a very populous tribe, which is divided into the following three categories: *Natagés, Lipiyanes*, and *Llaneros*. They contain the Comanches. . . . They also attack Spanish settlements, joining for this purpose with the Mezcaleros and Faraónes with whom they have a close friendship and alliance (John 1991: 163).

The principal chief of the *Llaneros* from 1787 to 1790 was *Picax-andé Ynstinsle (Strong Arm)*, a *Lipiyan* who rose to the leadership of the three *Llanero* groups (Moorhead, 1968: 202-203).[2]

The problem with Cordero's information lies in the fact that he based his Apache study on military reports which, in relation to the Texas Apaches, were purposefully made contradictory in many instances. The blame can be laid at the feet of Juan de Ugalde, a tempestuous commander who fought his Apache wars like an Apache, collected a large amount of information regarding the Apache leadership, yet he obfuscated this data in order to misrepresent his actions to his superiors. Ugalde waged campaigns against the Upper Lipans, Coahuilan Lipans and Mescaleros without provocation, in contravention of established policy, and in spite of the fact that they had signed peace treaties with Ugalde's superiors (Moorhead, 1968: 70, 203-207). Tribal affiliations were twisted to suit the moment. Coahuilan Lipan chief *Bigotes*, consistently named as a Lipan by non-Ugalde sources from 1758 to 1763 and included among other Lipan chiefs by Ugalde in 1780, suddenly became a "Mescalero" rebel when Ugalde embarked on his Mescalero campaigns in 1781 (Dunn, 1912: 193, Cansio, 1763: 177, Ugalde, 1780: 7). An entirely new Apache "nation" appeared in the form of the *Llaneros (Cuelcajen-ne)* and *Lipiyans* when Ugalde undertook his Pecos campaigns. The insubordinate Ugalde was relieved of his duties in 1783, but the Viceroy placed him back in command in 1786 for a further five years of chaos (Starnes, 1996: 616-617). Ugalde's superior, Jacobo Ugarte, was also occasionally guilty of errors regarding tribal affiliation (Moorhead, 1968: 249).

Documentary evidence prior to and after Ugalde's tenure supports the division of the Lipan bands along east/west, upriver/downriver lines. The existence of Mescalero Apaches in the Texas Big Bend and *Bolsón* of Coahuila is also confirmed. Documents also consistently associate the *Natagés* with the Lipan tribe in a political alliance and place the *Natagés* along the Pecos River. However, the identity of the *Llaneros (Cuelcajen-ne)* and *Lipiyans* poses an interesting conundrum.

An examination of *Llanero* territory and *Lipiyan* chief *Picax* provides some clues. *Lipiyan* and *Llaneros* territory in 1796 (upper Colorado to Pecos Rivers) was the same territory assigned to the *Ypandes* by Fr. Santa Ana in 1743. Santa Ana also noted an alliance of the *Ypandes* with the *Natagés* which was later reflected in Cordero's *Llanero (Cuelcajen-ne)* "nation." The "Prairie Men" or *Llanero* band of Lipans inhabited territory west of Shackelford County, Texas (Gatschet, 1884: 55-56). This would place "Prairie Men" band territories along the upper Colorado River, as noted by Cordero.

Lipiyan chief *Picax-andé* was identified as a Lipan by New Mexico Governor de la Concha when the chief arrived in Santa Fe seeking a peace treaty and bearing a passport signed by Juan de Ugalde (Moorhead, 1968: 249). De la Concha might have mistaken *Picax'* tribal affiliation, but it is clear that the chief's visit was part of a larger plan. Just eight months prior to *Picax'* arrival in New Mexico, "two chiefs of the Lipan nation, accompanied by six other ruling families speaking for the rest of their class and nation" presented themselves in Santa Fe requesting a trade treaty and permission to trade at the Pecos Pueblo (De Anza, 1786: 341). Six months prior to the appearance of the two Lipan chiefs in Santa Fe, Lower Lipan chief *Zapato Sas* requested a peace and trade treaty from the Governor of Texas (Cabello, 1786c: 27-28). It seems that *Picax'* appearance was part of a coordinated Lipan strategy to undermine or duplicate Spanish-Comanche alliance treaties signed in New Mexico and Texas in 1785. Whether

Picax' participation can be traced to his Lipan roots or was merely the act of a Lipan ally cannot be known, but *Picax* and the *Lipiyans* never asserted themselves in this manner on behalf of the Mescaleros or *Natagés*.

When Ugalde negotiated a peace treaty with *Picax* along the Pecos River on July 10, 1787, he stated that *Picax* was the "principal chief of the "Apaches *[Natagés]*, *Lipiyans*, Lipans, Mescaleros, *Sendé*, *Nit-ajende* and *Cachu-ende* nations" (Ugalde, 1788c: 321). Moorhead equated the *Sendé* with the Mescaleros, the *Nit-ajende* with the Faraónes/Jicarillas and the *Cachu-ende* with the *Cuelcajen-ne* or *Llaneros* of the Cordero report (Moorhead, 1968: 238). However, Ugalde quickly clarified that *Picax* did not represent the entire Mescalero tribe, but only represented "some Mescaleros who, at the time, had incorporated themselves with him."(Ugalde, 1788c: 321). Nor was *Picax* the principal chief of the Lipan Apaches. When *Picax* ratified the Ugalde treaty, only three Lipan chiefs of the *"Western Lipanería"* accompanied him and acknowledged his leadership (Ugalde 1788c: 321). *Picax* did not speak for all the *Natagés*. In 1787, a *Natagés* chief named *El Natagée* was included among a group of Mescaleros seeking to negotiate a peace treaty in El Paso and at least two separate *Natagés rancherías*, who did not acknowledge the leadership of *Picax*, were reported near El Paso in 1790 (Moorhead, 1968: 242, 258). The historical record clearly shows that *Lipiyan* chief *Picax-andé Yns-tinsle* led an Apache coalition, composed of elements from the Mescalero, Lipan and *Natagés* tribes, whose primary purpose was to present a defensive barrier against southward Comanche expansion (Nelson, 1940: 438-439).

There are numerous clues in the reports of Ugalde's junior officers to connect the *Lipiyans* to the Lipans on the basis of possible kinship. In 1788, *Picax* "was camping with all the *Lipiyans* and three *rancherías* of Lipans near the junction of the San Saba and Colorado Rivers" when Comanches attacked the camp (Valdez, 1788: 397-398). In seeking assistance to revenge the attack, *Picax* turned to *Juan Tuerto*, a chief who was a full brother to Lipan chief *Bigotes*, and *Davinica-jaté*, son of Upper Lipan chief *Boca Tuerte; Boca Tuerte* was a nephew of Lipan chief *Bigotes* (Valdez, 1788: 398, Serrano, 1780: 35). [3] Although the Spanish reported that *Picax* married the sister of Mescalero chief *Alegré,* if the *Lipiyan* chief was the son of a Lipan mother, he would have been considered a Lipan Apache because the Lipans (and the Mescaleros) reckoned tribal affiliation through the female line (Ugalde, 1789: 270).

Ugalde's successor, Pedro de Nava, believed it was impossible to separate the Lipans from the *Lipiyans*, "their friends and relatives, [for they are] all the same nation with the same idiom, character, customs, physical features and dress." (De Nava, 1791c: 532) The *Lipiyans* do not seem to have been a Lipan band *per se*, but they do seem to have been a Lipan-affiliated group, perhaps containing an amalgam of Lipans, *Natagés* and other small Apache groups who inhabited the Pecos region. However, the predominant *Lipiyan* ethnic component was probably Lipan Apache, given *Lipiyan* participation in Lipan political strategy and *Picax'* primary association with known Lipan chiefs.

On the other hand, the term used by Cordero to describe the *Llanero* "nation," *Cuelcajen-ne*, is merely an alternate spelling of the Lipan term for their "Prairie Men" band *(Kól kukä 'n ndé or Prairie Men People)*. Based on Cordero's territorial range and linguistic identification, the *Llaneros* were a group separate from the *Lipiyans*. They were not a "nation" but a single Lipan band that allied with and acknowledged the leadership of the *Lipiyan* chief *Picax* during a specific historical era.

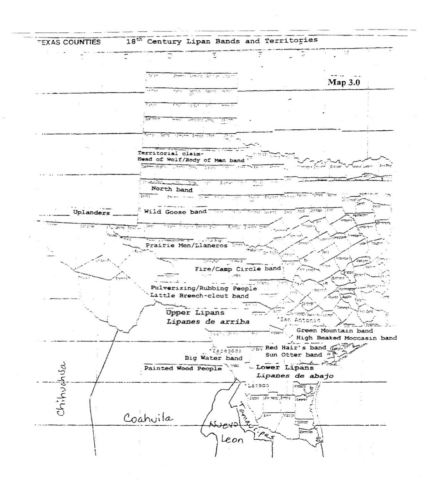

Lipan Bands

During the early eighteenth century, the Lipans were organized into two large tribal divisions—the Forest and the Plains Lipans—which were the result of dissention within the tribe after its migration into Texas. However, the Comanche entry into Texas and their ongoing war with the Lipans split the tribal divisions into a number of different bands, since smaller groups were better able to avoid Comanche attack.

During the historical period, the number of Lipan bands ranged from ten to fourteen, with some bands absorbed by others as they suffered decimation or a catastrophic loss of leadership. Bands would unite in order to wage war against the Comanches, then separate and return to their own territories in order to avoid Comanche retaliation. As bands were decimated in the late eighteenth and nineteenth centuries, remnants were consolidated into new bands. The groups of extended families within a band, who had once identified themselves with territorial, cultural or mythological features, moved away over time from an identity which represented a cohesive tribal culture. Group identity became personalized and tied to the distinctive adaptations of a leader. Thus, when the tribe fractured in response to severe military pressure after 1850, political organization naturally evolved into a "local group" form observed by Opler.

In 1884, a Lipan scout named Louis provided ethnologist Albert Gatschet with the only extant list of the names and territories of known bands. Many of Gatschet's territorial descriptions were given using Ft. Griffin (Shackelford County, Texas) as a geographic reference point (Gatschet, 1884: 55-56). [4]

Lower Lipan bands; Remnants of the Forest Lipan division
1. Red Hair band   *Tséṛal tuétahä^n*
This band was led by *Cabellos Colorado (Red Hairs)* and seems to have taken its name from him. Band territories lay southwest of San Antonio. In 1738, *Cabellos Colorado* was captured and imprisoned by the Spanish at Béxar. He was marched to Mexico City in chains and died in prison by 1740 (Basterra, 1739: 52). After the death of *Cabellos Colorado*, the Red Hair band was absorbed into either the Sun Otter band or the Green Mountain band. In 1884, Gatschet noted that the Red Hair band no longer existed as a separate political entity.

2. Sun Otter band   *Tcheshä'^{n}*
Gatschet noted that the first syllable of the band's name *(tche-)* was similar to the Lipan word for "river otter," *(tchá)*. The second syllable *(shä^n)* was rooted in the word for "sun" and had connotations of the sacred east. Gatschet also provided an alternate spelling of the band name as *Tcecä^n* and noted that the Tonkawas called this band *Tcá*. Gatschet termed the Sun Otter band the "San Antonio Lipans" (Gatschet, 1885: 33). They ranged from San Antonio to the Rio Grande, with their primary camp, *El Atascoso*, located about thirty miles south of San Antonio near the Atascosa River.

3. Green Mountain band   *Tsél tátlidshä^n*

The Lipan word *tsél* meant "mountain," while the word *tátlidshä^n* indicated a dark green color *(tátlidh)* associated with the sun *(shä^n)* of the sacred east. This band inhabited the lower Texas Gulf Plains, primarily along the lower Colorado, Guadalupe and Nueces Rivers, and represented a core remnant of the Forest Lipan division. Along with the chiefs of the Sun Otter band, the Green Mountain chiefs were responsible for establishing horses-for-guns alliances with east Texas tribes and acted as middle-men when horses stolen by other bands were funneled through to east Texas. On May 22, 1786, most of the Green Mountain chiefs were killed in a Tonkawa attack (M. Valdéz, 1786: 123). The Green Mountain remnants were absorbed by the High-Beaked Moccasin band.

4. High-Beaked Moccasin band   *Kóke metcheskó lähä^n*

Gatschet did not specify a territory associated with this band, as they most probably took their name from that their chief, *Zapato Sas (Tailored Shoe or possibly Bear Shoe).* [5] When the buffalo or cow hide was cut for a moccasin, this particular band cut the hide on the bias or at an angle across the grain. When the hide was drawn together at the top of the foot above the instep, instead of forming a bunch to be tied off, it formed a bird-like beak pointing toward the toes. The High-Beaked Moccasin band was a renamed incarnation of Green Mountain remants. When *Zapato Sas* took over band leadership in May 1786 upon the death of *Cuernitos (Little Horns)*, the amalgamated remnants were renamed after their new leader (Cabello, 1786b: 90-93).

Upper Lipan bands; Remnants of the Plains Lipan division
5. Fire or Camp Circle band   *Ndáwe χóhä^n*

The name of the Fire or Camp Circle band was rooted in the Lipan word for wheel *(ndá awĕ)* and indicated that this band pitched their teepees and *jacals* in a circular fashion (Gatschet, 1884: 8). Since the word "wheel" would have been a linguistic adaptation made after contact with the Spanish, the usage in the band name probably referred to the geometric form of a circle, a concept that would have been familiar to the Lipans prior to Spanish contact. The second word in the band name *(χóhä^n or qóhä^n)* probably derived from the Lipan root word for fire *(kó)* (Gatschet, 1884: Schedule 4). The Fire or Camp Circle band inhabited areas west southwest of Ft. Griffin from the San Saba River to the Rio Grande.

6. Pulverizing or Rubbing band   *Tchó^n kanä^n*

The name of this band was reflective of the use of a *metlatl* or grinding stone known in Lipan as a *se'tchesh* (Gatschet, 1884: 9). The band ranged from west of Ft. Griffin to the west side of the Rio Grande on the Mexican side of the river. Gatschet noted that they were "probably extinct now [1884]." (Gatschet, 1884: 56) This band was probably led by *Pastellano (The Baker)* after 1750. When *Pastellano* and most of his band were killed by Spanish troops from El Paso in 1762, the remnants of the Pulverizing band were absorbed into the Little Breech-clout band (Cansio, 1763: 177-178).

7. Little Breech-clout band   *Tcha^n shka ózhäyĕ^n*

Gatschet used a Spanish phrase, *taparrabos chiquito (tiny loincloth)*, when describing the name of this Lipan band. As was the case with the Red Hair band and the High-Beaked Moccasin band, the name of the Little Breech-clout band was representational of both a particular Lipan stylistic aspect as well as the name of the band chief, *Poca Ropa (Scant or few clothes)*. It is impossible to know with certainty if the chief took his name from the distinctive clothing style or if the distinctive style flowed from an adaptation created by the chief for his particular band. The Little Breech-clout band inhabited territory along the lower Pecos River of Texas (Gatschet, 1884: 55).

8. Uplanders   *Tāzhä'^{n}*

Gatschet noted that the Uplander band was also known by the Spanish designation *arriba*, meaning "upper." His second informant, a Lipan scout named Juan, was a member of this band (Gatschet, 1884: 55). The Uplanders lived along the upper Rio Grande in southern New Mexico, probably in the Organ or Sacramento Mountains. In October 1790, Spanish documents recorded Upper Lipan *rancherías* in that area, although the group migrated to the upper Nueces River of Texas to hunt buffalo (Wade, 2003: 213-214).

9. Prairie Men   *Kó ^{c}l kukä'^{n} or Kó ^{c}l kahä'^{n}*

The name of this Lipan band was rooted in *kó ^{c}lká*, the Lipan word for prairie (Gatschet, 1884: 27). The Prairie Men inhabited territory west of Ft. Griffin along the upper Colorado and Concho Rivers and ranged west to the Pecos. This band represented the primary remnant of the Plains Lipan division which had pushed the Jumanos from the Concho River valley in the late seventeenth century. By the late eighteenth century, this band was known as *Llaneros* and inhabited territory which constituted the front lines of Comanche expansion in west Texas. Alliances with other Apache groups, such as the *Lipiyans*, *Natagés*, Mescaleros and Faraónes, were only natural given the perilous location of the Prairie Men's territorial range.

10. Wild Goose band   *Te ^{c}lkóndahä^n*

The band name was rooted in the Lipan word for wild goose *(te ^{c}l)* and is reminiscent of a Lipan myth, "The Battle with the Wild Geese." In this myth, a group of Lipan raiders came upon a camp of people who had been troubled by attacks of wild geese. The geese enjoyed fighting—"dancing up and down," brandishing their wings as shields and "they could kill with their pecking." (Opler, 1940: 46-47) The name of this Lipan band was probably based on a particular style of battle, using shields and arrows to "flap" and "peck at" the enemy. The Wild Goose band inhabited territory west of Ft. Griffin and were known as renowned fighters. Gatschet commented that "they fight all the time." (Gatschet, 1884: 56 and Schedule 12) In the late eighteenth century, it is possible that this band was incorporated with the Prairie Men band, forming a combined *Llanero* group.

11. North band   *Shä-ǟ*

Gatschet noted that the North band "lived on the other side of a big mountain, other side of *Dapéshte* River; now at Washita River Agency (Ft. Sill Reservation), abt. 300 Lipans." (Gatschet, 1884: 56) The *Dapéshte* River is not included in the ethnologist's list of Lipan place names, a list which encompasses most of Texas' largest rivers. [6] However, the word *Dapéshte* contains the root word *pesh,* or stone knife, and the prefix *Da-,* which indicates the color brown, so the reference seems to be to a river which contained brown flints along its banks (Gatschet, 1884: 16).

Gatschet's location of the North band of Lipans at the Washita Agency of Oklahoma indicates that the North band ranged, in the mid-nineteenth century, in areas of northwestern Texas also inhabited by the Kiowa Apaches since the Kiowa Apaches were the primary residents at Washita in 1884. Between 1855 and 1860, a group of approximately 100 to 300 Lipan Apaches sought to escape military pressures exerted against the Lipan tribe in Texas and took refuge with the Kiowa Apaches prior to the placement of the latter tribe on an Oklahoma reservation. When the Kiowa Apaches were placed on a reservation near Ft. Sill after 1865, the Lipan North band remained with the Kiowa Apaches and also occupied the Washita settlement. However, the scanty records that do exist seem to indicate that the North band was composed of only about 100 persons by 1884, rather than the 300 persons estimated by Gatschet (Sjoberg, 1953: 80).

Mexican Lipan bands
12. Big Water band   *Kû'ne tsá*

This band inhabited the Mexican side of the Rio Grande River, primarily northern Coahuila, and took its name from that river *(Kuné tsé)* (Gatschet, 1884: 55, 33). Louis, Gatschet's primary informant, was a *Kû'ne tsá* member. The Big Water band was originally formed in 1751, when a group of Lipans broke away from their kin inhabiting areas west of San Antonio and moved across the Rio Grande into northern Coahuila near Zaragosa. They ranged south into the Santa Rosa Valley. Their primary camps were along the Escondido and San Rodrigo Rivers as well as camps located in the Santa Rosa Mountains and in the mountain range known as *Sierra El Burro.*

By 1850, the Big Water band lived in a fixed settlement at Hacienda Patiño. An attack by Mexican Army troops in 1869 sent a portion of the band fleeing to join the Mescaleros in New Mexico (Chebahtah and Minor, 2007: 3-5, 32-33). Band remnants returned to Zaragosa but in 1903, the Diaz regime "took their land away from them and [threatened to] send them to a place in South America." (Carroll, 1908) Thirty-seven Lipans were taken into custody by the Mexican Army and imprisoned in Chihuahua City. This group was sent to join their kin on the Mescalero Reservation (Ball, 1988: 267-270). The balance of the Big Water Lipans fled to Texas or into the Santa Rosa Mountains of Coahuila.

From 1750 to 1903, the Big Water band remained the primary cultural repository for the Lipan people, retaining the old ways and purest form of shamanistic belief, although it also adapted much from both the Hispanic and native inhabitants of northern Mexico. This band's incorporation of peyote rituals adapted from the Carrizo Indians was a Lipan cultural feature passed along to the Mescalero Apaches and, ultimately, to the Comanches and Kiowas, forming the foundation of the present-day Native American Church.

13. Painted Wood People   *Tsésh ke shénde or Tséč kecénde*
Gatschet noted that this band "lived at Lavon, Mexico . . . [and] may be extinct now [1884]." (Gatschet, 1884: 56) Gatschet's locational note was probably a reference to *Laván,* Coahuila, a small ranching settlement located between Zaragosa and Morelos. The settlement does not appear on modern maps, but Mexican anthropologists attest to the fact that the settlement still exists. The area is also the site of rock art, which local residents attribute to the Lipan Apaches. [7] Berlandier (1828) noted that the Lipans were skillful painters and sold buffalo hides painted with "hieroglyphic" designs (Ewers, 1969: 128). The name of the Painted Wood band echoes this aspect of Lipan culture and also provides a clue as to one possible means by which the Lipans recorded the celestial observations necessary to predict eclipses (See Chapter 16).

Band representing an aspect of early Lipan history
14. Heads of Wolves, Bodies of Men band   *Tsés tsē'mbai*
Gatschet noted that this band "lived about sundown," and in a northwesterly direction from Ft. Griffin (Gatschet, 1884: 55). This geographic location would place band territory far above the Colorado River, possibly in the Lubbock, Texas area. Gatschet did not state that the band had been extirpated by 1884, but it is hard to see how they could have survived in eighteenth century Comanche territory. It seems probable, given the mythological aspects embedded in the name, that this band was not a historical Lipan band of the eighteenth century but was included in Gatschet's list on a purely representational basis to indicate an early Lipan presence in north Texas prior to the advent of the Comanches.

Population Estimates

A number of eighteenth and nineteenth century outside observers attempted to estimate the total Lipan population, but the large number of bands and their vast territorial range—stretching across Texas into New Mexico, as well as extending across the Rio Grande into four northern Mexican states—made it virtually impossible for one observer to be aware of, much less estimate population figures for the entire tribe.

In any discussion of Lipan tribal population totals, the North band and the Heads of Wolves band must be separated out. The Heads of Wolves band probably represented an ancient territorial claim stretching back to the Lipan entry into Texas in the 1600's. The North band's presence in northwest Texas is not confirmed by the historical record until after 1855 and it is unclear whether the North band represented a band which existed prior to 1850 or was a break-away group which sought refuge with the Kiowa Apaches and adopted the "North" designation around 1855 or 1860. In addition, this discussion of Lipan population figures will be confined to a total of ten bands, using the assumption that the High-Beaked Moccasin band was a later Green Mountain incarnation containing the same population and that Red Hair's group was absorbed by another band after his arrest in 1739.

In the eighteenth century, there were only two instances where reasonably accurate Lipan population totals were calculated. In 1761, Fr. Diego Ximenez was the first Spaniard to confirm that the Lipan tribe was composed of at least ten bands (Ximenez 1761b: 195). He was also the first Spaniard to meet with band chiefs from both Texas and northern Mexico, giving him a much wider appreciation of the extent of Lipan territories. The priest made a number of estimates of the Lipan population both before and after founding two missions for the Lipan Apaches on the Nueces River of Texas, basing his estimates on his discussions with band chiefs. In 1762, he estimated the Lipan population to total 5,000 men, women and children (Ximenez, 1762: 113-115). In 1763, he estimated the population to be at least 3,000 persons (Ximenez, 1763a: 140). In 1764, Fr. Ximenez reported that the Lipan totaled "4,000 males and females of all ages." (Ximenez, 1764: 175) However, Ximenez admitted that he was not acquainted with all the Lipan bands, and his figures might be a low in light of statements made by Lipan chief *Turnio (the Squint-eyed One)*, who disclosed that his band alone contained, "400 men (warriors only) without including women and children of either sex." (Rabago, 1762b: 201) *Turnio's* count seems to represent one of the larger Lipan bands (totaling about 1,200 men, women and children).

An average Lipan band contained "300 persons capable of bearing arms." (Cansio, 1763: 177). This statement indicates that an average band contained 300 adults, or approximately 150 men and 150 women. If a corresponding number of children were included, the average Lipan band would contain about 450 persons. Using this figure and a multiplier of ten bands, a total eighteenth century tribal population can be fixed at about 4,500 men, women and children.

This calculation finds validation in a series of meetings held in Monclova (Coahuila), San Antonio (Texas) and Chihuahua (Nueva Vizcaya) from December 1777 to September 1778, as Spanish military commanders met with Commanding General Theodoro de Croix to devise a strategy for dealing with the Apaches. The Monclova meeting determined that there were about 5,000 Apache warriors among the "*Lipanes* from above, Apaches *Lipanes* from below, Mescaleros, *Natagés*, Faraones, Navajos and Gileños." (Juntas de Guerra, 1778: 53) This figure represents at least 1,400 Lipan warriors, or a total population of 4,200 persons. [8] However, Brigadier Mendinueta and Lt. Col. De Anza argued in Chihuahua that they were "of the opinion that [the total number of Apache warriors] is much larger than 5,000 men." (Juntas de Guerra, 1778: 53) While Mendinueta and De Anza did not speculate as to exactly how many Apache warriors they believed existed, a conservative estimate for a total Lipan population would still fall between 4,000-6,000 persons.

By the dawn of the nineteenth century, the Lipan tribal population had declined in numbers, due in great part to smallpox epidemics which periodically swept through Lipan *rancherías*. The smallpox epidemic of 1780 was particularly severe, with a disease epicenter of south Texas. In 1798, the San Antonio and south Texas bands each contained a total of about 300 persons, a decline from an average of 450 persons early in the eighteenth century (Lafuente, 1798: 156).

By 1820, Juan Padilla estimated that there were only 700 Lipans still residing in Texas (Hatcher, 1919: 56). In 1828, José Ruíz estimated the Texas Lipan population at 450 persons (Ewers, 1972: 6). Berlandier estimated the Lipan population to be 400 families and 600 men, or a total of at least 1,200 people (Ewers, 1969: 128). From 1845-1852, a number of different estimates were made as to the total Lipan population, but in each case, the observer was only aware of a portion of the tribe. Butler and Lewis, who negotiated treaties with the Texas Indian tribes in 1846, "estimated the Lipan with 125 members, a figure which may have been derived from treaty attendance." (Opler, 1975: 170) Opler and Ray, in their 1975 Lipan study for the Indian Claims Commission, concluded "that the population of the Lipan remained stable or increased in the 1845-1855 period between 500 and 1,000 [persons]." (Opler, 1975: 171)

While estimates of the population of the Texas Lipan bands varied wildly in the mid-nineteenth century, the population totals of the bands inhabiting Coahuila and southern New Mexico were virtually unknown. In 1868, two Mexican Lipan groups led by *Costalites* and *Gicori Soli* were estimated to total 80-120 persons (Brown, 1868). A decade later, Mexican Army officers estimated a single Lipan *ranchería* contained no more than 35 or 40 people (Moffitt, 1879).

The earliest reservation census data shows only seventeen Lipans living at the Oakland Agency of Oklahoma after 1880 (Irvine, 1880). After 1865, about 100 Lipans lived with the Kiowa Apaches at the Washita Agency in Oklahoma. By 1940, that number had been reduced to an estimated thirty-five persons (Carlisle, 1996: 212).

In New Mexico, the first Mescalero census (1885-1886) listed twenty Lipan Apaches, only 1.7% of the total Mescalero Agency population. By 1904, the total number of Lipans at the Mescalero Agency had risen to 108 persons with the birth of children and the inclusion of additional Lipans placed on the reservation from 1886 to 1903 (Mescalero Reservation Census, 1886-1904). [9]

What happened to the once numerous Lipan Apaches? How could a tribe that once numbered from 4,000 to 6,000 persons in 1778, and which contained a Texas population estimated to be at least 500 to 1,000 persons in 1855, be reduced to less than 250 persons by 1904? Smallpox certainly took its toll, as did Lipan deaths occurring during raids and military attacks. The Lipan birthrate was probably never high even when the bands were at full-strength (Ball, 1988: 213). However, all these factors still do not fully explain the great diminution in Lipan population.

One explanation can be found in Gatschet's 1884 ethnographic notes. In his comments on the Sun Otter band of San Antonio, he noted, "Some are there now." (Gatschet, 1884: 33) This author contends that a case can be made that small groups of extended families, in response to epidemics and military pressure which splintered their bands, simply faded into the Hispanic populations of Texas and northern Mexico. After 1800, most Lipans bore Hispanic surnames and spoke Spanish. The Lipans traditionally disguised themselves in Hispanic clothing so as to pass unseen among the general population. The existence of Lipan Apaches in San Antonio in 1884, a date when the core groups comprising the Lipan reservation populations were already in place, proves that not all the Lipans were placed on reservations and supports the thesis that conventional wisdom, which credits the virtual extinction of the Lipan Apache tribe in the late nineteenth century, is wrong. At least a small portion of the tribal population evaded military custody in Texas and refused to submit to reservation life after 1880.

If Lipans in south Texas and around San Antonio were able to blend into the Hispanic population, one must wonder if that was also the case with many of the Mexican Lipans. Again, Gatschet provided an explanation. He also noted that in 1884, there were 200 Lipans living in the Santa Rosa Mountains of Coahuila, a location about thirty miles south of Zaragosa (Gatschet, 1884: 33). At least three major Mexican Army campaigns and eleven U.S. Army cross-border incursions were directed against the Coahuilan Lipans from 1873 to 1881. Conventional wisdom credits these military actions with the extirpation of most, if not all, of the non-reservation Lipan tribal population. However, conventional wisdom is wrong in this case. Gatschet's informants stated there were still 200 Lipans in Coahuila three years after the last military campaign. The very fact that thirty-seven Zaragosa Lipans were thrown off their land, imprisoned in Chihuahua City and brought to the Mescalero Reservation in 1903 proves the argument that Lipan remnant groups remained in Mexico after 1881.

Today, the Lipan Apache Tribe of Texas is composed of persons who claim descent from the many anonymous Lipan extended families who never entered a reservation, but who blended into the Hispanic populations of south Texas and northern Mexico. [10] Although this group represents only a small fraction of the total possible descendants of the once-numerous Lipan Apaches, they represent a growing awareness among borderland peoples of their proud Apache heritage.

Chapter 11

Political Organization: The Lipan Chief

Personal Qualifications and Role of the Chief

Each Lipan band was led by a chief *(náshneta* or *nanitá)* who, through general consensus within the band, was deemed to be "the most respected and admired of the heads of the families." (Opler, 1975: 8) [1] He was a respected individual who "earned his prominence through performance and personal qualities. . . . Many of the families that clustered about his were present because of their faith in his sagacity and successful exploits." (Opler, 1975: 15)

In contrast to a man's merit as the measure of leadership, Manuel Merino (1804) believed that an Apache band's choice of chief was conditioned on which man could marshal the largest family faction (John, 1991: 150). The actual process of reaching a consensus on a chief was probably a combination of both factors. A man had to possess sterling qualities in order to be recognized as a Lipan leader, but having a large number of family supporters also didn't hurt.

However, even a highly esteemed candidate for leadership was not immune to criticism and challenge by other men. Berlandier recorded the following conversation among a group of young Lipan warriors in 1828.

> During my stay in Laredo, I heard some malcontent Lipans grumbling about their chiefs and murmuring against their nomination. 'There they are captains,' they said, 'and they have only little scars. But I, who am covered with scars, am nothing.' (Ewers, 1969: 39)

In order to obtain the standing and prominence necessary to be recognized as a Lipan chief, a man had to possess a number of meritorious qualities. He not only had to be a shrewd and valorous war leader, but he had to be a persuasive conciliator and peacemaker. "A successful leader had to be sensitive to currents of opinion; often he summed up a consensus and paved the way for a popular course of action, rather than attempting to impose a personal point of view (Opler, 1975: 8-9).

The skill necessary to reconcile opposing factions within a band was perhaps more important for a Lipan leader than a reputation for bravery in battle, since the Apache concept of revenge could destroy the harmony of the camp and splinter the group. If an individual caused grievous injury or insult to another, the offended party could declare a blood feud. The Lipan chief had to have his finger on the pulse of the community to such a degree that he could persuasively intervene in a judicious manner before events reached such a dire end.

A thorough knowledge of tribal mythology and legend was also necessary before a man could be acclaimed a Lipan band chief. One of Opler's Lipan informants explained this aspect of Lipan leadership.

My father said that before a man can be a chief, he has to know all about the chief's ways in the time when the birds and animals spoke. He has to know how they acted; he has to know all these stories of the chiefs among the animals and birds. Before he talks a great deal or gives orders he should know all about these stories and study them well. These are the 'chief stories. . . .' A man gains his chieftainship by all these (war) deeds. But there is another way to become a chief. If a man knows the traditions about Killer-of-Enemies and about the eagle, if he knows these two things, he becomes a chief without even being in a fight. (Opler, 1940: 8)

In addition to a thorough knowledge of myth, a Lipan band chief had to tender the utmost respect and deference to the band's holy men and women, thereby acknowledging the preeminent role of shamanistic power and ritual in community life. A Lipan chief could also benefit from a claimed ability to access supernatural power. "[I]t was well to have a leader, no matter how sagacious, who had access to divine guidance when the best human efforts seemed unequal to the problem confronted." (Opler, 1975: 8)

To a large extent, the Lipan chief was "the spokesman for the group and the one who sensed and summarized sentiment." Any coercive power he possessed was held at the will of his followers. A Lipan chief was only as successful as his skill in interpreting community sentiment and mitigating friction within the group allowed him to be.

He had no way to enforce an unpalatable decision; he had to understand what his followers were willing to do. No other family head was obliged to follow him blindly or to remain with the group; therefore serious misjudgments or unpopular counsel might cost him his position or a portion of his followers (Opler, 2002: 11).

Typical decisions made by a Lipan band chief fell into three general areas: economic, social and political. A band chief might decide to move the camp to a different location because of poor hunting. He also had to determine and announce, after consultation with the band's holy man, the appropriate time and location for the buffalo hunt and tuna harvest. While small groups often decided to hunt deer or trade hides, the band chief still assumed overall responsibility if such ventures did not reach a successful conclusion. While the band chief might not specifically direct a group of raiders to steal livestock, the trade in stolen horses was carried on with the complicit knowledge and assistance of the chief, who had to forge alliances with other Lipan bands and other Indian tribes in order to be able to trade stolen horses for guns. The band chief also had to be mindful of the general health of his population. Repeated deaths or epidemics called for intense shamanic consultation and decisive measures, and the chief was charged with making sure the band followed shamanic recommendations in an exact manner. Social ceremonies involving the entire band, such as the girl's puberty ceremony, were sanctioned by the band chief, although the arrangements were usually carried out by the girl's extended family. Finally, the

Lipan band chief acted as the final authority in matters of raiding, war and peace. Although any man could step forward and propose a raid, a holy man could exercise a veto over the project if his Power told him that the raid would be unsuccessful. If this occurred, the band chief would then be called upon to validate the holy man's decision and propose an alternative route or raiding destination. If a Lipan band declared war, the chief acted as the voice of the community in declaring war and negotiating peace.

Aspects of Leadership and Authority

The issues surrounding the extent of a Lipan chief's authority and the inheritability of that authority were viewed by the Lipans in a different manner than the same issues were viewed by the Mescaleros. Morris Opler took the position that both tribes had the same view and practice. When examining aspects of Lipan chieftainship, he stated,

> Leadership was in keeping with the diffused social conventions. The chief of the local group was a respected and important individual, but his role was that of an esteemed adviser, rather than that of one who exercised arbitrary authority (Opler, 1975: 15).

In reference to both Lipan and Mescalero chieftainship, Opler noted, "With so much emphasis on performance, it is obvious that leadership was not hereditary, though a leader's son of estimable qualities probably had an advantage." (Opler, 1975: 9) While Opler's statements were certainly applicable to Mescalero leadership, the historical record paints a very different picture of the authority of the Lipan chief and his ability to pass his office to his offspring.

Fr. Diego Ximenez was the first Spaniard to closely observe Lipan band chiefs in a non-military situation, and his comments in 1761 and 1764 on Lipan leadership are illuminating.

> [The Lipans] . . . have many chiefs. This quality [title] is inherited. . . . He who gets a reputation of being bold is joined by several others who elect him chief without any ceremony other than joining him. The valiant practice polygamy; the others are not permitted to do so. . . . [The people] are subordinate to the chiefs. The chiefs punish them even with the death penalty whenever they are powerful enough to do it and not because there is an ability or a commitment. All of them are free; they go from one settlement *(ranchería)* to another whenever their chief does not have the strength to oppose. . . . They recognize one chief as their leader. He is in charge of all their affairs. The chief condemns traitors to the great fire. The innocent also go with the criminals (Ximenez, 1761a, 1764: 26-27, 177).

The observations made by Fr. Ximenez paint a very different picture than the model proposed by Morris Opler. Whereas Opler believed a chief to be a naturally recognized leader who rose to chieftainship through selection not inheritance, a man who was an esteemed advisor but whose role did not include the exercise of arbitrary power, Fr. Ximenez described Lipan chieftainship as a position which could be inherited and a chief's role as one with considerable arbitrary authority, albeit with a constant check provided by general consensus. The historical record supports Fr. Ximenez, providing numerous instances of inherited chieftainship among the Lipan Apaches.

However, the priest and Opler did agree on one aspect of Lipan leadership. A man first came to the attention of his peers through braveness and boldness on the field of battle. He was then "joined by others" who "elect him chief without any ceremony." (Ximenez, 1761a: 27) This described the process within the band as consensus began to build around one candidate for leadership. A candidate who had the largest extended family and associated relations (and thus had the highest approval rating) and was able to win the support of the majority of family heads, was generally acknowledged by the entire band to be its leader.

Fr. Ximenez noted there were three benefits flowing from the position of leadership. The first benefit was the possibility that the position could become hereditary if the chief had a son with enough ability and charisma to succeed his father. This would allow the older chief to retain the wealth and power he had accumulated within his extended family. Each generation of leaders had to win over their "constituents" through sagacity, good judgment, war bravery, a thorough knowledge of band territory so that all food resources could be utilized without exploitation, a thorough knowledge of myth, and a shrewd confidence and forward-thinking that assured advantage in dealing with tribal outsiders. These qualities were a necessary component of leadership and if a chief possessed them, his people could then rejoice in a steady flow of favors, raid booty and ample food sources. A rough system of checks and balances assured that each band chief, whether selected by consensus or through inheritance, possessed at least some of the qualities mentioned above. The freedom of each extended family to leave one band and affiliate with another acted as a strong check against a weak leader. If a young man inherited a chieftainship and was too indecisive or pushed too strongly against general opinion, he could soon find himself without any followers.

A second benefit flowing from a position of leadership was the ability to accumulate wealth and thus the ability to support multiple wives. A band chief who planned and executed a successful war or large-scale raid could count on receiving the best horses and booty. Although the chief knew that his personal possessions would be destroyed upon his death, his extended family would have the use of horses and booty distributed lavishly within the family while the chief still held his position of leadership. When enough wealth was accumulated by a chief to support multiple wives, the possibility of alliances with other powerful extended families both within the band and in other bands became a possibility. The wealth and authority necessary for some Lipan band chiefs to approach and ally through marriage with other tribes such as the *Natagés* is a testament to the structure and position of the Lipan leadership and illustrates that a powerful Lipan band chief could be much more than just an "esteemed adviser."

A third benefit flowing from leadership was power. The chief received the subordination of his people and held the power of life or death over them. But Fr. Ximenez was anxious to point out that a chief's power was not that of a despot. His wording is important in understanding the nature of the power of a Lipan chief. The Lipan people chose to become subordinate to their chief and he, at times, could order the death of someone within the band. The chief, however, could not rule as a tyrant, nor did the Lipans have a system of laws mandating a death penalty for an offense. The chief could condemn a "traitor" to death ("the great fire" of death that awaited the heathen) only because this was the general wish of the population. This interpretation of the priest's words is made clear in his sentence, "The innocent also go with the criminals." If the consensus of the band (validated by shamanic interpretation) was such that a person or persons had breeched custom to such an egregious degree that death was the only remedy, then the chief was obliged to order death. An example of such a situation would be the death of both an adulteress and adulterer.

Individual Lipan Chiefs

The names of the Lipan band chiefs are a colorful combination of Spanish characterizations of the man's notable physical features and a smattering of Spanish baptismal names acquired when the chief was nominally baptized. *Josef el Manco (Joseph the One-Armed)* is one example. Other chiefs' names are a direct translation of the Lipan name into Spanish, such as *Maiz Malo* or *Bad Corn.* In a few instances, we even have the chief's name in the Lipan language. *Cusax-ques* was the Lipan name, or possibly title, of Chief *Josef Chiquito.*

One interesting feature is the addition of the suffixes *-cillo* or *–lillo* at the end of some names. This odd usage seemed to indicate that the chief with the suffix attached to his name was an adopted son (or descendant of an adopted son) who inherited the chieftainship. For example, Chief *Xavierlillo (Little Xavier)* inherited the chieftainship of his band from his father *Josecillo (Little Jose)*, who was, in turn, a Christianized Manso Indian who had been adopted by a Lipan chief and rose to the leadership of his band (i.e. a captive who married the daughter of a band chief) (Weddle, 1968: 341). The suffix *–ito*, however, indicated a direct blood relationship between two generations of chiefs. Chief *Boca Tuerte's (Crooked Mouth)* son was known as *Tuertecito (Little Crooked).*

During the nineteenth century, there are some faint hints among the Mexican Lipans that the names of some eighteenth century chiefs were carried over for at least two or more generations, probably because the original name had been associated with a family or clan identification symbol. The Mexican Lipan named *Caro Colorado (Red Face,* born ca. 1825) carried the *Colorado* designation seen in the names of *el Bermejo (The Reddish One,* ca. 1790) and *Cabellos Colorado* (ca. 1740). Similarly, a Lipan named *Blanco* (born 1846) carried the designation indicating the color white, as seen in the name of *Cabellos Blanco* (ca. 1763). The name of Mexican Lipan shaman *Chevato* or *Chivato* (born 1852) echoed that of Mexican Lipan chief *Pedro el Chivato* (ca. 1784). The Mexican Lipan named *Boneski* (White Tooth, born 1835) recalls the name of the *Natagés* chief *Big Tooth* (ca. 1790). [2] There is also strong evidence that the naming patterns within the family of Mexican Lipan chief *Bigotes* carried a family or clan identifier of a shoe. *Bigotes'* brother and brother-in-law both carried the designation *Quijiugusyá* (Shoe). *Bigotes* was also known as *Taguadas Chille* or Squeaky Boots (Serrano, 1780: 35). [3]

Lipan Bands and Associated Chiefs

One of the primary reasons the Lipan Apaches were able to survive and thrive for almost two centuries in the face of near-constant attack can be traced directly back to the abilities of their leaders. The shrewdness and forward-thinking of the Lipan band chiefs, their ability to turn setbacks to their advantage and their skill in playing more powerful groups against each other were qualities demonstrated time and again. These were men who, through their cunning, preserved their tribe and culture in the face of near-overwhelming odds.

Table 11.0   Lipan Bands, Their Chiefs and Lines of Succession, 1738-1874

Note: (S) = Son

Band	Chiefs and Their Successors*	Approx. Length of Rule**
Lower Lipans (Remnants of Forest Lipan division):		
Red Hair band	Cabellos Colorado (Red Hairs)	1738-1740
Red Hair band absorbed into Sun Otter band after 1740		
Sun Otter band	Boca Comida (Mouth of Food)	1749
Sun Otter extended family groups ca. 1780:		
+ (1) Josef Grande el Manco (Big Joseph the One-Armed)		1779-1781
(S) Josef/José Chiquito aka José Antonio, aka *Cusax-ques*		1781-1821
(S) Cuelgas de Castro		1821-1842
(S) Ramón Castro		1844-1847
(S) John/Juan Castro		1845-1854
(S) Seuge/Simon Castro		1844
(S) Lamo/Lamos- possible son		1845-1852
(S) el Cojo (The Lame One)		1822-1828
(S) el Joyoso (Jeweled One) – son of Josef Grande		1779-1784
(2) Casaca (Riding Jacket)		1779-1787
(S) Casaca Chiquito, Casaquito (Little Casaca)		1787-1799
(3) Roque (Castle)		1779-1791
Sun Otter extended family groups ca. 1800:		
+ (1) Canoso (Old One) aka Canon, Canoso el Colorado		1787-1810
(2) Josef Lombraña		1791
(3) Xavier aka Malave (Evil One)		1791-1808
(4) Moreno (The Dark One), aka *Tuclax-y elté*		1791-1833
(S) Magoosh – successor and possible son; fled to Mescaleros		1850-1900

Band	Chiefs and Their Successors	Approx. Length of Rule

Green Mountain band   Green Mountain extended family groups ca. 1740-1760:
+ (1) Cuero de Coyote (Coyote Hide)	1740
(2) Cabellos Blanco (White Head)	1763

Green Mountain extended family groups ca. 1760-1780:
+ (1) Panocha (Corn Pudding) aka Panocha Rivera	1762-1786
Panocha died in battle May 22, 1786	
(S) Panocha's son- died in battle, May 22, 1786	
(2) Manteca Mucho (Much Butter) aka el Gordo (Much Fat)	1755-1779
(S) Pisana (One who leaves a footprint); died of measles	1779-1787
(S) el Pato Blanco (White Duck); died of measles	1779-1787
(3) Cuernitos (Little Horns) - died in battle May 22, 1786	1785-1786
(S) el Cibolo (The Buffalo)-successor and possible son	1785-1787
(4) Borado Zapato (Embroidered Shoe)	1762

Green Mountain absorbed into High-Beaked Moccasin band after May 22, 1786

High-Beaked Moccasin band   High-Beaked extended family groups ca. 1800:
+ (1) Zapato Sas (Tailored Shoe or Bear Shoe)	1786-1791
(S) Juan Maria Sas	1821-1840
+ (2) El Flacco (The Thin One)	1821-1843
(S) Flacco the Younger- killed 1843	1840-1843
(S) Flacco Chico (Little Flacco) aka John Flacco	1844-1854

Upper Lipans (Remnants of Plains Lipan division):

Fire/Camp Circle band   Pintas (Spotted One)   1754
Fire Circle extended family groups ca. 1760:
+ (1) Cavezon (Big Head) aka Cabello Largo	1760-1790
(S) el Valazo (The Wounded One)	1790-1791
(2) Turnio (Squint Eye)	1762
(3) Boruca (Chatterbox)	1762-1772
(4) Teja	1762

Fire Circle extended family groups ca. 1780:
+ (1) Boca Tuerte (Crooked Mouth)-died of smallpox	1775-1781
(S) Tuertecito (Little Crooked) aka *Davinica-jaté*	1781-1791
(2) Casimiro aka *Dabeg Silipete*	1780-1788
(3) Maiz Malo aka Maiz Feo (Bad or Ugly Corn)	1780
(4) el Viejo (The Old One)	1780
(5) Josecillo (Manso Indian captive)	1775
(S) Xavierlillo	1775-1790
(S) He of the Red Feather aka Bloody Feathers	1791

Fire Circle extended family group ca. 1800:
+ (1) Coyote	1851

Pulverizing band   Pulverizing band extended family groups ca. 1750:
(1) Casablanca (White House)	1754
+ (2) Pastellano (The Baker); chief and most of band killed in 1762; survivors absorbed by Little Breech-clout band	1754-1762

Band	Chiefs and Their Successors	Approx. Length of Rule
Little Breech-clout band Little Breech-clout extended family groups ca. 1780-1850:		
+ (1) Poca Ropa (Scant Clothes)		1775-1788
(grandson) Yolcna Poca Ropa		1822-1828
(2) Shanaca		1851
War chief- Manuel Hernandez		1851
Uplanders Unknown, see Note below		
Prairie Men/*Llaneros* Chiquito aka El Chico (Little Boy) aka *Tacú*		1754-1759
Prairie Men extended family groups ca. 1800:		
+ (1) Chiquito		1848-1855
War chief- Chapota		
(2) Manuel		1851-1853
Wild Goose band Unknown, see Note below		
North band Unknown, see Note below		
Heads of Wolves band Unknown, see Note below		

***Mexican Lipan bands*:**

Big Water band Big Water extended family groups ca. 1750-1800:		
+ (1) Bigotes (Mustached One) aka *Daguné* (The Consoled One)		1754-1781
aka Taguadas Chille (Squeaky Boots)		
Died of illness, possibly smallpox, after August 1781		
(S) El Quemado (The Burned One)-successor, possible son		1781-1798
(2) el Bermejo (The Red One) aka Bigotes el Bermejo		1787-1790
(3) Pedro el Chivato (Pedro the Goat)		1784
Big Water extended family groups ca. 1860:		
+ (1) Costalites		1866-1874
(2) Gicori Soli		1868
Painted Wood band Painted Wood extended family groups ca. 1800:		
+ (1) Dátil		1845
(2) Juan Sames		1838

*   Successors are persons named as sons in archival records unless otherwise noted.
** These dates represent only years in which the chief is named in archival records.
\+   Principal band chief

Note: The following 18th century chiefs have an unknown band affiliation but were associated with Upper Lipan bands: el Cojo (The Lame One, 1762), el Lumen (The Light, 1762), Pajarito (Little Bird, 1775), el Cielo (The Sky, 1775; may be same as el Lumen), and el Flacco (The Thin One, 1775). Upper Lipan band chiefs of the 19th century: Yekehtasna (1850), Kehrauch (1850), Peso Sitn (1853). Chiefs with unknown band affiliation: Jacinto (1790), Agá or Dagá (1790-1799), Juan Jose (1799), Cara Humilde (1799), Bautista (1799), Ayatinde (1791), Caboe (1821), Juan Novale (1825), Roan (1844-1854), Quaco (1851), Jose Manuel (1852).

(Sources: *Provincias Internas* and *Historia* volumes in the *Archivo General de Indies* and *Archivo General de Mexico*; Béxar Archives; Opler, 1975: 253-254; Gatschet, 1884: 55-56; Brown, 1868, Rodriguez, 1995: 71)

Chapter 12

Lipan Apache Raiding

Raiding Culture

Lipan raiding culture was inextricably linked to the concept of "harvesting" resources within the bounds of territory over which the tribe claimed dominion. The Lipan ritual used to claim dominion over the land—uprooting grass, drawing water and pouring it over a pile of collected rocks—sealed the tribe's possession of the land and, by extension, implied a right to "harvest" any resources found within its boundaries (Rabago, 1762a: 189). When the Lipans claimed a homeland at Many Houses, they not only claimed the physical terrain of central Texas (its rivers, hills and trees) but they claimed dominion over all its resources. They believed that those resources (deer, buffalo, cactus tuna) existed solely to provide the tribe with the food items they desired and thus could be "harvested" whenever the Lipans wished to do so. The Zuazua history was careful to note, and to reiterate, that the Lipans claimed the land around San Antonio long before the Spanish arrived, even though historical facts suggest otherwise. This claim must be understood in a figurative, not a literal, sense as a belief in an implied right of dominion over the San Antonio area which was used to justify the tribe's later actions *vis-à-vis* Hispanic and Anglo "interlopers."

Within the bounds of territory claimed by each band, any human interlopers, and the possessions and livestock they brought with them, were subject to Lipan dominion and its corresponding right of capture or "harvest." The Lipans believed that because they had staked their claim on the land, they had a corresponding right to search out any resource within their territory and claim it as their own, regardless whether that resource was a herd of deer or a herd of Spanish horses. What the Spanish considered a theft, the Lipan saw as a right.

After 1700, the constant Comanche threat and the need to seek protective alliances forced the Lipans to adopt an attitude of willing co-existence with outsiders who could be of use to the tribe. However, the Lipans tended to view this co-existence through the prism of their concept of dominion, and outsiders were "allowed" to enter and inhabit Lipan territory on the condition that they accept Lipan dominion over them. An ideal example of the behavior expected of outsiders could be seen in the later fortunes of the Jumano tribe. After the Lipans had driven the northern Jumanos from the Concho River Valley in the late seventeenth century, the Lipans claimed dominion over that territory. The Jumanos, however, were allowed to co-exist with the Lipans to such a degree that they joined a Lipan coalition against the Spanish in 1732 (Wade, 2003: 175).

Of course, the Spanish New World experience was also based on concepts of territorial conquest and dominion, so conflict was inevitable from the beginning. Yet, even if the bison herds had not become depleted and even if the Spanish had given the Lipans all the guns and horses they desired, the Lipan Apaches would have still raided, because they saw themselves as the sovereign masters of their territory and their concept of dominion carried with it a corresponding right to "harvest" or "capture" any and all resources.

Raiding Tactics

Any man could propose a raid. Status as chief was not required and the Lipan Apaches valued initiative. However, above initiative, the Lipans esteemed successful performance, so the man proposing a raid must also organize the raid in such a manner so as to ensure its success. This meant that a raider was constantly surveying the physical landscape around him, searching for *ranchos* which offered rich targets and seeking routes that offered the most concealment as the raiding party made its way toward the target and escaped after the theft.

The Western Apache word for raiding meant "to search out enemy property." (Basso, 1971: 16) Unfortunately, we do not know the Lipan word for the act of raiding, but a Lipan raid also generally focused on livestock and other property. A single location containing herds of horses and cattle—along with guns, ammunition, women and children—would have been considered by a Lipan raider to be a rich target indeed, yet this description applied to most Hispanic and Anglo ranches of late eighteenth and nineteenth century Texas and northern Mexico. All isolated ranches and small *villas (towns)* were at risk. Even the presence of a nearby presidio failed to deter Lipan raids, as the presidios were often undermanned and the troops inadequate. Nineteenth century Texas frontier forts, while containing troops better trained and equipped, were also inadequate to prevent Lipan raids. The life of a frontier cavalry soldier often consisted of a series of frustrating pursuits, trying to track a Lipan raiding party that had long since done its damage and moved on. Punctuating the boredom of the fruitless pursuit was the occasional ambush, terrifying in its sharp intensity.

Faced with the meticulous planning and surveillance that accompanied most Lipan raids, many Hispanic and Anglo ranchers were forced to choose between two bad options. The ranches of late eighteenth and nineteenth century Texas and northern Mexico were built as small compounds. Most of the ranch horse herd, or *remuda*, was kept at pasture, guarded by cowboys or horse herders. This job was particularly hazardous because a Lipan raid often involved killing the herders before the horses were stolen. Most of the *remuda*, however, was considered breeding stock and was differentiated from saddle horses, which were generally more valuable and were kept inside the ranch compound at night in a pen or stall (called a *barraca*) next to a house. If stables and pens were built next to a dwelling, there was a chance that the settlers could save their horses from Lipan theft if they posted a nightly guard, but this option was problematic because one never knew when the next night raid might occur and the Lipans were equally as likely to attack during daylight hours. In addition, the close proximity of the stables and pens also forced the rancher and his family to live amidst a cloud of flies and the possibility of disease. Most ranchers penned or tied only their most valuable animals directly adjacent to their dwellings each night and then gritted their teeth and endured the flies. The rest of the saddle horses were penned in enclosures at the edges of the compounds and guarded. The breeding stock *remuda* always remained at risk of theft.

By 1800, the ever pragmatic and resourceful ranchers of Coahuila and Nuevo Leon devised a simple solution. They began to leave their old, sick or inferior saddle horses in unguarded open pens while closely guarding their more valuable animals, hoping to trick the Lipans into stealing animals they were planning to sell in any event. In some cases, the trick worked and as long as the ranchers left their "bribe," the Lipans generally did not attack the family compound. "The Indians preferred to let the cooperative Mexicans live in order to provide them with future supplies of horses." (Ball, 1988: 213) In much the same way, the Lipans chose to allow a portion of a deer or antelope herd escape in order that a future supply of animals would be available. For every "bribe" horse left for the Lipans, corruption among the ranching community grew and the connection between Lipan raiding culture and their concept of dominion was strengthened. The practice of "bribing" was understood by Lipan raiders as an acknowledgement of their dominion over their territory and its inhabitants.

The corruption engendered by the Lipan shadow economy first operated on a personal level among frontier ranchers. Once border ranchers overcame their distaste and "bought off" the Lipans, thus minimizing losses that they figured would be incurred in any event, it was but a small step to "buying off" a corrupt government official to look the other way as they illegally branded *mesteño* cattle. The corruption engendered by the Lipan shadow economy was, by 1850, tacitly acknowledged by the town council of Zaragosa, Coahuila, who officially "adopted" the Lipans, offering them a safe refuge on their return from raids in Texas in return for the economic benefit flowing from the sale of the stolen horses in the local market (Brown, 1868, Schuhardt, 1878a). The town of Santa Rosa (now known as Melchor Musquiz, Coahuila) also had a similar "arrangement" with the Lipans, allowing them to live on ranches owned by Mexican smugglers (Anonymous citizen, 1878).

The Lipan raiding season, source of so much angst for every horse owner in Texas or northern Mexico, generally occurred in the late spring and summer, with May being the primary month in which raids were undertaken. Each raid could last from several weeks to several months. Merino noted that the Lipans and other Apaches carried out two distinct types of raids. The first type of raid was that conducted by a small group of men from one band. These small raiding parties were composed of from four to six men, although from ten to twelve men was more probably the norm. The second type of raid involved raiding parties from several different bands who combined to attack one rich target. This sort of cooperative effort might be undertaken through the agreement and coordination of several band chiefs and might occur when the target lay in territory familiar to the bands undertaking the raid (John, 1991: 155-156).

The Lipans were able to locate and target livestock herds through a combination of surveillance and superior tracking ability. "They can tell not only how long ago the tracks were made, but also whether they were made at night or day, whether the animal was loaded, and with or without a rider, whether it was being driven or was wild." (John, 1991: 160)

A raiding target was assessed in terms of the quantity and quality of the livestock, and the Lipans were excellent judges of horseflesh. Although a "bribe" of sick or inferior animals might be accepted, the Lipans usually sought to punish a rancher for this sort of effrontery. If the Lipans wished to attack a moving target, such as a group of settlers riding along a roadway, they employed skillful means of concealment, such as lying "along the side of their mounts, holding on by a leg and the mane in a manner so perfect that one believes he is looking only at a herd of wild horses. Then, when close enough, they fall on their enemies with an extraordinary velocity." (Ohlendorf, 1980: 270)

Although surveillance and pre-planning before a raid were deemed important, the Lipans and other Apaches excelled in avoiding pursuit after their theft and went to great measures to escape with their booty. Lipan captive Frank Buckelew (1866) noted after his capture, "Every part of [the raider's] trail was covered so completely that a searching party would have been at a loss to determine even the direction in which we were going." (Dennis, 1925: 42) After the successful completion of a raid, the raiders returned to camp with their booty. It was customary "for victorious Lipan war or raiding parties to sing when approaching the camps, that the people might come out and greet them." (Opler, 1940: 8) The booty was then divided up, with the band chief receiving a portion. Although the division of the spoils was often the occasion for disputes among the band, it also provided an opportunity for the band chief to distribute favors and garner support through his distribution of largess (John, 1991: 156).

Depredations

It is extremely difficult to grasp the full extent of a century (1732-1880) of Lipan depredations in Texas and northern Mexico, partly because of the secretive and shadowy nature of the activity and because the historical record is peppered with so many thefts attributed to the Lipans, that to calculate them all would be impossible. A more profitable approach consists of an examination of reports from four eras in order to perceive the scope of the problem posed by Lipan raiding.

Target area: San Antonio, Texas (1718-1731). This decade saw the founding of a presidio, garrisoned by fifty-three soldiers, at San Antonio in 1718 and the establishment of the *villa* of San Fernando de Béxar by fifty-six Canary Island settlers in 1731. [1] The soldiers, priests and settlers brought herds of cattle, breeding horses *(remudas)* and mules with them, as well as a lesser number of ride-able saddle horses shod with iron horseshoes. We do not know exactly how many saddle horses were owned by the soldiers and their families from 1718 to 1731, but a comparison can be made with the *villa* of Laredo, which in 1757 had a comparable population and contained 162 saddle horses, or an average of two horses per person (Bolton, 1903: 190). When the same ratio is applied to the early population of San Antonio, numbering about 150 persons, the result is a total of about 300 saddle horses for the period before the arrival of the Canary Islanders in 1731. The herds of breeding stock, or *remudas*, contained much larger numbers of horses. Although some of these horses could be ridden if necessary, most if not all were unshod and many were unbroken to the saddle. The *remudas* of Laredo, for example, were four to five times larger than the number of saddle horses (Bolton, 1903: 190). If the same proportion is applied to the San Antonio breeding herds, an estimate of 1,200-2,000 breeding horses can be made for the era from 1718 to 1731.

In 1723, only five years after the founding of San Antonio, and before the arrival of the Canary Islanders, Apache raiders came very close to forcing the abandonment of the new settlement. Cabello specified that the raiders were Lipans and *Natagés*, although contemporary documents only stated that the raiders were "Apaches." (Cabello, 1784, 104-105) The first significant raid at San Antonio occurred in 1722, when four raiders stole fifty horses, or about 15% of the garrison's entire saddle horse herd. The soldiers gave chase, caught the thieves, recovered the horses and returned with the heads of the raiders. [2] Not deterred, on the night of August 17, 1723, Apaches took eighty horses from inside a locked corral guarded by ten soldiers (Flores, 1723: 2). This theft resulted in a loss of 27% of the saddle-horse herd and represented significant economic damage, since the animals were not immediately recovered and the mission did not possess enough saddle horses to replace the stolen animals. If the raiders had returned in subsequent nights, the soldiers would have soon been without ride-able horses and it was a long walk to the nearest presidio for help.

Target area: Coahuila (February-June, 1776). When Don Jacobo de Ugarte y Loyola assumed his new post as Governor of Coahuila in 1769, he could boast of almost thirty years service to the King of Spain but nothing had prepared him for what he would soon encounter. By the spring of 1770, more than 3,000 Lipan Apaches were camped on the Texas side of the Rio Grande and they soon began to send raiding parties into Coahuila. The province was protected by a paltry 115 troops in three presidios, a force inadequate to prevent the theft of over 1,500 horses taken in Lipan raids from 1771 to 1772 (Moorhead, 1968: 27-28, 34). It took Ugarte only seven months to decide he did not like the Lipan Apaches. While the new Governor was visiting the Santa Rosa presidio in July 1771, Lipan raiders attacked at high noon, taking over 600 horses and killing one soldier between lunch and siesta. No wonder Ugarte recommended that the entire Lipan tribe be rounded up and shipped overseas! (Moorhead, 1968: 27, 44)

After a 1775 comprehensive Apache campaign led by Hugo O'Conor, the province of Coahuila was deemed to be rid of troublesome raiders but O'Conor had merely temporarily dislodged the problem. The following events occurred during a five-month period in early 1776 and represent a low level in terms of casualties and depredations. The surviving victims reported that the raiders were, in all cases, Lipan Apaches (Ugarte, 1776b, 496).

Table 12.0   Lipan Depredations in Coahuila (February-June 1776)

Date	Occurrence
February 1776	2 settlers killed, 2 mules stolen
March 1776	3 Tlaxcalan Indians killed; horse herd stolen from their pueblo
April 1776	Livestock stolen near *villa* of San Fernando de Austria.
May 2, 1776	1 settler killed, 1 female child captured at Santa Rita Spring; horse herd at *Rancho de San Yldefonso* stolen
May 17, 1776	A settler named Seles escaped from the Lipans after being held captive for 3 years. He reported a stampede of a dozen stolen horses which killed 8 Lipan raiders
May 28, 1776	A servant killed at a ranch near the Rio Grande.
May 29, 1776	4 shepherds killed, 2 children escaped
May 30, 1776	1 servant killed, another wounded in Santa Rosa Valley
May 31, 1776	Oxen stolen from ranch one league from town of Santa Rosa
June 6, 1776	1 peon killed near la Babia presidio; his herd of mares stolen
June 17, 1776	A portion of horse herd owned by the Mines of *Potrerillos* was stolen by a raiding party of about 15 men.
June 19, 1776	5 soldiers from la Babia presidio attacked by 25-30 raiders; 1 raider killed.

(Source: Ugarte, 1776a: 295-298)

Target area: Nuevo Leon (August-September 1791). Don Josef Tovar can rightly be credited with igniting a Lipan rampage across the breadth of Nuevo Leon the likes of which had never been seen before or since. The trouble started with two mules and four mares, all of which had been deftly taken out of a settler's locked corral during the night of July 10, 1791. The settler informed Tovar that the thieves were Lipan Apaches, so Tovar sent out a squad of twenty-nine soldiers with orders to find the thieves' trail. The soldiers found and followed the trail into Texas to the Arroyo San Miguel on the upper Nueces River. After reinforcements arrived, the soldiers attacked the camp of fifty Lipan raiders. In Tovar's glowing report to his superiors, he boasted that his troops had killed Lipan chiefs *Canoso* and *Josef Lombraña* and five raiders. Among the dead warriors was the son of *Xavierlillo*, "the one more terrible and blood-thirsty according to the public voice than his deceased father and [*Canoso* and *Lombraña*], although not in the same class (De Castro, 1791a: 64).

Tovar's superiors were elated at the news of the deaths of the three Lipan chiefs, since *Canoso* and *Lombraña* led large Lower Lipan *rancherías* and the son of *Xavierlillo*, known as Bloody Feathers, led a troublesome group of Upper Lipans. The "Heroes of San Miguel" were highly praised for their bravery. (Tovar, 1791: 77-85).

But Tovar had received faulty intelligence from the battlefield. Not only were *Canoso* and *Lombraña* still alive, they were furiously angry and vowed revenge. They chose the rich ranchlands of northern Nuevo Leon, about 100 miles southeast of Arroyo San Miguel, and blazed a bloody trail through the jurisdictions of *Vallecillo*, *Yguana* and *Punta de Lampazos*. In one month, over 300 howling Lipan warriors killed at least thirty-seven settlers, captured twenty-five men, women and children, and made off with 1,086 horses, 2,400 head of cattle and seven shotguns.

Table 12.1   Lipan Depredations in Nuevo Leon (Aug. 6-Sept. 6, 1791)

Location	Reported Results of Lipan raids
Rancho de Palmitos	Raiders "insult" the cowherds- 1 cowboy killed.
	1 cowboy and 6 women taken captive
Paraje de Palmitos	A family of 6 killed; only the father escaped
	8 horses and 300 head of cattle stolen
Real de Sabinas	1 man killed, 1 man taken captive; 200 horses stolen
Rancho de la Parra	2 men and 1 woman killed; 6 women captured
	5 shotguns and ammunition stolen
Rancho de la Escondida	1 man wounded; 2 shotguns stolen; 2 horses stolen
Rancho del Colorado	2 men killed, 2 women killed, 1 woman captured
Rancho del Ojito y Caracol	2 men killed, 1 captive recovered; 600 horses stolen
Rancho de las Tortillas	1 man killed, 1 man captured
Real de la Yguana	2 men killed, 1 man captured, 1 man injured
	70 horses stolen, 2100 head of cattle stolen
	3 Lipan raiders killed, 3 raiders injured
Yguana Road	2 men and a woman killed
Paraje de la Parrita	1 man killed, 1 man captured; 6 horses stolen
Rancho de Mojarrillas	1 man killed; 100 horses stolen
Real Punta de Lampazos	3 men killed, 1 man captured; 1 captive recovered
	100 horses stolen
Hacienda Carrizal	1 man killed
Rancho de los Lisondos	Unknown number of people killed; raiders also killed
	"cows, calves, chickens and dogs"
Unnamed ranch	Raiders interrupt a wedding dance; 1 guest shot in knee
Rancho de Villareal	2 caretakers killed; "the place ransacked"
Villareal Pass	3 settlers killed, 1 settler captured
El Dorado	Raiders assault and kill the wife of a Coahuiltecan Indian
	and the child of Basilio de la Cruz
Arroyo de la Pata	Settlers kill 2 Lipan horses
Ranch of Xavier Serna	Xavier Serna's father killed, 1 child captured.

(Sources: San Juan Bautista, 1791: 155-156; J. Ramon, 1791: 141-148; De Castro, 1791b: 249-253)

Target area: Nueces County, Texas (1849). The following losses were reported in a depredation claim filed by Col. H.L. Kinney, a large south Texas landowner. These losses occurred in 1849 on or near various Nueces County ranches owned by the Colonel. Two witnesses filed affidavits stating that the thieves were Lipan Apaches in all cases except the fight at San Becinta, which was an attack by a combined Comanche and Lipan raiding party. In just one year, in one Texas county "claimed" by the Lipans, and on ranches owned by just one individual, at least seven or more people were killed, one child was captured, 501 horses and mules and 250 head of cattle were stolen.

Table 12.2   Lipan Depredations in Nueces County, Texas, 1849

Location of theft/attack	Property Stolen	Value	Total Value
Alazan Ranch	100 horses	$ 25.00/head=	$2,500
	250 head cattle	$ 5.00/head=	$1,250
Tolosa Ranch (2 cowboys killed)	250 horses & mules	$ 20.00/head=	$5,000
Bannaco Blanco Ranch	73 horses & mules	$ 40.00/head=	$2,920
Rancho del Oso ("some" people killed)	21 horses	$ 25.00/head=	$ 525
Unnamed Kinney ranch	18 horses & mules	$ 25.00/head=	$ 450
San Becinta (1 man killed)	8 horses, saddles, bridles	$ 50.00/head=	$ 400
Attack at La Mesa	6 "best quality" mules"	$100.00/head=	$ 600
(2 men killed; 1 child captured)	1 wagon & contents	$200.00 =	$ 200
The Motts	18 mules & 6 horses	$ 75.00/head=	$1,800
Corpus Christi Road	A mail carrier killed; horse, saddle and pistol stolen		
	7 wagons broken, damaged	$ 20.00/each=	$ 140
	Loss of 4 rifles & 6 pistols	$ 14.00/each=	$ 140
	Loss of one Colt six-shooter	$ 40.00/each=	$ 40
	Total Value of Claim		**$15,965**

(Source: Kinney, 1861: 51-53)

It is easy to see why a stereotype of the Lipan as a "bloodthirsty thief" quickly developed, but what drove the Lipans to raid in such an intense and brutal manner? In many cases, they needed to deter pursuit and retaliation. They needed to buy time in order to funnel their stolen livestock into their shadow economy. A stunning, brutal attack left the victims reeling in shock, unable to launch a quick response. It is telling that the only military group feared by the Lipans was the Texas Rangers who, because they were organized as small, well-armed local militias, were not only able to launch a quick response but possessed an intimate knowledge of the terrain that enabled them to use many of the Lipan raiders' tactics against them.

The frontier of Texas and northern Mexico could, indeed, be a very dangerous place. Ranching was never an easy way to make a living, but the toughness and resilience required of a ranching community was sorely tested year after year in the face of the magnitude of personal and economic losses suffered at the hands of the Lipan Apaches.

Chapter 13

Captives

Captives Taken during a Raid

Thirteen-year old Francis Monroe (Frank) Buckelew was well acquainted with the hardship and loss that was part and parcel of Texas frontier life. Born on October 3, 1852 in Union Parish, Louisiana, he had been brought as a two-year old child to Texas by his parents, who were looking for "more land and 'more elbow room.'" (Dennis, 1925: 11) The family settled in Cherokee County in 1854. Two years later, his mother died. His father remarried, but died soon thereafter. The orphaned Frank and his sister Sousanna were sent by their step-mother to their father's brother, Berry Buckelew, whose homestead lay in the heart of Lipan country on the Sabinal River in Uvalde County. Frank and his sister were raised by their uncle and his wife until January 1866, when Uncle Berry was killed by Indians while bringing several wagon-loads of goods back to the small settlement on the Sabinal (Dennis, 1925: 19).

After Uncle Berry's death, Frank Buckelew and his sister were hired out to a neighboring rancher, James B. Davenport, whose ranch lay further upstream. In March 1866, Frank Buckelew and a slave named Morris were sent with a team of oxen to plow a field some distance from the ranch house. At some point after the field had been plowed, a large bell hanging from the ox's neck fell off and was lost. Frank and Morris were sent back to look for the missing item. As they searched in a thicket of trees, something caught the boy's eye.

> Looking around, I thought I saw a hog, but a second glance convinced me that it was a man and an Indian, with war paint on his face, feathers in his hair, and a dirty greasy frock-tail coat on his body. At this moment he raised up with his hands high in the air (in one he held his bow, in the other his arrows), gave his blood-curdling war whoop and seemed to sail right at us. Morris gave one wild grunt and, with wild terror, ran with all his might. I started off with him, and was making fair headway when a voice behind me caused me to check my speed. Looking back I beheld to my horror, an Indian advancing toward me with an arrow in his powerful bow and pointing it directly at me. Realizing that further effort to escape at this time would be useless, and could only result in my death, I stopped in my tracks and turned my face toward him. When he saw I was making no farther [sic] effort to escape he assumed a more leisurely gait.
>
> A period of more than fifty years has failed to erase from my memory . . . the exciting scenes of this day March 11, 1866. . . . Then [the Indian] tapped me rather sharply on the head and said, *'Vamos (Let's go).'* We went back to the thicket . . . and when we reached the thicket we were suddenly confronted by three other fierce-looking warriors. Without any ceremony whatever, the four savages began stripping off my clothes, never stopping until every thread had been taken off. (Dennis, 1925: 27-29)

The Lipan warriors took the young boy to the leader of the raiding party.

It was evident to my mind, from the action of the four savages, and from the bearing of the stranger, that he was more than an ordinary warrior, for just as I approached him he rose from the rock on which he was sitting, with an air of haughty dignity, characteristic of his race, extended his hand to me saying, 'Howdy! How old you be? You be American or you be Dutchman? You be American me killie you; you be Dutchman me no killie you.' Being afraid to tell my exact age, as I had often heard that Indians would not keep a boy captive alive who was over ten or twelve years of age, as his chances to escape were much greater than those not so old, I replied that I was ten years old, which I considered true in one sense, but untrue in another, as I was nearly fourteen. To the second question, I told him I was American, and he said, 'You be American, me killie you.' I said, 'I can't help it if you do, I am an American.' This reply in all probability saved my life. I later learned from a friend, Mr. Charles de Montel, who was on friendly terms with the Lipan Indians, and well versed in their history, that at this time they were greatly incensed at the 'Dutch,' a name improperly applied to the German people, on account of the conduct of a party of Germans from Stringtown. Had I not told the truth in this instance, their contempt and hatred for the German people would very likely have caused them to kill me. Yet the sly old chief pretended that he was mad at the American people. This shows the reader how treacherous they were.

The old chief stood for some time as if in deep study, when he said, 'Heap big ten year old boy.' Without waiting for me to argue my case further, he very kindly and politely introduced himself to me as *Custaleta*, a war chief of the Lipan Indians. (Dennis, 1925: 30-32) [1]

The Lipans made a marked distinction between captives taken during a raid and captives taken in warfare, a distinction also noted by Frank Buckelew who attributed his survival after capture to correctly identifying himself as an American rather than a "Dutchman." If Buckelew had claimed to be part of a group against whom the Lipans had declared war, he probably would have been brought to the main Lipan camp, tortured and killed.

The Lipan practice of taking captives during a raid showed many general similarities to the captive-taking practices of other southern Plains Indian tribes (Comanches and Kiowas, for example), and was identical in many respects to the practices of other Apache tribes, particularly the Western Apaches and Mescalero Apaches. All these tribes raided for captives, who were then either integrated or "adopted" into the tribe and assigned a status based on kinship or blood relationship, or were viewed as slaves (chattel property). All of these tribes also acknowledged the capture with ritual or ceremony.

There were, however, several fundamental differences between Apache captive-taking and the practices of other southern Plains tribes. Unlike the Comanches and Kiowas, the Lipans never made captive raiding a "core cultural element."(Brooks, 2002: 180) Lipan raiding priorities were focused primarily on stealing horses and the capture of children was a secondary strategy. The Lipan raiders who took Frank Buckelew continued on after he was captured, killing several cattle and stealing horses before they finally returned to the main camp (Dennis, 1925: 46-81).

The grandson of Mescalero Apache chief *Natzili* attributed the taking of child captives to the lack of success in stealing horses. As he explained,

> The wise *ricos (rich men)* [in Mexico] were shrewd enough to understand the Indian's ways and could afford to keep their corrals filled with horses for their raids. They knew that if the Indians met with no resistance and got a good supply of mounts they would not disturb the hacienda nor its inhabitants. . . . If the Mexicans were uncooperative or too poor to cooperate, the Indians stole their women and children. If the boys were young enough, they could make good warriors of them (Ball, 1988: 213).

The root of the fundamental difference in Apache captive-taking practices lay in the Apache matrilineal social construct. Since lines of descent, tribal affiliation and even residence were determined by the mother, Apache women generally had greater freedom and power in the decision-making process within each extended family than many other southern Plains Indian women. An Apache mother had a great deal of veto power over choice of future sons-in-law, since they would support her once she was widowed. Some of the jealousy of Apache husbands, noted by outside observers, probably stemmed from the Apache woman's freedom and ability to voice her own opinions. Because Apache women held a great deal of power within their families, an Apache man's status was not completely centered upon his control of the women and children in his family, but was leavened by the power of the female hierarchy.

Lipan women also led many of the rituals associated with raiding and captives. Before each raid, the older Lipan women left the camp and went to a secluded location, where they chanted through the night, calling upon supernatural powers of protection for the raiders. When the raiders returned to camp, the older women would again leave the camp and chant through the night, "thanking the Great Spirit for the success of [the] raid." (Dennis, 1925: 112) If captives were taken during a raid, the women of the band led the ritual that began the process of assimilation.

As the raiding party neared the main Lipan camp, Buckelew begged his captor, *Custaleta*, for his freedom, but *Custaleta* replied, "When you be big Injun, me givie you my girl for wife," an indication that *Custaleta* intended to assimilate Buckelew into his band through marriage (Dennis, 1925: 41). As the raiding party came in sight of the camp, they were approached by *Custaleta's* wife, who "was chanting a weird welcome to us."(Dennis, 1925: 82) As wife of the band chief, *Custaleta's* wife led all the women and children in rituals associated with the entry of a captive into the camp and the claiming of that captive by the women of the band. The ritual was intended to symbolize the status of the captive as being below that of even the youngest tribal member. Buckelew was dragged from his horse and forced down a gauntlet of women and children, all of whom struck him with quirts, sticks and clubs. *Custaleta's* wife then performed a ritual intended to convey the message that the captive's life now lay in his captor's hands, and most particularly, in the hands of his wife.

> The old squaw who had whipped me with the quirt came forward carrying a long dangerous-looking knife. She motioned me to follow her.... She passed some distance beyond the village to a small open space, where she sat down on the ground and motioned for me to lay my head in her lap, which I did. The whole tribe followed us, and the old squaws, the boys and girls, sat down and forming a large circle and leaving us in the center. The warriors stood outside the circle and a deathlike stillness reigned on every hand. Suddenly the old squaws began [a] mournful hissing chant, and the boys and girls joined them in this chant or weird song. . . .
>
> The chanting ceased and when all was quiet again, she pulled my head back leaving my throat exposed and raised her knife high in the air. . . . She began leisurely to draw the knife back and forth across my throat, just barely touching the skin, each time flourishing the knife high in the air before repeating the stroke. . . . When she tested my courage to her satisfaction she raised my head from her lap, and signed for me to raise [sic] to my feet. The circle of savages now broke and all followed us back to the village, the old squaw conducting me to my captor's wigwam, and after giving me to understand that this wigwam was to be my future home, she gave me my supper of dried beef and tallow, and then showed me my bed (Dennis, 1925: 82-87).

Apache matrilineal societal structure influenced the tribe's choice of preferred captives. The Lipan preference for older boys (from ages nine to thirteen) allowed them to be rapidly assimilated into the family. A boy's potential as a future son-in-law could be quickly assessed based on observation of his skills and how rapidly he assumed a role as a successful hunter and warrior. While young girls were also captured, from the sketchy records that exist regarding female captives, it does not seem that many were fully assimilated into the tribe. Most seem to have been integrated as slaves. In instances where a female captive was not assigned slave status and where a kinship relationship was acknowledged by the captor, the girl or woman was generally married to another captive (Opler, 1940: 241-242). This makes sense in a matrilineal society, where blood relationships are measured through the woman. There seems to have been some discrimination practiced by Lipan women, who tended not to champion the adoption of a captive girl into the family. Once adopted, the female captive would, upon marriage, draw down the pool of potential spouses available for Lipan girls. Yet the same Lipan mothers looked favorably on a young male captive who showed promising skills and rapid assimilation, since such a young man would be an attractive son-in-law.

In a fragmentary list of eighteen captives turned over by Texas Lipan chief *Cuelgas de Castro* in fulfillment of an 1822 treaty obligation, only one quarter, or five, of the recovered captives were *mujeritas* or young women. Three quarters, or thirteen, of the recovered captives were young or adult men. Of the young women, three of the five could remember their hometowns, an indication that they were not taken captive while still a child. Only two girls had been captured while still so young that they could not remember where they had come from (Cuelgas de Castro, 1822). These statistics indicate that of the five captive young women, only two had been held by the Lipans for any length of time, and thus only two of the five would have been assimilated into a Lipan band.

One might assume that, although the Lipans tended to discriminate regarding the age and sex of their captives, over time the Lipan population would become heavily Hispanicized due to the assimilation of large numbers of Hispanic captives. There are only three known cases of Anglo boys held captive for a substantial length of time and all three boys were redeemed and returned to their families before they married Lipan women (as far as is known). However, the large numbers of Hispanic captives taken in the eighteenth and early nineteenth century would certainly lead to the assumption that many Hispanic captives were assimilated, resulting in a mixed Hispano-Lipan population by 1880. Since this was the case with the Comanche population, it is logical to question if the same situation can be found among the Lipan Apaches.

When seeking the degree of Hispanization of the Lipan population, what little data that does exist points to an opposite conclusion from that drawn from a study of the Comanches. The Hispanic surnames (Villa, Venego, Rodriguez, Mendez, Zuazua and Carillo) borne by the thirty-seven Mexican Lipans brought to New Mexico from Chihuahua in 1903 cannot be considered evidence of intermarriage. Augustina Zuazua's surname, for example, was adopted from a Juarista hero of the Mexican War of Reform (1854-1856). Every peace treaty signed by the Lipans from 1770 to 1880 required them to turn over their captives and, although the records do not give the names of individual redeemed captives, they do indicate that the Lipans generally complied. Buckelew noted that *Custaleta's* band was holding eight Hispanic boy captives in 1867, but a treaty negotiated with the Mexicans led to their release (Dennis, 1925: 121-122).

Buckelew's commentary on the choices made by the eight freed Mexican boys is also illuminating and displays the psychologically fluid state of captivity. "Then the boys were told of their release and that they could go, but could remain with the Lipan if they wished. Three immediately expressed their desire to return, while five chose to remain with their Indian masters." (Dennis, 1925: 122) Buckelew was also asked if he wanted to return home, but feared a trick and opted to remain. Buckelew related a second incident which helps to explain why some Hispanic captives might have chosen to remain with the Lipans.

> The tribe was visited by a young Mexican dressed in an extra fine suit of clothes, with his hat decorated with gold ornaments. I could not help noticing his costly apparel, for his general bearing was above that of the ordinary Mexican. We soon learned that one of the Mexican boys that chose to remain with the Lipans was his brother. After seeing his brother dressed so nicely, and hearing of the wealth of his father, the captive decided to go home with his brother. The Indians all expressed their regret at seeing him leave them, and the squaws all kissed him goodbye and wept openly (Dennis, 1925: 129).

The choice to stay with the Lipans, and eventually assimilate into the tribe, was often the easiest choice for a captive to make. Many captives believed that their entire families had been killed. Buckelew, for one, was told this. Thus, they had nothing or no one to go back home to. Others, captured at an early age, knew no other family other than the family of their captor. Some Hispanic children, particularly if they had been captured because their families were too poor to provide large numbers of horses for Lipan raiders, probably would not have relished the thought of returning to a meager subsistence existence. Given the delicate interplay of captive psychology combined with issues of wealth and status both inside and outside the tribe, it is easy to see how some Hispanic captives would have preferred assimilation through marriage into their Lipan band. However, from a statistical point of view, of the eight captives mentioned by Buckelew, four returned home and four chose to stay with the Lipans, providing evidence that, while there was some Hispanicization of the Lipan population, the phenomenon was probably not as widespread as that seen in the Comanche population, where distance and political circumstances resulted in most Hispanic captives remaining with their Comanche captors.

Yet the effect of the assimilation of one Hispanic boy child into an Apache family could be extensive, particularly when measured over a lifetime. Marcus Musquez, captured as a small boy in 1826 by the Mescalero Apaches, was not restored to his Mexican family until 1879 when he was recognized by his brother, Don Miguel Musquez Davila, among a group of eight-one captured Mescaleros. Although "almost blind and decrepid [sic] with age," Marcus Musquez was forcibly separated from the other eighty Mescaleros, most of whom were his family and descendants, including his son, Mescalero chief *Alsata* (Hood, 1879). Lipan captive Jeff Smith noted in his captivity narrative that the band holding him captive "seemed to like Mexican captives because when they brought them in they could raise them up and no one could tell them from full blood Indians." (Smith and Hunter, 2005: 189) Thus, from the sparse evidence that exists, it seems reasonable to believe that, while some Hispanic captives were assimilated through marriage and that their assimilation could have far-reaching effects over time, at least half and possibly more than half of the Hispanics captured by the Lipan Apaches either escaped or were redeemed and restored to their families prior to any assimilation into the tribe.

The Life of a Lipan Captive: Assimilation of the High Status Captive

The answers given by Frank Buckelew to the two questions posed by his Lipan captor both saved his life and determined his status as a captive. When Buckelew admitted he was an American, he not only categorized himself as a raid captive, rather than a war captive, but he exhibited an honesty that weighed in his favor once his Lipan captor determined his status. By informing *Custaleta* that he was ten years old, Buckelew also placed himself in the age range of preferred male captives, which was another point in his favor. In fact, Buckelew's knowledge of Lipan custom regarding captives was probably what prompted *Custaleta* to immediately assign him a high status as a potential future son-in-law, although once Buckelew was brought to the Lipan camp, he was not "adopted" by *Custaleta* or his wife, but by the wife of his original captor, a raider named *Bezaca* (Buckelew, 1868: 258-260).

From the moment of capture, the Lipans began to scrutinize and assess the value of their prize, and the captive's fate and status often rested on the attitudes and behaviors he exhibited during the first hours of his captivity. A captive who showed himself capable of maintaining a presence of mind during the violence of his capture was deemed to hold more value than a hysterical captive, who was often killed on the spot if he or she could not be wrestled into submission.

Frank Buckelew's narrative provides valuable insight into Lipan treatment of high-status captives. These were captives who met several important criteria— they were generally older boys (nine to thirteen years of age) who, through their behavior, had shown that they could be considered potential members of the tribe and assimilated, at some future date, through marriage. In the interim, the high-status captive was integrated into the Lipan family of his captor through adoption and the establishment of a kinship relationship.

Once Buckelew was brought to the main Lipan camp, he underwent the beating ritual symbolizing his entry into the band as a low-status captive. After the first twenty-four hours, Buckelew was dressed and painted by his captor's wife. This was done "before the whole tribe [who] had quite a lot of fun at my expense." The women then pierced his ears with long thorns and inserted "a pretty pair of Indian ear rings."(Dennis, 1925: 88) Buckelew was instructed, on his second day of captivity, to call his captor and his wife "Pa" and "Ma," indicating his adoption by this couple. Buckelew was also told to call their daughter his "sister." (Dennis, 1925: 88-89, 122)

When Buckelew had been with the Lipans for about two weeks, an event occurred which signaled the future status planned for him. While Buckelew had been adopted into the family of his captor, Chief *Custaleta* had obviously been impressed with his potential as a Lipan warrior and wanted to assimilate Buckelew into *Custaleta's* family through marriage to a granddaughter.

> I noticed there was great rejoicing in the camp, and the old squaw began chanting her weird song. I looked toward the river and saw *Custaleta* and his men approaching. I ran to him; he dismounted and took me by the hand and led me to his own wigwam. The whole tribe gathered around us, and while we talked he tried to teach me his language, and I learned to speak several words plainly. Soon he called his little granddaughter to him and had her stand beside me, and very solemnly said, 'Me givie you this girl; she be your wife when you be big Injun.' I thought he was a very poor judge of a wife for me. I liked another girl in the tribe much better, but had no desire for either to be my wife. (Dennis, 1925: 93-94)

Buckelew's entry into the life of the Lipan camp mirrored the sequence of events which occurred after his capture. At first he was assigned tasks that would have been done by slaves and only later did he "work his way up" and begin training as a warrior. He was set to doing menial work such as helping the women plant corn along the river bottom and tending his adopted father's horse herd of over 100 animals. Because Buckelew was "adopted" by his captor's family, he was not forced to undertake any task. If he had slave status, however, force and punishment would have been used to compel him to work.

Later in his captivity, Buckelew began training as a warrior. "Frequently they made the small boys fight in a sham-battle. The boys used the warriors' shields, small bows and blunt arrows. I was urged to take part in these battles." (Dennis, 1925: 106-107) Buckelew's riding skills also tested when he was placed on the back of a wild bronco; he was thrown to the ground and knocked unconscious (Dennis, 1925: 110-111). Many Comanche and Apache captives described being thrown or tied on the back of a wild horse in order to see how well they could ride or how much potential a male captive possessed as a future warrior. While the test was not always used to determine a captive's status, it was, in many cases, used to determine a captive's fate, since a captive who could not ride a horse with some skill was a liability. However, the choice of words used by Buckelew to describe this riding test is illustrative of his status as a captive. "The Indians were anxious to teach me their art and skill in riding bronco horses." (Dennis, 1925: 110) A process described by some captives as a cruel means of death at the hands of Indian captors was described by Buckelew as an "art and skill" the Lipans were anxious to teach him.

Assimilation of the Low-Status Captive

In order to distinguish the Lipan treatment of a high-status captive from that afforded a low-status captive, one must turn to a comparison of the captivity experience of thirteen-year old Frank Buckelew with that of nine-year old Jeff Smith, who was captured by a combined Lipan-Comanche raiding party on February 26, 1871. Within days of his capture, Jeff Smith was sold as "a menial . . . for several horses and possibly a blanket or two." (Smith and Hunter, 2005: 186)

Before turning to an examination of the Smith narrative, however, a strong note of caution is necessary. The captivity narrative of brothers Clint and Jeff Smith contains a number of serious problems, particularly relating to the claims made in the case of Jeff Smith. The narrative claims that Jeff was traded by his Lipan and Comanche captors to Geronimo, the Chiricahua Apache leader. Once with Geronimo, the narrative states that Jeff Smith was taken as far north as the Rocky Mountains, and possibly Utah, where he met the noted Sioux chief Sitting Bull. After being held as a captive of Geronimo for two years, Jeff Smith escaped in Mexico during a battle between Geronimo's band and Mexican troops. Smith was discovered by the Mexicans, who took him to a nearby town where he waited until he was brought back (in the spring of 1873) to his parents' home northwest of San Antonio (Smith and Hunter, 2005: 186-213).

Unfortunately, Jeff Smith's claims cannot be substantiated by any historical evidence and, in fact, fly in the face of evidence that does exist, particularly with regard to his redemption. In 1871, Geronimo was just beginning his rise to leadership within the band of Chiricahua led by his brother-in-law *Juh*, whose son *Daklugie* stated that his father was in Arizona in May 1871 (Ball, 1988: 26-27). It seems very improbable that *Juh's* band would have been camping with the Comanches in Texas at approximately the same time *Daklugie* tells of the Nednhi robbing stagecoach payrolls in Arizona. In addition, the claim that the Chiricahuas ever hunted or camped with a Sioux band led by Sitting Bull is, frankly, preposterous. Other serious problems in the narrative center on the geographic references, which are abysmally inaccurate. Finally, Jeff Smith's description of his redemption in Mexico is completely at odds with official dispatches from the U. S. Consul at Piedras Negras, who paid the ransom for Jeff Smith.

In 1869, Consul William Schuhardt requested authorization to buy back any white captives brought by Mescalero, Lipan or Comanche raiders to the town of Zaragosa (Coahuila), where the Apaches and Comanches were preparing to sign a peace treaty with Mexican authorities. The peace treaty contained provisions mandating the Indians turn over their captives and Schuhardt wanted to be prepared to buy the captives from the Mexican government so that they could be repatriated to the United States (Schuhardt, 1869). In March 1873, Schuhardt received the following information:

> Doctor A. Adams, an American resident of Zaragosa (San Fernando) a Mexican town 36 miles from here [Piedras Negras], communicates to me that he has received information through Ramon Perez, a Mexican of that place that from three to four hundred Indians are encamped in the cañon San Rodrigo, about two days riding north from Zaragosa. . . . [T]hat the said party is composed of Lipans, Mescaleros and Comanches, that they had recently returned from a campaign into Texas, bringing a large drove of horses and mules with them. The said Ramon Perez also saw in the camp of these Indians a boy, which he thinks is German and about eight years old, but to whom he was not allowed to speak. The Lipan who had the boy in possession said he had bought him from the Comanches (Schuhardt, 1873a).

On May 8, 1873, Consul Schuhardt informed the U.S. Secretary of State that "the said boy was since ransomed from the Indians at the price of one hundred and fifty dollars and sent home to his father, H.M. Smith, a resident of Comal County, Texas, who is unable to pay the ransom money, being very poor." (Schuhardt, 1873b) As the Consul's communications make clear, Jeff Smith was held, at the time of his redemption in 1873, by the same Lipan raider who had, in all probability, captured him in 1871 and who had bought him as a slave from his Comanche co-raider for several horses and a few blankets.

In spite of the obvious flaws in Jeff Smith's story, his captivity narrative still possesses some value. It contains several passages that seem to leap out of the story as authentic memories of Smith's captivity among the Lipans, particularly when compared with Frank Buckelew's experience. Once Jeff was brought to the Lipan camp by his captor,

> I was given a bow and arrows and taught how to use them, and I mingled freely with the children of the tribe, but was made to carry water and wood, and help herd the horses, help grain all kinds of skins, cut switches for arrows, go on buffalo hunts to help carry in the meat, ride horses in races, and make myself generally useful. . . . When a buck or a squaw would tell me to do a certain thing, and I could not understand what was wanted, they would get me by the ear and pull it hard, and then point toward whatever it was they wanted (Smith and Hunter, 2005: 188-189).

As a slave, Jeff Smith was deemed to be chattel property, forced to work at menial of tasks such as carrying water and wood. He was also assigned the most dangerous tasks. Smith described a bear hunt.

> [The hunters] sighted two big bears and four cubs some distance away, so they sent me [unarmed] around them while they concealed themselves behind some trees, and when the bears caught sight of me they would run toward them [the hunters] and be easily killed." (Smith and Hunter, 2005: 189-190)

The mention of a bear hunt and the eating of bear meat is further evidence that Smith's captors were Lipans and not Chiricahuas, as the Chiricahuas and Mescaleros avoided all contact with the bear and the eating of bear meat.

Redemption and Restoration

The Spanish in Texas attempted, after 1778, to create a monetary fund *(Fondo de Mesteñas)* for the redemption of Indian captives, but the small amount of money collected was never sufficient to redeem the large numbers of captives. Spanish commander Phelipe de Neve estimated in 1784 that the Texas Apaches and Comanches were holding at least 152 captives, mostly Spaniards or Christianized Indians (De Neve, 1784: 48). Needless to say, the Spanish never amassed enough revenue to redeem large numbers of Lipan captives.

More successful, however, were treaty obligations which forced the Lipans to turn over all their captives. A 1791 treaty negotiated by Pedro de Nava with Lipan chief *José Antonio* contained a typical redemption provision—"That the Lipans will deliver all the Christian captives that they have, inasmuch as they are able to do so, some by way of ransom, and that they ask about captives held in other *rancherías*." Chief *José Antonio* responded, "At present they do not have any captives in the *rancherías*; however, they will make a diligent search of the rest that live far away and bring [the captives]." (De Nava, 1791a: 569)

An 1822 treaty with Lipan chiefs *Cuelgas de Castro* and *Poca Ropa* was more successful in redeeming captives. Article 3 promised that a newly-independent Mexico would turn over all Lipan prisoners being held by the Mexican government. Article 4 stated, "In the same way, the Lipan chiefs will deliver the 24 prisoners of war [i.e. captives] that they have and also promise to commit these to the care of the Government Commissioner." (Bustamante, 1822) Pursuant to this pledge, Chief *Cuelgas de Castro* turned over eighteen Hispanic young men and girls. The fate of the six remaining "prisoners of war" was never disclosed (Cuelgas de Castro, 1822).

The escape of a Lipan captive and his return to his biological kinsmen could bring about symbolic redemption and literal salvation for his community, as seen in the story of Lipan captive Marín Ortiz or *Ateaikai,* a name bestowed by his Lipan captors. The tale records events surrounding an 1849 Lipan raid on the town of Santa Rosa, now known as Melchor Muzquiz (Coahuila).

> In years past, the Lipan Indians used to raid Santa Rosa. In one of these raids they kidnapped a male child and raised him as if he were an Indian. One time, when the child had already become a young man, the Lipans had a war council and decided to attack Muzquiz. The attack would occur on midnight of Christmas Day. The Indians knew that the people from Santa Rosa would be attending the *Misa de Gallo,* the midnight mass in the local church, and because of the weather the doors to it would be closed. The Indians would shoot an arrow on fire at the wooden roof of the church. As the people came out of the burning church the Indians would shoot them.
>
> After the war council, the Indians went to sleep. The young man remembered that he was from Santa Rosa. He waited until the men in the war party were asleep and slowly and carefully rolled away until he got to his horse. He led the horse by the bridle until he was a prudent distance away from the Indians and then mounted it. He rode into Santa Rosa late at night yelling. People came out to find the source of the commotion and found the young man, who by now spoke only in broken Spanish.
>
> The young man explained, in his broken Spanish, to the people of Santa Rosa what the Indians were planning. The men from Santa Rosa organized themselves and soon a large contingent of them had mounted their horses and went to where the young man told them the Indians were sleeping. The Indians were at a place about 25 kilometers to the north of Santa Rosa called *La Rosita.*
>
> When the men from Muzquiz got to *La Rosita* the sun had not yet risen. They waited without being noticed. As soon as there was enough sunlight to aim their rifles, the men of Santa Rosa killed all the Indians. (Bedolla-González, 2001: 16).

The redemption of Frank Buckelew from Lipan captivity demonstrated the efforts made by local Texas communities to redeem their children, as well as the lack of effective governmental or military assistance in the decade after the Civil War. Frank Buckelew escaped from *Custaleta's* band near the village of San Vicente (Coahuila) after a captivity lasting about a year. An American engineer, working on an irrigation canal along the Rio Grande, heard that a nearby Lipan band held a captive Anglo boy and sent a Mexican employee to San Vicente to ascertain the truth. Once at the village, the employee was joined by a local Mexican man who spoke English and had previously communicated with Frank

Buckelew. Together, they spirited the boy away from the Lipans and brought him to the engineer who paid the two men a reward. After a stop at Ft. Clark, Buckelew was brought back to Bandera (Dennis, 1925: 133-153). Friends and neighbors in Uvalde, Medina and Bandera counties raised money to reward the boy's saviors.

> Nearly every man we met from [Uvalde] to Bandera gave ten dollars or signed a beef steer, which was valued at ten dollars. More than fifty head of steers and some money was subscribed by those good people as a reward for my release (Dennis, 1925: 146-147).

The capture of Frank Buckelew in 1866 did not bring any response from the government of Texas, which was in disarray and just beginning the task of Reconstruction. There was no military effort to "punish" the Lipan Apaches for kidnapping a frontier child. Rather, an attempt was made on the county level to seek some sort of justice for Frank Buckelew. In the fall of 1867, a Bandera County grand jury indicted *Custaleta, et al,* for the kidnapping of Frank Buckelew. Bond was set at $5,000, but "the case never came to trial for lack of the appearance of the defendants."(Dennis, 1925: 160)

Neither a grand jury indictment nor money raised for rewards could stop the violent Indian attacks in Bandera, Uvalde and Medina counties. A year prior to Frank Buckelew's capture, thirteen year old Herbert Weinand was captured by Lipan Apaches near Castroville (Medina County, Texas). The U.S. Consul at Piedras Negras received information that the Weinand boy was spotted in a Lipan-Mescalero camp in Mexico in 1873 and the child was redeemed by a Mexican merchant for $100 and returned to his father (Schuhardt, 1873a, Richards, 1868: 262-263). From 1866 to 1876, seven persons died and six were wounded in additional Indian attacks in these three southwest Texas counties. Many of the attacks were believed to have been perpetrated by the Lipans, as they searched for Frank Buckelew in order to reclaim him as their captive (Dennis, 1925: 21-23, 147-178).

As for Frank Buckelew, the determined optimism that carried the orphaned boy through his Lipan captivity also stood him in good stead as he grew older. In 1870 he married and worked as a cowboy, hunter, shingle cutter and rancher in the three southwest Texas counties he had known since childhood. The former Lipan captive died in 1930 and was buried in Wichita County, Texas. [2]

The redemption of Jeff Smith provided a more poignant, yet unstated, acknowledgement of his captivity experience. When Jeff was brought back to his family in May 1873, his father did not recognize him at first, but he was recognized instantly by his older brother Clint, who had been recovered from the Comanches on October 24, 1872 and returned to his family. Jeff noted that "we two boys were pretty wild at first, and had no manners of any kind except those which we had learned from the Indians, and that did not fit very well in polite society." (Smith and Hunter, 2005: 211-212) Jeff Smith went on to work as a cowboy on ranches northwest of San Antonio and served in a military unit drafted from Kendall County in World War I, yet his life was forever changed by the two years he spent as a captive of the Lipan Apaches.

> After Jeff 'came home,' he still lived as an Indian in many respects. I don't know how or why, but he and my grandfather, Thomas Beddon Whitworth, were friends. I think they both grew up in the same general area as boys and just stayed life long friends. . . . Quite often, Jeff would come visit [my grandfather and his wife during the early years of their marriage], maybe to hunt or maybe to get away and enjoy some peace and quiet. I recall hearing Grandpa Tom tell stories of Jeff always sleeping outside under a big tree— winter, summer, spring or fall—he slept under that tree when he came to visit. Sometimes, if it was raining or real cold, he would come indoors, but even then, he would only sleep on the hard floor with only his blanket. Jeff followed the Indian customs in many ways, sometimes making folks uncomfortable, but my grandmother didn't pay any attention to it and just went along with it. He didn't like to sit at their table to eat, choosing instead to sit 'Indian style,' eating in the corner or outdoors. [3]

The muddled tale of Jeff Smith's Lipan captivity, as told to his interviewer, was likely heavily influenced by his dementia, which had become noticeable by 1927 (the year the first edition of his captivity narrative was published). The details might have become garbled in Smith's mind, but he never forgot that terrifying moment of capture as he was swept up by cruel-faced men and thrown across the saddle of a horse. Jeff Smith died in 1940 and was buried in the Coker Cemetery, Bexar County, Texas.

Table 13.0   **Known Captives of the Lipan Apaches, 1734-1873**

Date Recovered	Name	Circumstances
1734	Juan de Sartuche	Captured near San Antonio, died during escape attempt
1734	Andrés Cadena	Captured near San Antonio, died during escape attempt
1743	Florencio (surname unknown)	Interpreter for Fr. Santa Ana
1761	Joseph Antonio de Trujillo	Captive many years; interpreter for Fr. Ximenez
1791	Juan Jose Nalasco	From Revilla, Nuevo Leon, age 22
1791	Maria Ynés Timoteo	From Vallecillo, Nuevo Leon, female
1822	Juan Pablo Rodriguez	Shoemaker from Monterrey, Nuevo Leon
1822	Felipe Flores	From San Fernando (Zaragosa), Coahuila
1822	Florencio Gutierrez	From Yguana, Nuevo Leon
1822	Marcos Bustillos	From San Fernando (Zaragosa), Coahuila
1822	Antonio Fernandez	From Nava, Coahuila
1822	Cesario Adame	From Villa Cienegas, Coahuila
1822	Fabian (surname unknown)	From Santa Rosa, Coahuila
1822	Another boy who does not know his surname	
1822	Juan Garcia	From Sardinas, Coahuila
1822	Pablo Estrada	From Yguana, Nuevo Leon

Date Recovered	Name	Circumstances
1822	Esteban Romero	From San Antonio, TX
1822	Felix de la Parra	From Revilla, Nuevo Leon
1822	Jose Maria de la Parra	From Sabinas, Coahuila
1822	Felipa	From Sabinas, Coahuila, female
1822	Encarnacion	From Sabinas, Coahuila, female
1822	Joaquina	Does not know where she is from
1822	Guadalupe	Does not know where she is from
1822	Lina Espinosa	From Laredo, TX, female
1851	Crescencio Arrellanes	From Morales, age 14, captive 3 yrs.
1851	Pedro Gallegos	From Sabinas, Coahuila, age 16, captive 3 yrs
1851	Luciano Guerrero	From Los Alamos, Coahuila, age 18, captive 2 yrs
1851	Ultimio Herrera	From Guerrero, Coahuila, age 18, captive 4 yrs
1851	Valentin Sanchez	From Cuevas, age 7, captive 3 yrs
1851	Chapita Flores	From Camargo, Tamps, age 18, captive 2 yrs
1851	Jesus Huerfano	From Cienegas, Coahuila, age 12, captive 2 yrs
1851	Eliseo Cortez	From Monclova, Coahuila, age 11, captive 4 yrs
1851	Agapito Cortez	From Monclova, Coahuila, age 14, captive 4 yrs
1851	Mariano Ramos	From Geronimo, Chihuahua, age 19, captive 5 yrs
1851	Balthazar Chapa	From San Elissa, age 16, captive 3 yrs
1851	Pedro Rodriguez	From Ramada, age 18, captive 3 yrs
1851	Massadonia Perales	From Cienegas, Coahuila, age 18, captive 2 yrs
1867	Frank Buckelew	Captured in Bandera Co, TX, 1866, age 13
1873	Herbert Weinand	Captured in Medina Co, TX, 1865, age 13
1873	Jeff Smith	Captured in Comal Co, TX, 1871, age 9

(Sources: Urrutia, 1738: 23; Cuelgas de Castro, 1822; Santa Ana, 1743a: 67; Rabago, 1762a: 187; De Castro, 1791d: 285; Mexican Captives, 1853-1854; Dennis, 1925; Smith and Hunter, 2005)

Chapter 14

Lipan Apache Warfare

Unlike a raid, whose primary objective was the taking of booty in the form of livestock or captives, Lipan Apache warfare was rooted in revenge and had, as its primary objective, the taking of enemy lives. The Lipan waged war in a manner similar to other Apaches, yet adapted elements, such as the ritual cannibalism of war captives, which differentiated the Lipans from other Apache tribes. In the same way, Lipan warfare also contained practices such as scalping, familiar to many Plains tribes. However, Lipan culture did not contain many of the institutionalized rituals and organizations used by Plains tribes to give social recognition to war deeds. As was true with so many features of Lipan Apache culture, their warfare rituals and practices were unique, reflecting a skillful blend of adaptations within an Apachean model.

Because Lipan warfare was generally based on revenge, or a desire to return evil for evil, the Lipans waged war in deadly earnest, eschewing such practices as counting coup. Lipan status was based on diffuse elements of a man's performance, with battlefield heroism constituting only one aspect of a man's reputation. Lipan bravery in warfare was recounted in songs sung before a victory dance, and occasionally a warrior's deeds passed into legend, but a more telling acknowledgement of Lipan heroism, and its ties to rank and status, could be seen in the names and war injuries of Lipan chiefs such as *Josef Grande el Manco (Big Joseph the One-armed)* and *el Valazo (the Wounded One)*.

The mind-set of the Lipan warrior was just as important as his deeds. A fatalistic attitude of self-sacrifice was highly esteemed. In one legend collected by Opler, an old Lipan chastised a young warrior who questioned his decision to stop and rest at a location within view of an approaching enemy, "'Hm, you're always a coward. You always want to live a little longer.'"(Opler, 1940: 231) In 1788, Lipan chief *Boca Tuerte's* son, *Davinica-jaté*, described the war deeds of *Lipiyan* chief *Picax-andé Yns-tinsle* from a Lipan point of view, stressing not only his bravery but his self-sacrifice.

> At daybreak, Comanche Indians attacked [a combined *Lipiyan* and Lipan camp] in large numbers, and *Picax* the *Lipiyan* ordered his people and their families not to go out of their tents. 'For what reason should they all die?' he said thusly. With great effort, *Picax* went up on horseback as the Comanches tried to throw them loose and destroy them, but *Picax* and the Lipans succeeded to the contrary, killing thirteen including two brave [Comanche] chiefs. We have never seen a man like the *Lipiyan* chief, since within sight of his nation and the Lipan nation, he killed four Comanches at the point of a lance. (Valdez, 1788: 397-398).

The revenge basis of Lipan warfare could take as many forms as the resentful mind of an individual could allow. The most common scenario for a declaration of war was at the urging of the family of a slain Lipan. During the period of family mourning, emotions were raw and, in many cases, as the family continued to think about their loss, they became "very angry and sorry," demanding that their band chief declare war to avenge the unjust death of their loved one (Opler, 1940: 253). In most cases, war was declared against the Comanches. Hostilities between the two tribes lasted throughout the eighteenth century to about 1840. Fr. Ximenez noted in 1761 that the Lipans "go to war frequently with the Comanches, whom they hate. They make three or four campaigns a year." (Ximenez, 1761a: 26)

In rare cases, the Lipans declared war on the inhabitants of towns and settlements based on their refusal to supply the Lipans with gunpowder or other perceived injustices. Several hundred warriors, under the leadership of a single war chief, would mass and launch attacks seeking to seize weapons and inflict casualties. Lipan war-related attacks on Zaragosa, Coahuila (1763) and Laredo, Texas (1790) resulted in the Lipan seizure of entire arsenals but few Spanish casualties (Zaragosa, 1763: 1-10; Menchaca, 1790: 401-404). However, on the morning of October 12, 1844, over 400 Lipan warriors descended on La Palmita, Nuevo Leon, a small settlement of 200 persons. Eighty-three residents were killed and fifty to sixty women and children were taken captive. The warriors moved on to attack the nearby towns of La Laja and China before they were dispersed following a pitched battle with the Mexican Army at Vaquerias, Nuevo Leon. Lipan warriors also attacked the *villa* of Mier, Tamaulipas, at about the same time. [1] The circumstances under which the Lipans declared war reached a climax in 1879. Beset by a series of military campaigns launched by the Mexican Army in Coahuila, with coordinated U.S. Army assistance, the Mexican Lipans declared, "they will never make peace again and from this time forward they will war with the whole world." (Moffitt, 1879)

Waging War

The Lipans believed that they had been taught how to wage war by their primary spirit deity, Killer-of-Enemies.

> He made ready to go after his enemy. . . . He had a quiver full of arrows, a war club, a spear, and a shield. He met the enemy. He had a big fight with them.... Killer-of-Enemies was the one who told them to take scalps. He was the one who taught the Apache. . . . He always brought back something to show his mother, to prove what he had done. He scalped some of the monsters he killed. . . . Killer-of-Enemies was the one who started all the things that the Lipan did later. That's why the Lipan went out raiding after horses and fought their enemies when they met them (Opler, 1940: 36-37).

Lipan warfare utilized many of the same tactics used in raiding, particularly the ambush, and was conducted with a grim determination. "They never lose control, even when they are surprised and have no means of defense. They fight to the last breath and generally prefer death to surrender." (John, 1991: 156) In 1787, the *rancheria* of Lipan chief *Zapato Sas* was attacked by 400 Wichita warriors who drove away most of the Lipan's horses. But a total of 480 Lipan warriors, on foot and armed with 400 guns, managed to repel the Wichitas in an all-day battle with only one Lipan casualty (Pacheco, 1787: 71-72).

> [The Lipans] act with the same intrepidness on the attack, but with the difference that, if they do not quickly achieve the advantage they seek and see luck turn against them, they think nothing of breaking off their attack and fleeing. With this in mind, they plan a retreat in advance, including the direction they will head for their safety (John, 1991: 156).

The identity of the war chief was often concealed when a Lipan war party encountered the enemy, so as to protect their leadership (Opler, 1940: 274). Smoke signals, using several sotol sticks to start a small fire, were often used by Lipan scouts to report enemy positions (Opler, 1940: 223).

Once war was declared, the Lipan camp was immediately placed at risk of a retaliatory enemy raid. The women and children made immediate preparations for defense, should the camp be attacked, or to flee, if the enemy were detected nearby. Lipan women did not fight on the battlefield with their men.

> They could have done it if they had wanted to, but they didn't want to. The men didn't want them along. They would only get in the way and make it harder. However, if they are in camp, and the camp is attacked, they show their bravery; they fight fiercely then (Opler, 1940: 238).

If the camp was attacked, relatives were expected to remain and defend their kin at all costs, but reckless bravery was not demanded of a non-relative (Opler, 1940: 226). Although they did not take part in battle, Lipan women played an important role in warfare, as acknowledged by many Spanish commanders who fought against Lipan Apaches.

> [E]ven if perhaps they do not wage war in the same manner as the men, they do help with it. In whatever action the Apaches undertake, as has been seen, in fact women form the regular reserve corps. They drive the *caballada (horse herd)* while the men attack our troops and finally even when they are of no use except to increase the bulk of the parties, the enemy has managed to emphasize their objective, i.e. to make themselves more feared, a well-founded idea (Juntas de Guerra, 1778: 53-54).

Indeed, Lipan women posed a fearful threat to all captives taken during raiding or warfare, since they led the rituals associated either with the integration of a captive into the tribe or the killing of a captured enemy.

When prisoners were taken in the course of warfare for revenge, it was difficult to quiet the anger of the relatives of the Apache whose death had started hostilities. The lives of such prisoners were usually forfeit. They turned them over to the women who stabbed them in the throat (Opler, 1940: 256).

When the demands of honor and revenge had been satisfied, the Lipans often made peace with their enemies. If the Lipans were victors, they received the vanquished chief and his entourage in the Lipan camp with "a firing of salvoes and ringing their arms." (Galván, 1753b: 18) Military allies were also greeted in the same manner. Ugalde described the ritual greeting as a "fusillade of fire with a high speed echo, while [the Lipan warriors] advanced and filed by, firing by hand with no communicated sign." (Ugalde, 1788b: 350)

The ceremonies to formalize peace began with speeches indicating the Lipan desire for a peaceful relationship. The Lipan would dig a hole in the surface of the ground with his finger, creating a hole about four inches deep. He would then spit into the hole, followed by the enemy chief, and the hole would be covered up. This ritual was intended to symbolize the burying of troubles between the two antagonists (Opler, 1940: 244-245). In 1749, in order to symbolize a Lipan and *Natagés* peace with the Spanish at San Antonio, the Apaches dug a large hole in the town plaza. They placed a live horse, bows and arrows, a lance and a war club in the hole. After dancing around the edge of the opening three times, the chiefs, joined by the entire population of San Antonio, grabbed handfuls of dirt and covered the hole, burying the horse alive. "By this, the chiefs meant that they had had enough of war, which they buried here. When that was said, the chiefs howled and our people pronounced three cheers for the King." (Cabello, 1784: 111-112)

Ritual Aspects of Warfare: The *Mitote*, a Prelude to War

Much of Lipan life was governed by ritual, and the conduct of warfare was no exception. Prior to setting out on the warpath, the Lipans ate a communal meal. Following the meal, the *ranchería* held an all-night dance which they called a *mitote*, a Spanish word meaning "a raucous, noisy dance." (Cobos, 2003: 152) The Lipan *mitote* ritual was first described by Ximenez in 1761.

In order to make war they do their dances *(mitotes)* in which they all get together to eat. They do not get intoxicated and hate all hard liquor. They do not use intoxicating herbs. They meet the Comanches near their homes (Ximenez, 1761a:27)

In 1788, Ugalde provided two descriptions of *mitote* rituals as practiced by the *Lipiyans* and Lipans. The *Lipiyan* ritual, which was led by chief *Picax* but which also included Lipan participants, began in quiet splendor after a communal meal but soon escalated to a fever-pitch of dancing and chanting.

At 8 p.m. a large number of men and women formed in a large semi-circle facing their chief *[Picax]* and lit up *luminarias* of the Moon (festive lights), placing them at proportionate intervals. At the head of the line of lights was a wrapped object *(el Sarao)* that they called *Mitote*. With extraordinary ceremony, they made screams and chants whose sole object was for the destruction and whipping of their enemies, the Comanches. At daybreak . . . the dance, which lasted all night long without intermission, ended and the people retired (Ugalde, 1788a: 324).

Ugalde also witnessed a Lower Lipan *mitote* ritual performed at *el Atascoso* (Atascosa County, Texas), which he described as a communal feast honoring visitors. However, since Ugalde was visiting the *Atascoso* camp in order to enlist the Lower Lipans in a war against the Mescaleros, it seems likely that Ugalde was honored in the capacity of a military ally, rather than a simple visitor. The meal was followed by a dance, which began once darkness fell, celebrating the anticipated victory over their enemies (Ugalde, 1788b: 352).

The use of festive lights was a *Lipiyan* adaptation which was not practiced by the Lipan tribe, which restricted the *mitote* ritual to a meal and dance, but Fr. Ximenez hinted that the Lipans also used an effigy in their *mitotes* (Ximenez, 1764: 177). However, the ritual goal for both groups was the same- to unite the community in a common purpose as a prelude to war and to call down, through dance or chant, supernatural assistance in assuring a victory.

Scalping and the Scalp Dance

Just as the Lipan culture hero, Killer-of-Enemies, taught the Lipans about raiding and warfare, so he also taught them to take the scalp of their enemies (Opler, 1940: 36). The Lipan had no special manner for removing the scalp, other than to cut around the top of the head, but their myths contained specific instructions on the preparation of the scalp once it had been removed:

> [H]old all the hair, build a fire, turn the flesh side toward the fire and burn and dry off the flesh, being careful not to burn the hair; then to put a stick through two holes made in the scalp and to hold the lower end of this stick. They did not say how long the sticks should be (Opler, 1940: 49).

Once the Lipans removed the scalp of an enemy during or after a battle, they mounted the scalp on a pole. Some Spaniards even shaved their heads so as not to provide ready targets for Lipan scalp-takers during an attack (Cabello, 1779a: 87). If a scalp could not be had, the Lipans were not averse to "decorating their lances with full beards taken from white settlers (particularly red beards)." (Haas, 1964)

After a battle in which scalps were taken, Lipan warriors would begin to sing as they approached their home camp, in order to give notice to their band that they were returning victorious. The warriors would then line up and carry the scalps into camp, to the acclaim of the people. Once back at camp, the warriors sat in a circle to sing their victory song. As they sang, they slapped their thighs or a sage-filled buckskin pillow. After the warrior's song, the entire camp celebrated with a victory, or scalp dance (Opler, 1940: 48-49).

A victory, or scalp dance, was often confused by outside observers with the *mitote*. These were two separate dances, with the *mitote* performed as a prelude to warfare, and the scalp dance performed as a coda or a finale after the battle. The performance of the two dances—to begin war and to celebrate its victorious conclusion—and the communal meal before the *mitote* and after the scalp dance, were part of the symbolic circle of ritual binding the tribe together.

Unlike the *mitote*, which was performed whenever war was declared, the victory or scalp dance could only be performed under certain circumstances, depending on the number of war casualties. If a band chief was severely wounded during battle, his camp would often eschew a scalp dance in deference to the precarious medical condition of their chief, even if the Lipans had won the battle in which the chief was injured (Opler, 1940: 227). However, "[if] the [Lipan] Apache scored an impressive victory, the death of one or two of their own number in the fight need not have prevented the celebration." (Opler, 1940: 252) A Lipan victory, or scalp dance, began with drumming. The scalps taken in battle were brought into the dance circle, where dancers twirled and gyrated with the scalps in their hands (Ximenez, 1761a: 27).

War Captives and Ritual Cannibalism

The taking of captives had always been a component of Apache warfare, since it represented a war tactic designed to humiliate the loser and complement the foundational basis of warfare which was rooted in revenge. Berlandier acknowledged that the Lipans were "skilled at warfare," but also noted,

> Their cruelty is so hideous as would never be accepted as historic fact. They kill their prisoners with the most frightful tortures. Their women, in particular, vie with one another in inventing new torments for the unfortunate wretch whom the fortunes of war deliver into their hands (Ewers, 1969: 129).

Only one description exists of the Lipan ritual cannibalism of war captives and that description was provided by Fr. Juan Agustín de Morfi, a Spanish historian who toured Texas in 1778-1779. In Fr. Morfi's commentary on the *Apaches Lipanes*, the priest painted the following gruesome picture of the fate of Lipan war captives.

> When on their way they surprise an enemy, man or woman, who is not a child, or an old man, they guard them carefully, and take them to the *ranchería* for the celebration of their great fiesta. The captor convokes the many captains of the nation, and when those who come are gathered he delivers to them the captive, that each one may torment him at his will and in his turn. Some throw them out naked, into the fire, from where they are soon taken out; others wound

them with diverse sharp pointed instruments; some cut off a piece of flesh, roast it and eat it; they apply glowing coals to the most sensitive parts of the captive's body; but they all take care to feed the prisoners so they shall not die inopportunely from this diversity of cruelties.

The day assigned for the conclusion of the feast arrives; they carefully clean all parts of the body of the captive, then conduct him in a procession, to the place of torture, singing some military songs. They bind him securely to a tree, or stake, which they have prepared. The boys then go out to shoot arrows at him, so as to familiarize themselves in youth with inhumanity and barbarity; when they become tired of this brutal amusement, they follow the warriors, who with arrows, pikes, lances and knives, slowly take the prisoner's life. Immediately, and before the victim had breathed his last, they all fall upon the wretched victim, open his belly, take out his entrails, which they throw into the bushes, cut pieces of flesh from the victim which they keep for other feasts, or send to the absent, or eat immediately, raw, or roasted, according to the furor of taste which dominates each of them.

This infamous scene finished, they begin the victories, the Captain lauding the captor, to whom all the other members of the feast give something of importance, as horses, rifles, chamois or tanned deer skins *(gamuzas)* or beautiful buffalo skins. These praises and presents stimulate a powerful desire in the others to emulate [the deeds of the captor] that incites them to refine their cunning and treachery, to surprise their enemies and win similar approval (Chabot, 1932: 18).

How much of the Morfi description can be believed? No scholar has ever addressed the issue of their ritual cannibalism, yet this element in the Lipan treatment of war captives was attested to by so many eighteenth and nineteenth century sources that it must be believed. Morfi's description falls completely within the context of other Lipan ritual practices, so it must be given credence.

The Lipan Apaches made age distinctions with regard to war captives. Only adult males and females were taken, since their purpose was not to be assimilated into the tribe (as would have been the case with a child) but were considered physical tokens of a war victory and, as such, were to be sacrificed. The distinction made in the case of an "old man" is puzzling, since the historical record contains no instances of the Lipans seeking out older male captives for tribal assimilation. However, an elderly male captive from an enemy tribe might well have been a shaman. Any Lipan distinction that spared the life of such a captive might have been due to their fear of unleashing malevolent supernatural power through the death of such a man. The Morfi description also makes it clear that ritual cannibalism was a tribal communal rite involving a number of bands, since he stated that "many captains of the nation" were convoked and the war captive turned over to those band chiefs who gathered for the ceremony.

The nature of the ritual practiced by the Lipans also becomes apparent in the Morfi description. The Lipans were not seeking to ingest any admirable supernatural qualities possessed by their enemies which would then transfer and become manifest within themselves. Because Lipan warfare was grounded in revenge, they were seeking the total annihilation of the enemy, annihilation so complete that even the flesh of the enemy was destroyed. The enemy, however, was unclean and tainted. Thus, the captive was thoroughly washed before the final ceremony. It was imperative that the war captive be ritually and physically cleansed before being consumed, since the Lipans, as indicated by the tinge of the sacred in their tribal name and through correct adherence to ritual, lived in a "pure" state (Opler, 1940: 270).

Ritual cannibalism does not fall within an Apachean model and the Morfi description contains no clues as to the source from which the Lipans could have adapted the practice. The first historical reference was made in 1743 by Fr. Santa Ana. After noting that the *Pelones Apaches* (i.e. Forest Lipans) were under increased Comanche pressure which displaced them from their lands along the Red River, the priest described a fierce battle between the two groups in which a single Comanche was taken prisoner. "The victors consulted about the fate of this one enemy and, on this occasion, fear overcame their ferocity and their desire to cannibalize him." (Santa Ana, 1743a: 66)

The Karankawas and Tonkawas are two Texas Indian tribes which were historically associated with the practice of ritual cannibalism. The Lipans had horses-for-guns alliances with elements of both tribes, but a Lipan adaptation from these sources is problematic. The Karankawas inhabited the Texas Gulf coastal region from the lower Colorado to the lower Nueces River and probably practiced ritual cannibalism. However, Ricklis noted the ritual was performed on "enemies killed in battle," an indication that the victim was already dead (Ricklis, 1996: 147). This stands in contrast to the Lipan practice as described by Fr. Morfi. Additionally, the historical record does not indicate a sustained Lipan presence in Karankawan territory until a decade after the Santa Ana reference, although the Cocos, one of five Karankawan groups, were Lipan allies after 1750 (Cabello, 1784, 114).

The Tonkawas present a more likely Lipan adaptation source, but this option is also problematic. The Tonkawas were historically associated with the upper Trinity and the Brazos-San Gabriel confluence in the early eighteenth century and are now believed by scholars to have been a consolidation of diverse fragments of a number of tribes, including the Mayeyes (Chipman, 1992: 20). The Mayeyes were Lipan allies after 1750. In 1745, Fr. Dolores, who founded a mission on the San Gabriel River, noted generic "Apaches" in the region, although these Apaches cannot be definitively identified as Lipan Apaches (Chipman, 1992: 150). However, given the proximity of the Brazos-San Gabriel confluence to *Pelones Ypande* territory noted by Fr. Santa Ana in 1743, it is certainly possible that the Lipans had early contact with some of the diverse groups comprising the later Tonkawa tribe. The Tonkawas were also known to practice ritual cannibalism based on a revenge motif, which mirrored Lipan practice, although all historical sources which mention Tonkawa ritual cannibalism date from the nineteenth century (Hester, 1991: 82-83). Until more is known about the group composition and cultural practices of the early Tonkawas, an adaptive link to the Lipans cannot be definitively proven.

Early references to Lipan Apache ritual cannibalism do not confine the practice to the *Pelones* or Forest Lipan division of north central Texas. In 1763, Lorenzo Cansio noted in a report regarding a trip made by several Spanish priests from New Mexico to the San Saba River of Texas that they had encountered *los Ipanes (the Lipans)* north of the Pecos River. Cansio reported that a Lipan camp containing about 300 adults had been attacked by the Comanches.

> The Lipans resisted being tamed; at about 3 p.m. the combat ended resulting in the death of all the Comanches and one Lipan, with many injured. . . . The result was a celebration of the Lipans with a fiesta for a time of 20 days and they ate a Comanche woman prisoner (Cansio, 1763: 178).

Juan de Ugalde also reported a case of Lipan ritual cannibalism in 1779. After successfully repelling a Comanche attack, a San Antonio area Lipan band "lifted the tedium . . . by lancing [one Comanche prisoner] various times and cutting pieces of his meat, which they took off of the body, to celebrate their jubilation by having a banquet of him." (Ugalde, 1781d: 48)

In 1783, Lipan chief *Zapato Sas* rode into the Béxar presidio with 80 warriors and one Comanche prisoner. The Spanish were trying desperately to determine just which Indian tribe had murdered Don Fernando de Veramendi and five other Spaniards, and *Sas* brought in one of the killers. The Comanche confessed to being a member of a raiding party which murdered the Spaniards but, as he was questioned by the presidio Captain,

> He became so rattled that he could not answer. . . . Thereupon his captors [the Lipans] led him away in order to go and join the rest in their camps and to dance the *mitote* with him and with the smoked flesh of his companions, which they were carrying (Béxar, 1783: 167-168).

By 1828, several Spanish observers noted that the Lipan Apaches were moving away from ritual cannibalism of war captives, probably because they had established an uneasy peace with the Comanches after 1818. Three members of an 1828 Mexican scientific expedition to Texas noted that the Lipans were in the process of renouncing cannibalism. José María Sanchez asserted that the Lipans "were the last ones to give up eating human flesh." (Castaneda, 1926: 249) This assertion was echoed by Berlandier, who added commentary from his perspective.

> Some of these people sometimes eat the flesh of enemies they have killed in battle, but they indulge in these cannibalistic orgies only to satisfy their vengeance and appease their wrath. They are now gradually renouncing these barbarous customs, and in their last war they devoured only a few men they captured at Espíritú Santo [Goliad, Texas]. The Lipans are the last of the native peoples to give over these horrible feasts (Ewers, 1969: 129-130)

Perhaps the clearest picture of Lipan ritual cannibalism was the commentary made by José Francisco Ruíz, a third participant in the Mexican scientific expedition. Ruíz confided in his diary,

> In my opinion, the southern Lipans are the most cruel [sic] of all the barbaric nations I know. They mete out harsh punishment to their prisoners. I have been told by some of these Indians that they sometimes eat those they kill in war. This practice is not very common, and it is done more in revenge, or to assuage their fury (Ewers, 1972: 7).

Ruíz properly categorized Lipan cannibalism as a unique ritual of war, the practice of which was probably never commonplace. Yet the ritual consummation of the enemy provided the Lipan Apaches with complete retribution, satisfying through the complete annihilation of the prisoner, the cries for vengeance rising from the aggrieved family of the slain.

Chapter 15

Lipan Apache Religion- Overview

Lipan Apache religious belief began with the assumption that both the miraculous and the mundane lived in the same place at the same time. The world was alive, crackling and humming with supernatural power seeking to manifest itself, to channel itself into human form. Although each Lipan possessed some supernatural power by virtue of their membership in a tribe whose very name embodied a tinge of the sacred, some members were able to open a direct channel to the supernatural power residing both in the natural world and in the universe. Such persons were called healers *(curanderos)*, herbalists *(herbolarios)* or sorcerers *(hechiceros)* by the Spanish. For purposes of this discussion, they will be called shamans.

Although the word "shaman" is not of American Indian origin, it is the best term to convey the general character of Lipan religious practice, as well as the best descriptive term for Lipan religious practitioners. However, a note of caution is necessary. Many modern-day Lipan Apaches prefer to call their religious practitioners holy men and holy women, eschewing the term "shaman" because of its New Age connotations. [1] Thus, when the term "shaman" is used in this discussion, it is used only an historical sense to indicate an eighteenth or nineteenth century religious practitioner who opened a direct channel to the supernatural. Any New Age mysticism currently attached to the concept of shamanism had no place in the ancient (or modern) Lipan Apache mind.

There were two categories of Lipan holy persons, or shamans. Some tribal members (men or women) performed rituals to channel the supernatural power residing in the natural world to assist in making effective an herbal or folk medicine cure. These holy persons can be termed "curative shamans," since they used their enhanced power to help the individual, primarily through healing rituals. According to Gatschet, the Lipan term for a male curative shaman was *tésä^n* and the term for a female curative shaman was *tchä^n ki^n tésä^n*. The cure produced by such healers was called *isémá nila* (Gatschet, 1884: 26).

Other tribal members acted as mediums, channeling the supernatural power of the universe which resided in the spirit deities, and directing that power in order to benefit the larger community. Such male shamans (for these rituals were performed only by men) can be termed "mythic shamans," since they accessed the power of larger-than-life spirit beings whose exploits were preserved in Lipan mythology. Mythic shamans used effigies to impersonate spirit deities and were well versed in astronomical observation. The general Lipan term for "spirit deity" was *yáta seta (god who is in the sky)* (Gatschet, 1884: 61, 72). [2] One man could combine the functions of both a curative and mythic shaman.

The only instance of anthropological analysis of Lipan religion was a cursory treatment by Morris Opler, centered upon an examination of Lipan curative shamanism. In any hunting or gathering society, the injury or debilitation of tribal members through disease was a threat to the entire community, as they would not be able to perform tasks necessary to both feed their families and the larger group. Opler believed that Lipan shamanism grew out of the need to cure injury and disease so as to preserve the labor force and thus the food supply. A curative shaman was highly valued.

> [The tribe's] mobile and active life and the negligible surpluses that their hunting and gathering practices permitted [caused] the Lipan . . . [to be] beset by specters of illness and the hardship it entailed. Such grim prospects were countered on the practical and ethical side by precepts of sharing and generosity, and the religious system emphasized curing rites conducted by shamans who sought the aid of supernatural powers in the healing of their clients (Opler, 1975: 16)

However, while Opler's analysis of Lipan curative shamanism is supported by historical references to the practice, the historical record presents a much broader picture of the totality of Lipan religious practice. In Opler's comparative analysis, he noted that Lipan culture "corresponded in broad pattern in almost every respect" to that of the Mescalero Apaches. By extension, this connection also applied to the area of religion (Opler, 1975: 14). For example, Opler tied Lipan practices to the Mescalero vision quest, where individuals sought to channel supernatural power for their own success, courage and protection (Opler, 1975: 13). However, the vision quest seems to be a nineteenth century Lipan adaptation from Mescalero practice, rather than a core element of Lipan religious practice from earlier eras. Eighteenth century sources stated that the Lipans called upon the power of the universe (i.e. mythic shamanism) rather than power derived from a vision quest.

Opler also would have presumably characterized Lipan religion as "evangelical or devotional shamanism," a characterization he made after a study of Mescalero religion (Opler, 2002: 29). However, by definition alone, Lipan religion was not evangelical, as it was not focused on preaching as opposed to ritual. In fact, the opposite was true. Lipan religion was all about the rituals necessary for channeling supernatural power. It was only secondarily dependent upon the pronouncements of religious practitioners.

Lipan religion was only partly devotional, particular when "devotional" is used to mean the private practice of religion. Such private religious practices as the vision quest were only one aspect and late adaptation of the totality of Lipan religious practice. Although Opler collected a stunning array of Lipan myths (*Myths and Legends of the Lipan Apache Indians*, 1940), he seemed to assume that the supernatural deities figured largely only in myth and ceremony and that their major importance lay in the past. This assumption is contradicted by captive Frank Buckelew, who described a Lipan ceremony marking a lunar eclipse. Buckelew's description makes it obvious that the Lipan Apaches, as late as

1866, believed that their major spirit deities were active, very much alive and still held supreme importance in tribal ritual (Dennis, 1925: 112-113).

All Lipan religion was concerned with accessing supernatural power to assist and protect the individual and the tribe. However, Lipan religion was not people-centered, but Power-centered. The Lipans did not fervently pray and then assume that their spirit deities heard their prayers and would respond. The Lipan shaman presented himself as a spirit medium, and the spirit deity, who was always seeking a human channel, sought him out in order to manifest itself in human form. If bad consequences resulted after a shaman accessed supernatural power, the blame fell on the shaman, who was believed to have erred in the proper performance of the ritual. Supernatural power was never to be blamed, because that power was eternal and never varying in its characteristics. The power of an owl, for example, was always of an evil nature because the owl was associated with death. The power of the sun was always good because it was associated with the primary spirit deity, Killer-of-Enemies.

Just as the Lipan trade economy was carried out on two simultaneous levels, one of which was of an open or public nature (hides for food) and a second level which was of a secretive nature (stolen horses for guns), so the Lipan Apaches conducted religious ceremonies on two levels. On a surface level, Lipan shamans channeled the supernatural power of the natural world for curative purposes. Fr. Morfi (1779) noted that some Lipan curative shamans handled snakes, indicating that they were channeling the supernatural power possessed by the snake in order to effect a cure (Chabot, 1932: 18-19). These rituals were generally focused on ailing individuals, although communal curative rites were also performed during epidemics. Lipan curative shamans also combined their knowledge of herbal cures with Hispanic folk medicine practices prevalent along the Rio Grande. It was this aspect of Lipan religion that was seen most often by outside observers, leading them to assume that curative shamanism constituted the bulk of Lipan religious practice.

There was, however, a second, secretive level to the Lipan form of shamanism which sought to access the power of the natural world. Some curative shamans boasted they were witches or could cast evil spells. This aspect of curative shamanism reflected some aspects of New Mexican pueblo culture but was probably more heavily influenced by Hispanic folk magic. The individual vision quest was also a private, secretive ceremony, where young boys who indicated a willingness to seek shamanistic power ascended a mountain and prayed for four nights, seeking an infusion of power from the natural world. The ceremony was secretive in the sense that it was held away from camp and the outcome was always in question. No one knew which, if any, young boys would be selected by Power (Chebahtah and Minor, 2007: 57-58).

Lipan mythic shamans also performed rituals on two levels. On an open, public level, the shaman erected an effigy, called a "flesh-colored idol" by Fr. Diego Ximenez, before the band went to war, prior to a buffalo hunt, or during a severe epidemic. As the mythic shaman performed rituals using tobacco smoke, he opened himself as a channel for the supernatural power of a spirit deity, as represented by the effigy "idol." Once a channel was established, the mythic shaman then issued predictive statements, such as the location of the enemy, the location of bison herds or how many persons would live or die during an epidemic (Ximenez, 1761a: 26-27).

Yet, Lipan mythic shamans also performed rituals of a hidden, secretive nature that are only hinted at in the historical record. They were able to successfully predict total eclipses of the moon and possibly the sun. The peyote ceremony, a feature of Lipan religion from about 1780 on, was another example of a secretive ritual in which mythic shamans accessed the supernatural power of the universe, through the ingestion of peyote, in order to make predictions.

The dual nature of Lipan ritual practice—open and secretive, curative and mythic—was merely a reflection of the dual nature of the relationship the Lipans saw between the world they lived in and the world of the supernatural, a relationship between a world of shadow and a world of light.

Chapter 16

Lipan Apache Religion- Mythic Shamanism

Mythic Framework: The Spirit Deities

The Lipans believed there were two realities existing simultaneously: the "real" world peopled by mythic figures possessing vast reservoirs of supernatural power, and the "shadow" world peopled by the Lipan Apaches (Farrer, 1991: 108-111). [1] Their emergence myth began with the Lipans living in darkness below the earth. When the first humans were sent up to look upon the world above, four men were chosen, indicating the sacred nature of their task. Of the four men, one man named Mirage was chosen "from whom were to be made the things of the earth as we know it now. . . . They put up Mirage in the form of a ball. . . . That ball of mirage became a part of this earth." (Opler, 1940: 14) This detail, and the particular name given to this man, was a direct reference to the "shadow," or "mirage" nature of the earth later peopled by the Lipans. When they emerged onto the earth, the Lipans emerged from the darkness into the light, but it was a hazy, out-of-focus, half-light reality. The Lipans called it the "shadow world." It was a pale comparison to the clearly focused, brightly lit or "real" supernatural power of the mythic figures who would act as teachers and protectors of the tribe. Just as their tribal name indicated a continuous journey toward a better knowledge of the sacred, so the Lipan Apaches believed that their journey on earth was conducted in shadow and haze, as they moved from an out-of-focus existence toward the pure light of "reality" embodied in the sacred power possessed by powerful mythic figures.

For the Lipans, such mythic figures as Killer-of-Enemies were not spirits from the misty past, whose exploits merely served to explain the origins of many cultural features. Killer-of-Enemies, associated with the sun, was eternally existent, a pulsating reservoir of supernatural power that remained available to the Lipans much like an open electrical current, reaching out to the Lipans and waiting to be accessed by a human medium, or mythic shaman. The "real" world was that of illuminating supernatural power which could be tapped into by shamans who, because they were deemed acceptable vessels or channels by the mythic figure, received an outpouring of the supernatural power in order that the mythic figure might manifest itself to assist and protect the Lipan tribe.

A mythic shaman performed a far weightier role than that performed by a curative shaman. The power of the universe was perceived to be much greater than the power of the natural world. A mythic shaman was the only channel by which the awesome "real" power of a Lipan mythic figure could assert itself in the "shadow" world of everyday life.

The Lipans believed their myths in their most literal sense and form. They were not viewed merely as symbols of larger truths and struggles or as simple explanatory culture tales. For the Lipans, their mythology was a literal re-telling and rationalization of past events with larger-than-life figures who, while they were no longer present upon the earth in human form, still existed as embodiments of culture and supernatural power to be accessed by the Lipans through their shamans and the use of effigies in order to "illuminate" the shadow world of everyday events with the transcendent power of the universe.

There are hints in this mythic aspect of Lipan religion reminiscent of Hopi Katchinas (who visited mankind in impersonated form), or the Chiricahua and Mescalero pantheon of Mountain Spirits. However, the Lipans never elevated spirit impersonation to cult status, and their pantheon of spirits contained only two primary figures—Killer-of-Enemies (associated with the sun) and his mother Changing Woman (associated with the moon). Lesser-known Lipan spirit deities—such as Wise One (brother of Killer-of-Enemies and associated with water), Walking Rock (associated with old age), Cowbird (associated with the horse along with Bat Boy and Crow Boy), the Clown and the Crow (associated with hunting) and Big Owl (associated, along with the Raven, with death)— did not figure largely in Lipan ceremony.

Before turning to an examination of specific Lipan mythic figures, it is appropriate to ask whether Lipan mythology ever contained the concept of a single, all-powerful creator God. Killer-of-Enemies and Changing Woman were not the creators of humanity. That work had been done prior to their arrival on the earth. It is interesting that the Lipan emergence myth begins with the statement, "In the beginning they were going to create human beings," although the identity of "they" is never revealed (Opler, 1940: 13). By the nineteenth century, the Lipans used the term *yáta seta (god who is in the sky)* to refer to the Christian God, but this usage was a late adaptation. Traditionally, the Lipans never worshipped a single, all-powerful creator nor did they view their primary deities in formalized fashion as gods or goddesses.

Killer-of-Enemies and Changing Woman were seen as powerful supernatural culture heroes who came to earth. They "took the lead" after the Lipans emerged in the north, leading the people as they circumnavigated the edges of the earth searching for a home. These mentoring spirits taught the Lipans their culture and then returned to the sun and the moon, remaining constantly available to assist or protect the Lipans through an infusion of supernatural power.

It is best to let the Lipans tell the story of Changing Woman and Killer-of-Enemies in their own inimitable style. We enter the story as the Lipans are journeying in a clockwise fashion around the edges of the circular earth.

> The moon and the sun took the lead then. They were with the people. The sun is the man, the moon is the woman. The moon they call Changing Woman.
> Changing Woman was living at this time. Every time she had a child, the monster, Big Owl, would come. He would see tracks and say, 'There is another child.' He would come and eat the children. He did this several times before Killer-of-Enemies was born. Killer-of-Enemies was going to come soon.

The woman lay down. It rained and the rain entered her body. Then a child began to develop within her. The child was going to be a great person. In four days he came. After the child was born she put him under the fire place. She dug a trench there and reared the child under there, for Big Owl visited her. . . .

Soon the boy was strong. He could do anything now. Then his mother made him a little bow and arrow. It was for the little boy so that he could kill anything that came to fight him. Then Big Owl didn't bother him any more. When he was told that the boy belonged to Thunder he [Big Owl] was afraid.

The boy was now grown up. . . . [He was Killer-of-Enemies]. He was a great one. Nothing was impossible to him. But he asked for a little help; he prayed. That was to show that no matter how strong we are we must ask for a little help. It was to show the human beings. . . .

Two children were born to Changing Woman. One was called Killer-of-Enemies . . . and the other was called Wise One. Wise One was the younger boy. Killer-of-Enemies was hidden in the fire place. Wise One was hidden in a pool of water (Opler, 1940: 16-17, 22-23).

How would the Lipan Apaches have understood the myth regarding the birth of Killer-of-Enemies? The myth would have rationalized all the assumptions upon which the framework of Lipan religious practice rested. Killer-of-Enemies was a spirit entity born of two powerful supernatural forces—the Moon and Rain/Thunder. From birth, he was associated with the most powerful force in the universe (fire/sun). His younger brother, Wise One, completed the sacred set of four elements with his symbolic association to water. Yet, Killer-of-Enemies remained the most powerful force, and as such, he could do all things.

The Lipans would have extended this concept to a predictive knowledge of the future. Hence, a mythic shaman who channeled the power of Killer-of-Enemies would also gain a predictive knowledge of future events. The role of Killer-of-Enemies as teacher of the Lipans was set out in this first myth, and his first lesson was one of prayer. This episode reinforced the symbiotic relationship between the primary spirit deity, Killer-of-Enemies, and the Lipan people, who were being "taught" to subordinate themselves to him and to seek his power.

However, in the myth, the story of Big Owl played itself out against the backdrop of the birth and childhood of Killer-of-Enemies. The Lipans would have understood this tension as representative of the invisible struggle between good and evil, life and death. Big Owl, representing the malevolent supernatural forces of death, was overcome by the more powerful force of life/goodness, as represented by Changing Woman, Thunder and Killer-of-Enemies.

After a time on earth, Killer-of-Enemies removed himself from mankind and returned to his pure supernatural state as the sun. He joined his mother, Changing Woman (the moon). Before leaving the earth, his final instructions were to the shaman, who was instructed to pray and to teach the Lipan Apaches "the right way while the earth stands." (Opler, 1940: 33) This commandment was a mandate to the shaman and to the people to preserve their culture and rituals.

The Lipan Prediction of Eclipse

The use of planetary observation to predict eclipse is perhaps the most fascinating and most hidden aspect of Lipan religious practice. Even Farrer's study of the Mescalero Apache use of astronomy to time the ceremonial songs sung during the girl's puberty ceremony captured only a small segment of what was, for the Lipan Apaches, a much wider practice and usage (Farrer, 1991: 108-111). Because Lipan mythology stated that the primary Lipan spirit deities, Killer-of-Enemies (the sun) and Changing Woman (the moon), had left the Lipan people but were still "leading" them from a position in the universe, the worship of the sun and moon (and the supernatural power each possessed) remained of primary importance in Lipan religious practice. And, in order to properly worship these deities, they must be closely observed.

Lipan myth stated that as Killer-of-Enemies and Changing Woman left the earth, they made four promises to the Lipan people.

> These two said, 'We'll go ahead. We will separate but we will meet each other.' And when they meet there is an eclipse. Before they left the people they said, 'Nothing will disturb you people. Everything ahead is good for you people.' The sun and the moon said, 'We will take the lead now. We will keep on going. We will never stop, no matter what happens here on earth; we will always keep going.' The moon is Changing Woman and the sun is Killer-of-Enemies. When he left this world, he went back to the sun and he is there now (Opler, 1940: 16).

The first promise made by Killer-of-Enemies and Changing Woman was a promise to lead the Lipan people. The second promise was that the deities would, at times, come together in an eclipse. The third promise was one of prosperity and protection, while the fourth promise was a promise of eternal guidance. It was the second promise which formed the basis of Lipan planetary observation, since an eclipse was the celestial manifestation and validation of this ancient promise made by the primary spirit deities and indicated their continuing presence and watch-care over the Lipan people. It was imperative that the Lipans closely observe the movements of the sun and the moon in order to be able to predict an eclipse. And, when such an eclipse did occur, it was accompanied by Lipan ritual of the highest importance and solemnity.

The planetary aspects of Lipan religious practice were first noted in 1761 by Fr. Diego Ximenez who stated,

> They worship the sun, moon and best known stars. To these they direct their pleas and ask for help in their needs. They do not give them a fixed, determined or sensitive cult outside of the petitions. Each one selects the star he likes best (Ximenez, 1761a: 27).

Fr. Ximenez' comments are extremely important in understanding the precise nature of Lipan worship of their primary spirit deities, as well as the celestial observation necessary to complete that worship. The priest first listed the primary deities in their order of importance: the sun (Killer-of-Enemies), the moon (Changing Woman) and the "best known stars," by which we can assume he meant Venus, Saturn and Jupiter, which would have been assigned to the lesser deities. The Lipan worship of the sun and moon as spirit deities was confirmed by Fr. Morfi in 1779, who commented that the Lipans worshipped the sun (Chabot, 1932: 18). In 1828, Berlandier suspected the Lipans continued to worship the sun and the moon, although he was assured by a Lipan chief that this was no longer the case (Ewers, 1969: 130). Even as late as 1866, the Lipans celebrated a lunar eclipse ritual (Dennis, 1925: 112-113). The worship of the sun and moon as spirit deities, and the planetary observations necessary to predict eclipses and thus celebrate the most important rituals associated with these deities, continued to occupy the primary role in Lipan religious belief through the mid-nineteenth century, in spite of "civilizing" influences and missionary attempts at conversion to Christianity.

Fr. Ximenez observed that the spirit deities inhabiting the sun, moon and stars were objects of petitionary prayer, as the tribal collective prayed for assistance and protection. In his next sentence, however, the priest turned to the shamanic "cult," or formalized worship. He noted that it was not "fixed," meaning that the Lipans built no churches or other fixed structures in which they worshipped. His use of the term "determined" in describing the shamanic cult was meant to indicate that Lipan religion was not regulated. It did not possess a formalized, ordained priesthood, nor did it possess a single authority such as a Pope. A "sensitive cult," in the understanding of this eighteenth century Catholic priest, would have meant a cult characterized by orgiastic ritual (i.e. rituals of unrestrained indulgence). Fr. Ximenez was careful not to ascribe these sorts of rituals to Lipan practice. Finally, Ximenez noted the shamanic and individual specialization which characterized Lipan religious practice. Some mythic shamans might seek to access the supernatural power of the sun, others of the moon or of stars associated with minor deities. Fr. Ximenez was not dealing, in this description, with curative shamanism (he took up that subject later), but his words indicate that, in its earliest form, individual Lipan religious practice did not involve a vision quest seeking the power of the natural world. Rather, early individual religious practice involved the selection of a spirit deity ("the star he likes best") and the learning of necessary ritual so that an individual could properly channel the supernatural power of that deity.

What sorts of planetary observations would have been necessary for the Lipans to properly worship their primary spirit deities? In layman's terms, a solar eclipse occurs whenever the orbit of the moon transits, or crosses, between the earth and the sun so that the moon's shadow obscures the disc of the sun and sweeps across the face of the earth. The Lipans called this a meeting of the sun and the moon. The shadow cones cast by the moon are called the umbra and penumbra. Within the narrow area of the umbra, the eclipse is total, with the shadow disc of the moon appearing to move in front of and obscuring the disc of the sun. Within the wider surrounding region covered by the penumbra, the eclipse is only partial.

A lunar eclipse occurs when the moon moves through the earth's shadow and only at the time of the full moon, when the moon is on the side of the earth opposite to that of the sun. It appears much the same from all points on the earth from which it can be seen. The umbra, or total phase, lasts about two hours. From one specific geographic location, an observer might view about twenty lunar eclipses in a twenty-year period A total solar eclipse might be visible from the same location only once every 300-400 years (Britannica, 1992: 867-868).

Ancient cultures were able to predict a total solar eclipse by observing planetary movements over a long period of time. They noticed that, after a lapse of time equaling 18 years and 10½ or 11 days, the moon and the sun returned to very nearly the same relative positions. If the relative position had been a total eclipse, then they could predict another eclipse when the orbits cycled to the same point in 18 years and 10½ or 11 days. However, because of the rotation of the earth on its axis, the eclipse's umbra recurs each time in this cycle approximately 120° farther west on the surface of the earth. After three cycles (or 54 years and about a month), the longitude is repeated (Britannica, 1992: 867-870). The exact duplication of coordinates (longitude and latitude) does not occur but once every three or four centuries.

How would the Lipans have calculated the movements of the planets?

> Using a pair of notched sticks, one as a foresight and the other as a back-sight, an observer can determine the position of an object near the horizon with great accuracy. The sticks could be set in fixed locations to record the position of an astronomical body. When the body returned to its position between the notches, the astronomer could determine the length of its cycle. Perhaps a prominent feature in the landscape functioned as a natural foresight. (Aveni, 1980: 18)

In the nineteenth century, Alexander Stephen noted that the Hopi marked the passage of the sun across the zenith by observing where the sun rose or set relative to a prominent feature of the landscape. This technique was used to delineate a celestial solar calendar useful in determining the agricultural year (Aveni, 1980: 40 and figure 13). Although the Lipans practiced only a limited form of agriculture, solar observations would still have been useful in determining corn planting seasons and even ripening patterns for cactus tunas and other food sources spread over a large geographic area.

Were the Lipans able to predict both solar and lunar eclipses? Frank Buckelew recorded that the Mexican Lipan band holding him captive in 1866 had specific foreknowledge of a lunar eclipse (Dennis, 1925: 112). In 1788, *Lipiyan* chief *Picax-andé Yns-tinsle* was able to predict not only the day of a solar eclipse, but the hour (Ugalde, 1788a: 324-326). Even with the assistance of computer-generated ephemeris, modern astronomers are only able to predict the timing, within a few seconds, of a solar eclipse several years ahead. Long-range predictions are often confounded by irregular motions of the moon.

However, the *Lipiyans* were a Lipan-affiliated group and not part of the Lipan tribe proper. Yet it seems likely that the Lipan Apaches were also able to predict solar eclipses based on statements in their mythology. The Killer-of-Enemies myth cycle referred specifically to a solar eclipse when it stated the promise that Killer-of Enemies and Changing Woman would separate but meet each other. This describes the moon passing in front of the sun (i.e. solar eclipse), rather than the moon moving through the shadow of the earth (lunar eclipse). Although a narrow reading of Lipan myth might tend to support the idea that the eclipse promise was included merely to reassure the tribe when such natural events occurred, the Lipan ability to predict lunar eclipses would argue that they were also able to predict solar eclipses, since such solar predictions are calculated on a study of the moon's orbits. The Lipans must have discovered the saros cycle of 18/54 years in order to be able to predict a total solar eclipse which would occur within the umbra cast on one specific geographic location. It is also clear that the knowledge gleaned from planetary observation must have been passed from generation to generation, since the prediction of eclipse is only possible by observing planetary movements over a long period of time. This fact would argue for a loosely-organized group of observers, possibly mythic shamans, who observed the motions of the planets, recorded their observations, and then passed this knowledge along to the next generation.

The ritual ceremonies marking an eclipse were of the utmost solemnity and importance for both the *Lipiyans* and Lipans. A description of a *Lipiyan* solar eclipse ritual was preserved in Juan de Ugalde's diary of events surrounding a meeting between his lieutenant, José Menchaca, and the *Lipiyan* chief *Picax-andé Yns-tinsle* in the San Rodrigo canyon of Coahuila. Three Lipan chiefs and their *rancherías* traveled to Coahuila with *Picax* and the *Lipiyans*, although *Picax* placed the three Lipan chiefs under arrest as soon as they reached the canyon because "they had not done their duty in the battle which he had with the Taguaya [Wichita] nation." (Ugalde, 1788a: 322) However, both *Lipiyans* and Lipans joined together in a peyote ritual on February 28, 1788 and celebrated a *mitote* throughout the night of February 29th. *Picax* told Menchaca that he was going to be occupied with another celebration which would begin at dawn on March 1st and end at dusk. The chief suggested that Menchaca, who was anxious to bring the *Lipiyan* chief to Ugalde at the Santa Rosa presidio, postpone his travel plans for an additional three days. The chief also suggested that Menchaca not return to the *Lipiyan*-Lipan camp until "after the sun had crossed half the sky due to the celebration which was going to occupy him [on March 1st]." Menchaca watched the ritual from a nearby location (Ugalde, 1788a: 324).

[Picax] acknowledged that this function [ritual] belonged to the *Lipanes*, and that even though all Indians attended to watch it, it was them who should enter and render vassalage or tribute inside his great Chief's tent *(Supo que esta function era delos Lipanes, y que aunque concurria a verla toda la Yndiada, eran sol ellos los que Devian entrar a render el Vasallaje, o Tributo dentro dela los los que Devian entrar a render el Vasallaje, or Tributo dentro dela Tienda desu gran Capitan).* (Ugalde, 1788a: 325)

Although the ritual observed by Menchaca was *Lipiyan* in its particulars, the chief's words indicate that he borrowed a Lipan solar eclipse ceremony and adapted it for his own purposes.

> March 1, 1788. The sun had not yet completely risen when the Indian men and women, with their children (large, half-grown and small) occupied the space used the day before; they arrived with their bodies undressed from the waist up, their hair hanging down, shoeless and holding in their right hands a whip, a buckskin, a buffalo skin or some other tanned piece of everyday usage, and presented these things to the Chief.
>
> At mid-day, the people assembled and, as the sun went out, they all positioned themselves to a man on their knees, sitting on their feet; at the sound of a bell in the tent of *Picax,* they all inclined their heads to the ground and remained in this state, from that hour until one in the afternoon, without any chance to eat, drink or smoke or to do anything else except to enter four by four into the tent [of Picax], which was always closed and guarded by sentinels. After a short time, they left the tent without the gifts that they carried in their right hands, but with a daub of blue paint on the bridge of the nose, crossing the nose from the right tear duct to the left; it was also noticed that upon entering the tent, even the nursing children gave gifts, which, while not equal in value to those of the parents, had at least a fifth of their value, and thus they all presented something to their revered Chief (Ugalde, 1788a: 325-326).

There are a number of noteworthy details in Menchaca's description of this *Lipiyan* ceremony. Of primary importance is the fact that *Picax* was able to predict the date and hour of a solar eclipse which would be visible from the San Rodrigo canyon of Coahuila. *Lipiyan* territory was said to stretch from the Colorado to the Pecos Rivers of Texas, at least 250 miles north of the canyon. *Picax* also had foreknowledge that the solar eclipse would occur at midday, since he had warned Menchaca not to approach the Indian camp until after the hour of total eclipse. The *Lipiyan* ritual was one of submission and abasement, as indicated by the nakedness of the participants and the rawhide tribute which symbolized the people's removal of the protection offered by rawhide clothing. However, the over-arching ritual theme was not the religious worship of a solar deity, but submission and homage paid to a political leader, possibly as part of Lipan atonement for not doing their duty in battle with the Wichitas.

Nonetheless, several connections can be drawn between the *Lipiyan* ceremony and Lipan religious belief. The entry of the people into *Picax'* tent "four by four" (either on all fours or in groups of four, the Spanish meaning is unclear), can be linked to a Lipan belief in the sacred nature of the number four. The blue daub across the bridge of the nose also echoed the Lipan attribution of sacredness to the color blue (Opler, 1940: 30-31). The complete communal nature of the *Lipiyan* ritual meant that even nursing babies were obligated to make their obeisance to *Picax*. This small detail also calls to mind the Lipan insistence on a correct *cuenta (tally)* when clothing was given as gifts to Lipan chiefs after signing a peace treaty. Just as a complete and correct count was necessary before a Lipan chief would give his total commitment to peace, so a complete count of the entire camp population was necessary before they could give their complete and total submission to their political leader.

A fascinating description of a lunar eclipse ritual comes from the pen of Lipan captive Frank Buckelew, who described a ritual he witnessed between the time of his capture (March 11, 1866) and his escape (February 1867). The ceremony was performed as his captors were traveling between the Rio Grande and the Pecos and the lunar eclipse was probably observed at a location in Edwards, Val Verde or Terrell County, Texas.

> While I was with them I noticed the tribe making preparations, unusual in their nature, but of sufficient importance to engage the attention of all, old as well as young. Late in the evening, the entire tribe—men, women and children— marched to the foot of a low hill a short distance from the camp. In taking their seat on the ground they formed a vast circle inclosing [sic] an open space. In the center of this circle the musical instruments were placed. The same instruments were now used as in the dance, the drum, the long chain of disc-shaped bones and the smooth dry sticks. At a given signal, the musicians, or those whose duty it was to operate these crude instruments, took their position in the center.
>
> All was quiet and waited in breathless silence the coming event. Suddenly, by some common signal, the music began; it was different from that played during their dance. The music, the expression on their faces, in fact everything connected with the ceremony, depicted great solemnity.
>
> It was a cloudless night, and the moon was shining clear and bright. Soon the light of the moon began to fade until all was total darkness. The music continued, and at brief intervals the savages would join in with a low mournful chant, perfectly in accord with the expression and mood of the musicians. This ceremony was kept up until the moon emerged from the darkness and began to shine. Then all went back to camp and to bed.
>
> By some means, these savages had previous knowledge of this occurrence. The preparations made beforehand are sufficient evidence to show this. I knew at once that the moon was in eclipse, but had no knowledge of it before and as to how these simple savages knew it had always been a mystery to me. (Dennis, 1925: 112-113)

Much like the *Lipiyan* solar ritual, the Lipan lunar eclipse ritual required the participation of the entire band population, yet the lunar ritual was one of rhythmic drumming and chant, rather than a ritual of tribute, abasement and submission. The lunar ritual was tied to Changing Woman and its solemn nature was reflective of the prayer chants directed at the deity as she momentarily turned away. Through the chant, each band member implored Changing Woman to again turn her face upon her people. The ritual was led by musicians. The solemn drumbeats, the rattle of the bones (discs to symbolize the full moon) and the dull sounds made by striking dry sticks together provided the backdrop for the chant. Perhaps the chant included the following fragment collected by ethnologist Albert Gatschet: *"hāsaí tchetlē, nāna ān‛á onană einána einēyoná (translation: Ladder small, (unmeaning)* (Gatschet, 1884: 61). [2]

The concept of the use of a ladder as a means for spirit deities to descend to earth would have been an idea familiar to many Southwestern Pueblo cultures and a rare instance in Lipan culture of an obvious Pueblo influence. Although Gatschet's chant represents only one tiny fragment, it might indicate that the ritual manner in which the Lipans worshipped their spirit deities contained aspects more heavily influenced by Southwestern Pueblo cultures than previously believed by anthropologist Morris Opler.

The Use of Effigy and Totem

The Lipan use of effigy to impersonate a spirit deity was another Pueblo-influenced aspect of Lipan religious practice, reminiscent of Hopi Katchinas. Lipan effigies were used for two primary purposes: to provide a physical form used in shamanic ritual to encourage the manifestation of a spirit deity for predictive purposes, and to provide a form symbolizing the enemy to be used in warfare ritual.

In 1764, Fr. Diego Ximenez described the dual manner in which the Lipan used effigies. He first addressed the shamanic use of effigy to call down the supernatural power of the spirit deity through rituals using incense and tobacco smoke. The effigy itself was a flesh-colored torso (minus the head, arms and legs) made of animal hide. Since the lungs were located in the torso and the Lipan believed literally in the breath of life (i.e. that life began when wind or breath entered the body), the torso was the seat of life. A channeling of supernatural power, performed by the mythic shaman, would call down the power of a spirit deity, who would "come to life" inside the effigy. The effigy would then "speak" to the shaman in such a way as to provide prophetic insight.

> I believed they were heathens like all the others, without a King or God, until we managed to free a sorcerer from deception. He gave us an idol and other instruments used in the art of sorcery. There is no doubt that they have formal idolization. We do not know if they have churches or any other place designated for sacrifices but we do know they worship idols. The sorcerers seem to be the only ones who carry them. They apply incense to the idols with respectful ceremonies and during the ceremonies the sorcerers dispense smoke from their mouths. The idol is made out of animal hide, in the form of a human torso, well painted with flesh-colored paints. . . .
>
> The Devil speaks to the sorcerers through the idol, informing them where the enemy or bison can be found. Bison is their primary means of support. Through the idol, the sorcerers predict how many of the sick will live or die. . .
>
> In addition the people seek advice from the sorcerer on the following subjects: drought, storms, conjuration of evil spirits (Ximenez, 1764: 176-177).

In 1779, Fr. Juan Agustín de Morfi also addressed the Lipan use of effigy.

> They worship the sun, and other ridiculous figures made by their hands; and their cult neither perplexes them nor fatigues them, because all of their religious acts are reduced to placing tobacco and other herbs in their pipes, and smoking them, to blow the smoke to the dull (*torpe, clumsy or slow-witted*) object of their barbarous admiration (Chabot, 1932: 18).

Morfi's mention of pipes identifies the types of "instruments used in the art of sorcery" cited by Fr. Ximenez. Modern Lipan Apaches have eschewed the use of an effigy in seeking "advice on drought and storms," but continue the mythic shamanic tradition with *El Cortador da Nubes (Cloud Cutter-Rain dancer)*, an elder who chants and performs a dance whereby a knife is used to gently cut the clouds to release rain. [3]

The Lipans also used effigies to symbolize their enemies in warfare rituals, but these effigies do not seem to have been the flesh-colored torsos used to channel the power of spirit deities. Fr. Ximenez noted,

> We do not know the types of sacrifices they make, although we believe [the idol represents] the enemy they have killed in their *mitotes* or other festivals of sacrifice where an idol is among the procession and in many ceremonies involving execution by lance (Ximenez, 1764: 177).

The priest seems to be referring to the Lipan use of an object similar to the *Lipiyan el Sarao*, the wrapped object around which the *mitote* was danced prior to going to war. Fr. Ximenez also noted objects carried in procession during the Lipan ritual cannibalism of war captives.

The shamanic use of effigies was carried over, on an individual level, to the use of totems. Once an individual had been granted a vision quest, the power of one aspect of the natural world (his totem) was channeled into the human body, inhabiting the body and boosting the individual's normal power in dimensions associated with the totem. For example, a man who had received supernatural power through the bear in a vision would, it was believed, become ferocious in battle. Supernatural power through mountain lion would bring with it agility and an ability to perfect an ambush. Berlandier (1828) described the Lipan use of totems, contrasting Lipan usage with totems used by the Comanches.

> Ruíz says that superstition, while not as rife as it is among the Comanche, was nevertheless very widespread among the Lipans. These natives carry shrines with them of the sort the Comanche call *pouhahantes*, which are nothing but small animals or portions of larger ones which they have dried and which they believe possess supernatural powers. These objects are so various that it is hard to find two alike, and they depend entirely upon the taste, purposes, and ideas of the man who chooses to burden himself with these monuments to the ignorance of humankind (Ewers, 1969: 130).

Physical Manifestation of a Spirit Deity

In 1764, Fr. Diego Ximenez recorded one curious instance of what was believed by the Lipan Apaches to be an actual physical manifestation, in human form, of one of their spirit deities. This episode was the result of attempts by Spanish missionaries to convert the Lipans and "reduce" them to mission life and settlement in missions along the upper Nueces River of Texas. In almost every instance in which the Lipans settled near or entered missions, a smallpox epidemic swept through the Lipan *rancherias* shortly thereafter, creating a negative association, in the Lipan mind, between mission settlement and death.

> The Devil aided by sorcerers and bad Christians interferes with conversion. All the Indians state that they see an old man come and disappear. The old man advises them to have a continuous war with the neighboring nations and with the Spaniards. He emphasizes that they should never be baptized. Those that are will die shortly after the ceremony. He appears in battle, where he is killed. Later he reappears. The old man uses this episode to encourage others to fight promising that they will also live after death. After death they are to live among their people reunited; they are to reunite with the separated. He changes forms to convince the skeptical. He often appears in the form of a woman. The oldest Indian who has seen her says she is always the same age. Sorcerers advocate that the old man be trusted. Good Christians are quite helpful in handling this matter; on the other hand, bad Christians interfere with our plans (Ximenez, 1764: 178).

What is curious about the episode is the Lipan claim that a spirit deity manifested itself into human form apart from the flesh-colored torso or without being channeled through the body of a shaman. This would seem to indicate that the Lipans believed that their spirit deities could physically manifest themselves in times of crisis and move among the people. They could also change form at will and appear as either a man or a woman.

The identity of the old man is unknown. Perhaps he was Walking Rock, a minor spirit deity associated with old age and death, or perhaps he was Killer-of-Enemies in human form with acknowledgment given to his antecedents in the misty past. The male/female dichotomy of the apparition might have reflected the two primary deities, Killer-of-Enemies and Changing Woman (who was also said in myth to never age).

Mythological aspects aside, the curious episode related by Fr. Ximenez reflected an attempt by the Lipan shamanic community to assert themselves into the political arena and change the outcome of political decisions made by some Lipan chiefs to bring their bands into the Spanish missions. The shamans' warnings were successful, for the Lipan Apaches were never "reduced" to mission settlement nor did they accept wholesale conversion to Christianity.

Chapter 17

Lipan Apache Religion- Curative Shamanism

Curative Shamanism

The primary difference between a mythic shaman and a curative shaman lay in their clientele. A mythic shaman channeled supernatural power in order to make predictive statements on topics relevant to the entire Lipan band, such as the timing of the buffalo hunt, the location of the enemy and a prediction of the number of casualties sustained in an upcoming battle or raid. Such predictions were capable of altering the normal course of an annual migration or altering the course of warfare. Mythic shamans also probably functioned as celestial observers and predictors of eclipse, interpreting the movements of the planets as well as interpreting the will of the spirit deities.

A curative shaman's clientele was composed of individuals and his predictive statements were focused on the lives of individuals and extended families, rather than prophecy relevant to the entire band. His primary function was that of a healer. The Lipans believed that most illness was the result of the intrusion of a foreign substance into the body. In order to effect a cure, that substance must be removed by the shaman who would, in many cases, draw it out with his lips (Opler, 1940: 276-277). A shaman, who had been chosen as a channel by the supernatural power of the natural world, would call upon that power in the healing ceremony.

There was a great deal of specialization within the brother and sisterhood of Lipan curative shamans, for both men and women could seek to become mediums of natural power and masters of healing ritual. The specialization aspects of Lipan curative shamanism were first noticed by Fr. Diego Ximenez. He observed, "There are certain sorcerers *(hechiceros)* or liars but there are many hidden herbalists *(herbolarios)* or quacks *(curanderos)* who know various simples (herbal remedies)." (Ximenez, 1761a: 27) This comment would indicate that there were only a few mythic shamans, while most Lipan shamans were either herbal healers or mixed herbalism with folk magic. Some shamans dealt with illness and others dealt with the treatment of injuries, particularly gunshot, which was an occupational hazard in a raiding culture. Some shamans, upon receiving their power, also received the admonition to "always use it for good," while others received no such stricture and chose to use their power to cast and remove spells. The latter was always a popular feature in a culture where revenge could rear its ugly head in interpersonal relationships.

The reputation of a curative shaman rested upon his rate of successful cure. Opler equated the role of curative shaman with the role of chief. Both were leaders who rose to prominence naturally, rather than through election, and whose fortunes rose and fell according to their rate of success (Opler, 1975: 17).

However, as was also seen in the case of chieftainship, this generalization is too broad when applied specifically to Lipan practice. It does not take into account the fact that the Lipans believed a curative shaman was selected by supernatural power which sought to channel itself into him. It also does not take into account the family of *Chevato*, who was a fourth-generation Lipan shaman (Stewart, 1974: 218). [1] This would indicate that the role of shaman could be an inherited role, just as chieftainship could be inherited.

Nonetheless, successful cures and predictions were still the basis upon which a shaman's reputation rested and a shaman who could not cure and whose predictions were inaccurate soon lost clients. However, there did seem to be a brotherhood of shamans from various friendly tribes who were not averse to taking cases that confounded the curative abilities of Lipan shamans. Opler recorded one tale of a young boy who was taken to a Carrizo shaman after Lipan shamans were unable to cure him (Opler, 1940: 276-277).

Witchcraft

There was a strong undercurrent of witchcraft in the practices of some Lipan curative shamans. Fr. Morfi observed this aspect in 1779.

> There is among them a multitude of charlatans who practice medicine, and are like the priests of their divinities. They attribute to themselves the quality of witches and the knowledge of many natural secrets. They make believe that the *Demonio (Devil)* frequently appears to them, with whom they have familiar and intimate intercourse. The shameless audacity with which they profess these frauds, helped by the ability with which they manage their snakes, other skillful tricks and occasional successful cures, perpetuates the crude error of those miserable people, who hold them [the priests] as infallible in their divinations. (Chabot, 1932: 18-19)

It is impossible to know whether witchcraft practices had always been a core element of Lipan shamanistic practice, or whether they were adapted from Pueblo cultures or from Hispanic folk-magic practices of the northern Mexico. Fr. Ximenez does not ascribe the practice of witchcraft to Lipan religion and he, of all observers, was the most familiar with the tribe's ritual practices. However, Ximenez was also highly concerned with presenting the Lipans in the best light possible in order to win Viceregal support for his missionary efforts.

What can be stated with certainty is that by the late nineteenth century, many Lipans fleeing Mexico arrived at the Mescalero Reservation in New Mexico and soon gained fearsome reputations as witches (Carroll, 1908). This reputation followed them to Oklahoma, where some of the same Mexican Lipans settled on the Comanche and Kiowa reservation after fleeing the Mescalero Reservation in the early 1890's. A small core group of Lipans had been living with the Mescaleros since 1850 and this core group was never accused of witchcraft by the Mescaleros. A small group of Texas Lipans who were moved to the Oakland Agency near Ponca, Oklahoma in 1884 were not known as witches. Thus,

it becomes obvious that other tribes generally believed that witchcraft was practiced only by the Mexican Lipans. This would support the argument that Lipan
witchcraft was an adaptation from Hispanic folk-magic.

Smallpox

Although the Lipans were generally healthy, the one disease that proved to
be their scourge was smallpox. At least five epidemics are recorded as having
swept through Lipan camps within the last half of the eighteenth century. The
loss of life must have been substantial, since Fr. Morfi commented in 1779,

> If it were not for their having suffered from the smallpox and continual warfare,
> in which they live, they alone had populated these extensive lands to the detri-
> ment of the Spaniards, such being the fecundity with which they propagate
> their specie (Chabot, 1932: 19).

The 1780 smallpox epidemic was the most severe, decimating the tribal
population. The epidemic probably spread to the Lipans from the Tonkawas, a
tribe with whom the Lipans were at war. The Tonkawa leadership had been
decimated by the disease in 1779. By October 1780, the pestilence arrived at
San Antonio. Texas Governor Cabello reported, "I assure Your Lordship that
this plague is taking its great toll. Some Lipan-Apaches who arrived last night
tell me the same thing; that it is taking its toll among their people." (Cabello,
1780a: 63-64) By November, the plague spread to the mission of la Bahía (Goliad, Texas). There were so many abandoned Lipan corpses that Cabello feared a
new plague might arise "from the infestation of so many cadavers."

> One does not hear or see anything day or night except the tolling of bells
> and the sight of burials. The presidio is without medicament whatever or even
> anyone to administer it; nor is there even anyone who can perform bloodletting,
> whereby such an uncountable number of sick persons as have fallen victims at
> the same time to the said disease might be aided.
> Today I learned that a huge body of Lipan-Apaches, en route to relocate
> beyond the banks of the Nueces River, was seen to have to stop ten leagues [30
> miles] from this presidio. Victimized to such a great extreme by the smallpox
> and diphtheria—which are striking at the same time—these Indians are being
> decimated to a degree inexpressible. And so an endless number of them, now
> apostate, now heathens, have come to these missions, which have been inun-
> dated with such people. But their coming to the missions is not saving these
> people from nevertheless dying in great numbers. Since they have the custom
> of abandoning victims in the place where they lie, leaving the victims' horses
> and whatever else they owned, I feel that some new plague may arise from so
> many bodies of Indians and horses as that have died in the place wherein they
> have relocated. (Cabello, 1780b: 15-16)

As soon as smallpox appeared in a Lipan *rancheria,* the first response was to make immediate preparations to move the camp. "One can see the *rancherias* on the trail, seeking the emptiest, most deserted places they can find, abandoning the sick along the way and changing their camp every time one of them dies." (Ewers, 1969: 85)

Table 17.0   Known Smallpox Epidemics among the Lipan Apaches

Date Reported	Location	Details
Nov. 25, 1749	San Antonio	"Many Apaches asked for corn & tobacco, arriving here because of smallpox *(viruelas)* among the people"-Fr. Delores
Feb. 19, 1750	San Antonio	"Many Apache children died of smallpox *(viruelas)*" - Fr. Santa Ana
Dec, 26, 1764	Lipan Missions on Upper Nueces	Seventy-four children and adults baptized *in extremis* during smallpox epidemic. "The majority died." -Fr. Diego Ximenez
Oct. 20, 1780	San Antonio	"Lipan Apaches tell me that smallpox epidemic is taking its toll among their people."-Texas Governor Domingo Cabello
Jan. 31, 1781	San Antonio	"Lipans have been victimized to great extreme by smallpox & diphtheria which are striking at the same time."-Governor Cabello
Dec. 22, 1780	Coahuila	Mexican Lipan chief *Bigotes* and others seek herbal cures including *carrizalejo*- Juan de Ugalde
Feb. 8, 1781	Coahuila	Smallpox *(viruelas)* reported in Lipan *rancherias* - Juan de Ugalde
Oct. 16, 1798	Laredo, TX	"The smallpox *(viruelas)* epidemic goes through the Lipan population with a vengeance" - Conde de Sierra Gorda
1849-1850	San Antonio	Smallpox epidemic "in such a virulent form that few who took it survived."- Philemon Venego, Lipan

(Sources: Dolores, 1749a: 118; Santa Ana, 1750a: 140; Ximenez, 1764: 175-179; Ugalde, 1781b: 59-60; Ugalde, 1781b: 93-94; Sierragorda, 1798: 190; Cabello, 1781: 15; Ball, 1988: 269)

The initial response of Lipan curative shamans to the appearance of smallpox was to seek an herbal remedy. In December 1780, Mescalero chief *Patule* approached the Governor of Coahuila with a request. He reported that smallpox was ravaging the Mescalero camps as well as the camps of Mexican Lipan chief *Bigotes.* In the hope that the epidemic would "fade like running deer," *Patule* and *Bigotes* wished to move their *rancherias* into the interior of Coahuila to seek herbal cures. *Patule* specified that they wished to move to an area near the provincial capital of Monclova which contained black cherry trees *(capuli or capulin; Prunus serotina ssp. capuli)*, packsaddle grass *(zacate enjalma)* and reed beds *(carrizalejo)* (Ugalde, 1781a: 59-60). The mention of *carrizalejo* might be a shadowy reference to peyote acquired from the Carrizo Indians.

As the Lipans and Mescaleros searched for an herbal cure for smallpox in 1780, the Spanish also attempted to stem the tide of the epidemic. Berlandier reported in 1828, "A governor or vice-governor of the states of Coahuila and Texas vaccinated many Lipans and rendered great services to this people during the epidemic before the last one." (Ewers, 1969: 85) Berlandier was referring to the smallpox epidemic of 1780-1781.

In 1798, another smallpox epidemic swept through Lipan *rancherías* in south Texas. A report from Laredo, Texas indicated that the Lipans had found some success in finding herbal cures to treat smallpox, although the success of the herbal cures must have been greatly assisted by the vaccination effort of the previous decade. Spanish commander Conde de Sierragorda noted in a letter to the Viceroy, "although [the Lipans] have described the vomit as dark, there has been little of it and they have cured themselves well with *la Chaca*, or *Palo Mulato*." (Sierragorda, 1798: 190) The leaves, flowers and berries of *La Chaca* or *Palo Mulato* (botanical name *Bursera simaruba Linnaeus*) produce a purgative reaction when decocted into a tea. [2]

The Peyote Ceremony

There is no doubt that the primary Lipan cultural legacy still visible in modern life can be found inside a peyote tepee of the Native American Church. The story of how one major form of the peyote ceremony used by the Native American Church made its way from the Lipan *rancherías* of Coahuila to the ceremonial tepees of the Comanches and Kiowas (both former enemies of the Lipans), is the story of one family of Lipan shamans. This shamanic family introduced the use of peyote as a medicinal cure, participated in the development of a unique ceremony associated with ritual peyote use, and then spread the ceremony and ritual usage to the Mescalero Apaches and later to the Comanches. However, the late nineteenth century introduction of the Lipan peyote ceremony to the Comanches and Kiowas is the end of the story. In order to discover how the Lipans first began to use peyote, we must turn back to the year 1750 and look to the lands bordering the Rio Grande River.

The Lipans traditionally gathered, processed and ate many different cactus species growing in Texas and northern Mexico and the use of cactus as a food source was a staple of the Lipan diet. Around 1750, a group of Lipans broke away from their kin inhabiting the area around San Antonio and moved south across the Rio Grande into an area of Coahuila upriver from Mission San Juan Bautista and near the small town of San Fernando de Austria (later known as Zaragoza). The area they now claimed as their territory contained the largest concentration in the western hemisphere of an indigenous cactus species known today as peyote *(Lophophora williamsii)* (Stewart, 1974: 211-214). However, peyote was never used by the Lipan Apaches as a food source, in spite of its abundance, because of its bitter and nauseating taste when eaten.

Lipan Apache Religion- Curative Shamanism

A Mexican Lipan named *Dinero (Pa-na-ro or Penaro),* brother of the Lipan shaman *Chevato,* provided an important clue as to when and how the Lipans began to use peyote. In a 1918 sworn statement, *Dinero* testified:

> My name is *Pa-na-ro.* I am a Lipan Apache. I live five miles northeast of Indiahoma, Oklahoma, on my own allotment. I am about 57 years old. I knew about peyote before any of these Indians in the Oklahoma country knew about it. I first ate peyote in Mexico. My great grand-father was the first [Lipan] to make use of it in Mexico, and it was brought among the Indians here years after. It was used as a medicine at first, and no woman or young people ate it as they do now. It is called mescal-peyote in Mexico; here in Oklahoma it is called peyote. (Stewart, 1974: 218)

Dinero's statement contains three claims, all of which are validated by the sparse evidence available in the historical record. (1) *Dinero* indicated that his great grandfather was the first man to introduce the use of peyote to the Lipans; (2) that the introduction of peyote first occurred in Mexico and among the Mexican Lipans; and (3) that *Dinero's* great grandfather introduced the use of peyote through his role as a curative shaman, since the substance was originally used as a medicinal cure. An examination of these claims stakes out a timeline, and discloses elements of the origin of the Lipan peyote ceremony.

Dinero was born in 1860-1861 in a Lipan settlement at Hacienda Patiño, near Zaragosa, Coahuila (Chebahtah and Minor, 2007: 19-20). Counting back three generations would yield an estimated date range of 1750-1780 as the time period in which his great grandfather introduced peyote to his band of Mexican Lipans. The 1761 notation by Fr. Ximenez that the Lipans did not use intoxicating herbs would tend to push the date of the introduction of peyote toward the 1780 mark. The latter date is buttressed by a 1788 description of a *Lipiyan* peyote ceremony in which Lipans participated. Thus, we can assume that the Lipan Apaches were using peyote by 1788 (Ugalde, 1788a: 323-326).

Modern scholars generally accept that the Lipan s first acquired the use of peyote from the Carrizo Indians, but the location of that acquisition has been ascribed to both Texas and Mexico (Opler, 1938: 271-285, Stewart, 1974: 211-223). Some nineteenth century observers placed the Carrizos on the south Texas Gulf Coast plains and Opler believed that the Lipans acquired the peyote ceremony in Texas. However, the location of the Carrizos in south Texas (Carrizo Springs, Dimmitt County) was a result of later tribal migration. As early as 1735, the Carrizo Indians were known to inhabit an area of the northern Mexican province of Nuevo Leon near the town of Cerralvo (Jauregui Urrutia, 1735: 19). From there, they ranged east, following the Rio Grande River toward the Gulf of Mexico. By 1773, they were also present in the province of Coahuila at a mission dedicated to their settlement called *San Jose del Carrizo (San Jose of the Carrizo),* located along the south bank of the Rio Grande about thirty miles up the river from Cerralvo (Gerhard, 1920: 332). A nearby mission named *Mission del Dulce Nombre Jesus de Peyotes (Mission of the Sweet Name of Jesus of the Peyotes, founded 1688)* lay amidst the *lomerías (hills)* where the peyote cactus grew abundantly (Apuntes, 1998). Both missions were located fifty miles from the site of the main Lipan camps in Coahuila after 1750.

As the name of the *Peyotes* mission indicated, it was located in an area that contained abundant peyote, a small carrot-shaped cactus whose head protrudes above the ground about 1-2 inches. The protruding head, which is covered with tufts of silky hairs, is harvested and when dried, is called a peyote button. These buttons are the part of the plant which is consumed during the peyote ceremony. A chemical analysis of the plant shows that it contains nine narcotic alkaloids which cause physiological reactions of visual hallucination (particularly visions in color) and kinaesthetic, olfactory and auditory hallucinations. Although the peyote buttons are bitter and cause a gagging reflex when eaten, they produce no ill after-effects and are not addictive (McAllister, 1996: 174-175).

The nexus in Coahuila of Lipan camps (after 1750), a major source supply of peyote and the mission presence of Carrizo Indians is a strong argument for locating the transfer of peyote knowledge from the Carrizos to the Lipans in Mexico rather than in Texas. How, then, can the family of *Dinero* and *Chevato* be linked to this process?

Of extreme importance in *Dinero's* statement is the comment that his great grandfather originally introduced peyote to be used for medicinal, rather than ceremonial purposes. The severe smallpox epidemic of 1780-1781, which decimated both Texas and Mexican Lipan bands, was the probable inspiration for *Dinero's* great grandfather to seek to adapt the Carrizo use of peyote for Lipan medicinal purposes. *Dinero's* great grandfather would have sought to use this remedy in his role as a curative shaman, since the ingestion of peyote caused a gagging reflex which was believed to purge the body of harmful toxins (such as smallpox). The sharing of rituals between shamans of different tribes is noted earlier in this chapter, in the context of a Carrizo shaman curing a young Lipan boy when Lipan shamans were unable to help. It seems certain that this sort of sharing within the shamanic brotherhood, in response to the Lipans' search for a cure for smallpox, is what brought the use of peyote to the Lipan people.

Thus, all evidence ties the origin of the Lipan peyote ceremony to a smallpox epidemic. It was probably the terrible epidemic of 1780-1781 which began in Texas, spread to the Texas Lipan bands, and then crossed the Rio Grande and swept through the Mexican Lipan *rancherías*. About 1780-1784, a Lipan shaman (ancestor to *Dinero*) sought a smallpox cure from Carrizo shamans. He was introduced to peyote, the use of which he brought back to the Lipans as a medicinal cure. The cure seems to have been somewhat effective, because by 1798, when smallpox reappeared among the Lipans, the Spanish commander in Laredo reported that the Lipans were able to contain the epidemic through the use of their herbal cures.

The next area of inquiry, in an exploration of the roots of the Lipan peyote ceremony, is an examination of ritual form. Did the Lipans originally use the same form of ritual as did the Carrizos? The Carrizo peyote ceremony was first observed by the Spanish in 1649 who reported that the ritual consisted of the participants consuming peyote buttons during an all-night dance around a fire. No ritual tepee was mentioned (Fikes, 1996: 3-7). The dancers were accompanied by musicians playing the drum and shaking a gourd rattle filled with *usachito* seeds. By the eighteenth century, Carrizo peyote dancers wore bells attached to the leg below the knee (Salinas, 1990: 132-133). By the nineteenth century, Carrizo peyote dancers wore peyote buttons tied into necklaces and draped around their necks as they danced. The harvesting of peyote and the tying of peyote buttons into strings or "rosaries" was a common Carrizo (and Lipan) practice reported by Berlandier (Ewers, 1969: 62).

The first description of Lipan participation in a peyote ceremony came from the 1788 meeting of *Lipiyan* chief *Picax* and José Menchaca in the San Rodrigo canyon of Coahuila. However, since the ceremony was not initiated by the Lipans, but by the *Lipiyans*, early Lipan practice may have differed in many respects. The *Lipiyan* ritual was specifically described as a "religious ceremony" lasting from sunrise to sunset.

> February 28, 1788. Menchaca moved to a small hill that dominated the Indian camp and from there he observed at sunset a large number of people and a few household items from the *rancheria* in front of the largest of the tents. The people maintained a profound silence and being nude from the waist up, removed their shoes and with a step entered four by four into the indicated tent and stayed inside awhile, going out at last while others continued that ceremony, which appropriately began at sunrise, without having acted the fool *(chistado)*, eaten, drunk nor smoked. (Ugalde, 1788a: 323).

Further elaboration on the exact nature of the *Lipiyan* ritual was provided in a diary entry made several days later. Menchaca left the Indian camp "filled with admiration for the things he had seen."

> But the lieutenant departed from the encampment of the Indians without knowing what took place within the tent of the chief, nor the object of the ceremonies to which he had been a witness. Nor did he learn the reasons for the extraordinary grimaces without end *(sin fin de extraordinarios Visajes)* and the ridiculous movements *(ridiculos movimientos)* which they practiced there. (Ugalde, 1788a: 326)

The fact that Mendoza witnessed a *Lipiyan* peyote ceremony is validated by his mention of "extraordinary grimaces" and spastic, "ridiculous" bodily movements. These occurred as the bitter taste and hallucinogenic effects of the peyote, characterized by kinesthetic movement, became manifest.

The Lipan Apaches completely transformed both the Carrizo and the *Lipiyan* peyote ceremonies. They discarded the Carrizo element of dance, choosing instead to hold the ritual away from public view inside a ceremonial tepee. The Lipans restricted the ritual participants to exclude women. They retained the ritual time-frame, however, with the peyote ceremony being a ritual held over the course of at least one night. The Lipans also discarded the *Lipiyan* time frame (from sunrise to sunset) and clothing mandates (or lack thereof) and added the use of tobacco as a means of accessing the spirit of the peyote. The Lipan peyote ceremony also added food as a ceremonial conclusion.

By the time the Lipan peyote ceremony reached the level of cultural importance to warrant its adoption into myth (about 1800?), the element of song had been added to ceremonial practice. Interestingly enough, the myth did not ascribe the origin of the peyote ceremony to any spirit being, but to four human men who decided to experiment with the eating of peyote. This would reinforce the late eighteenth century origins of the peyote ceremony as described by *Dinero*, for if the ritual had been of much older vintage, one would expect the primary Lipan spirit deities (particularly Killer-of-Enemies) to have played a role in teaching the ceremony to the Lipan people.

The addition of the element of song or chant to musical accompaniment is reminiscent of the Lipan lunar eclipse ceremony and many of the features of the peyote ceremony seem to have been adaptations taken from the lunar eclipse ritual. Both were rituals performed only at night to musical accompaniment of drums and rattles. The dry sticks of the lunar ritual were replaced by a ceremonial staff in the peyote ceremony. Even late nineteenth century Comanche terminology for the name of the rite (the "Half Moon" ritual) seems to have been taken from the Lipan practitioners on the Comanche Reservation, and probably reflected the early lunar associations made by the Mexican Lipan band who originated the ceremony. However, what separated the Lipan lunar ritual from the peyote ceremony were the strict gender rules applied from the time of the origin of the Lipan peyote ceremony. Whereas the lunar ritual was a ceremony involving the entire band (men, women and children), the peyote ceremony was performed, from the time of its origin, only by men. Strict gender rules were enforced as to peyote ceremony participants. In addition, there were also strict rules governing the women who brought in the food at the conclusion of the ceremony (Chebahtah and Minor, 2007: 208-209).

The Lipan peyote myth is a faithful account of many of the details observed in a nineteenth century Lipan peyote ceremony. It was held in a ritual tepee and lasted throughout at least one night. The ceremonial leaders/singers (in many cases, four leaders indicating the sacred nature of the ceremony) were generally older men. A basket was filled with dried peyote buttons and placed inside the ritual tepee, generally on the north side of the interior. A fire pit was dug in the middle and one large peyote button was designated "Old Man Peyote" and placed on a raised mound to the west of the fire. The ritual leader entered the tent carrying a ceremonial staff and was seated behind the raised mound. He was followed into the tepee by the other peyote singers and then by the male participants. A peyote tepee could become crowded as twenty or more men pressed into the interior. Ceremonial songs were sung as the peyote buttons were consumed by the participants. Each participant then awaited the visions that would come with eating the peyote. As the songs were sung, they were accompanied by the sounds of a rattle. The ritual was concluded right before or at sunrise with the singing of the Morning Star Song. Smoke was offered up to the spirit of the peyote, the ceremonial drum was taken out and played, and the participants ritually cleansed themselves with water. The Meat Song was sung as the women entered the tepee with food, which they placed before the men (Stewart, 1974: 220).

Although Lipan shamans first used the peyote ceremony for medicinal purposes, the myth makes clear that the focus of the ritual quickly expanded beyond a curative function. Cures were still sought and would continue to be sought through peyote use to the present day, but the peyote ritual soon became central to Lipan ceremonial life. By the nineteenth century, the peyote ceremony was another method, in addition to the vision quest, for individuals to seek supernatural power to protect them during battle. The healing functions of the peyote ceremony had always been within the purview of Lipan curative shamans, but the ritual similarity with the lunar eclipse ceremony indicates that mythic shamans also used the peyote ceremony as a means of opening themselves as a channel for the supernatural power of spirit deities in order to make predictive statements.

So, how did a purely Lipan ceremony make its way from the Lipan *rancherías* of late eighteenth century Coahuila to the twentieth century Comanche and Kiowa Reservation of Oklahoma? The knowledge of the mystical and medicinal uses of peyote was carried by Mexican Lipan shamans as they were forced into exile after 1870. In order to trace the transference of the peyote ceremony, one must trace the movements of the Lipan peyote singers—from Mexico to the Mescaleros of New Mexico and, by 1895, to the Comanches. Opler noted that the heyday of Mescalero Apache peyote use was from 1870-1910 (Opler, 2002: 25). This period of time coincides with the residence of Mexican Lipan peyote shamans such as *Chevato, Dinero, Santavi, Shosh* and *Manuel* among the Mescaleros. The first three men left the Mescalero Reservation by 1893 and were brought to Oklahoma by Quanah Parker, who sought to establish a purely Native religion as an alternative to the aggressive missionary efforts of Protestant missionary groups on the Comanche and Kiowa Reservation. Parker put his own stamp on the Lipan peyote ceremony, primarily in consolidating a religious philosophy ("The Peyote Road") and in the use of terminology such as "roadman" to indicate the ritual leader. Yet the basic Comanche and Kiowa ceremony of the early twentieth century—the songs, the use of rattle and drum, the gender exclusivity—remained unchanged from nineteenth century Lipan practice.

It is fashionable now, in the twenty-first century, for pop historians to explore how the nature, practices or inventions of certain ethnic groups "saved civilization" or "saved the world." English curiosity and an eighteenth century passion for scientific inquiry, which led Edward Jenner to develop a vaccination for smallpox, is certainly one serendipitous case. However, the Lipan Apache contribution toward the saving of the traditional world of Native America was a gift of powerful proportions and of profound implications. The gift of the Lipan peyote ceremony, grounded in concepts familiar to all Native peoples—the supernatural power of the natural world, the purifying smoke used to pay homage to such power, the rattle, drum and the chant—became one of the few cohesive elements binding many Native peoples together during a time of profound cultural disintegration.

Sadly, this gift was made too late to help the Lipan Apaches. By 1905, their tribe was fragmented, their people dispersed to the four winds. What was once the bright flame of a Lipan cultural fire found burning within a peyote tepee had been reduced by the twentieth century to glowing embers, symbols of the scattered Lipan Apaches who remained the cultural repositories of the Light Gray People.

Notes

Preface
1. The counties surveyed were Medina, Webb (Laredo), Uvalde, Bandera and Kendall (Depredation Reports, 1867: 134-135, 141-142, 173-174, 203-204, 225-229).

Chapter 1   Translation and Meaning of Tribal Name
1. The Zuazua tribal history uses the word *kónicàà*, which Hoijer translated as "the Lipan [tribe]." However, Zuazua's term does not shed any light on the origins of the word "Lipan" and was probably a term used by the Lipans to refer to a group of people inhabiting a camp or *ranchería* since it is similar to the Lipan word for camp, or *gónka* (Hoijer, 1940: S1).
2. The Gatschet vocabulary is linguistically problematic in many respects. Gatschet did not use a modern orthographic system to record the sounds he heard and we can only assume that he heard Lipan words through the ears of an English-speaker rather than a Spanish-speaker (Gatschet, 1884: Schedule 7). Mooney's comparison vocabulary of Lipan and Mescalero is woefully abbreviated and incomplete. Although these clumsy first attempts to record the Lipan language are historically valuable, they leave the modern scholar guessing at pronunciations. Harry Hoijer's linguistic analysis of Athapascan languages, while extensive, is also somewhat thin in its examination of the Lipan language. In truth, we just do not know exactly what sounds Gatschet and Mooney heard when they asked their informants for the Lipan word meaning a light gray color. Hoijer never recorded the orthographic pronunciation of this important Lipan term, but the Chiricahuan verb stem denoting a quality or attribute of gray-ness, *libá (pronounced leh-pah* and meaning "he is gray") provides a clue (Hoijer, 1945: 22).
3. Mr. Chebahtah, of Lipan and Comanche ancestry, stated that his family believed the tribal name "Lipan" meant an ashy gray skin color. Author's interview with William Chebahtah, San Antonio, Texas, January 24, 2006.

Chapter 2   The Origin of the Lipan Apaches
1. The quote is a condensed and clarified version of a much longer tale (Opler: 1940: 13-16).
2. Jean Louis Berlandier linked the Kiowa Apaches to the Lipan tribe, calling them the "Plains Lipans or Lipans Llaneros" (Ewers, 1969: pp. 134-135 and notes 194, 195).
3. The contextual identification of the Rio del Norte with the Arkansas or Red Rivers is made by Ewers (Ewers: 1969: pp. 130-131 and note 184).

Chapter 3   The Zuazua History
1. Zuazua discusses both "Many Houses" and tepees, but uses different nouns to refer to each.
2. Photos of San Bernardo church and tombs can be seen in Weddle, 1968: Plates 7-10, Plates 16-17. An alternate meaning of "Circular House" could reflect the fact that the Big Water band was a group which broke away from, or was an offshoot of, the Fire or Camp Circle band.

Chapter 4   Early Lipan-Spanish Contacts in Texas
1. The other food items included meat, corn, cornmeal, beans and salt (Memoria, 1749: 207-211).

Chapter 5   Physical Appearance and Manner of Dress

1. Berlandier's estimates of Lipan height were made after his observation of a Texas Lipan band (Ewers, 1969: 129). The Mexican Lipans also averaged between 5'6" and 6'. Evidence of this fact are the heights recorded on several Mexican Lipans who enlisted as U.S. Army Scouts from 1883-1886. *Chevato* measured 5'10", his brother *Dinero* measured 5'8¼", *Magoosh* measured 5'7", *Shosh* measured 5'6", and *Jose Torres* measured 5'9" (Records of U.S. Army Continental Commands, 1883-1886). All of the men listed above appear on the Mescalero Census rolls (1885-1914) as Lipan Apaches.

2. To arrive at an estimate of gifts received solely by the two Lipan chiefs and their followers, the total amount of vermillion (25 lbs. 2 oz.) given to both Lipans and Comanches was divided in half (Lipan Gifts, 1807: 211-214).

3. The orthographic spellings of all Lipan words in the text are taken directly from Gatschet, who did not use a modern linguistic system to record what he heard. However, these words are included in the form in which Gatschet recorded them simply to give a sense of the Lipan language and are not meant to represent a modern orthography or linguistic analysis (Gatschet, 1884: 15).

Chapter 6   Lipan Apache Material Culture

1. Opler used the term "wickiup," but his description fits that of a *jacal* (Opler, 1940: 214). In the Lipan language, the exact terms for tepee and *jacal* are unknown. Gatschet's vocabulary defines the Lipan word *kówa* as "lodge or cabin," with a notation that the word *yéwĕ kórǎ* as literally translated to "skin lodge." The Lipan word *tanani-ai* or *kó'ra nani-ai* was translated as "canvas tent," while the word *kî* or *k'hi* meant "American house" (i.e. a fixed dwelling) (Gatschet, 1884: 8).

2. Two Lipan-style bows made by Frank Buckelew are in the collection of the Frontier Times Museum, Bandera, Texas (Dennis, 1925: 118).

Chapter 7   Lipan Apache Economic Culture: Hunting and Gathering

1. The town of Lipan is in Hood County (Hart, 1996: 212). "Lipan Flat" and "Lipan Spring" are in Tom Green County (Lipan Flat, Lipan Spring, 1996: 212). "Lipan Spring" is in Bell County (Lipan Spring, 1996: 212).

Chapter 8   Lipan Apache Economic Culture: The Shadow Trade Economy

1. The presidio commander's depredation report was made in conjunction with a report filed by the priest at the nearby mission of la Bahía. The mission reported a loss of 3,500 head of cattle (Piscina, 1762: 184-185).

Chapter 9   Lipan Apache Social Culture: Family, Kinship and Society

1. Opler contradicts himself on this point in his Chiricahua study (Opler, 1994: 74-79, 105).

2. The three letter-writers were *Picax-andé Yns-tinsle*, *Juan María Sas/Sais (son of Zapato Sas)* and *Chevato*. (Picax-andé Yns-tinsle, 1788: 372-374) (Sas, 1821: 2) (Chevato, 1889)

Chapter 10   Political Organization- The Lipan Band

1. Opler's study focused primarily on the Mescaleros, but he extended his remarks on societal structure to include the Lipan Apaches as well.

2. Juan de Ugalde translated *Picax'* name as "Strong Arm" and said it was pronounced *Pica-gande* (Nelson, 1940: 438).

3. *Juan Tuerto* was a Lipan who married a Mescalero woman and assumed leadership of her Mescalero group.

4. Caution must be used in taking Gatschet's orthography at face value, since he did not use a modern system. The band names are given exactly as he recorded them. This author adds the caveat that the actual or correct pronunciations and linguistic notations might have differed in many respects.

5. The most probable translation of the name *Zapato Sas* is based on the assumption that *Zapato* and *Sas* were Spanish words—*zapato (Sp. shoe)* and a corruption of a Spanish word *(sastré)* indicating both a tailor and the act of tailoring. An alternate translation would yield a half Spanish-half Lipan combination of *zapato (Sp. shoe)* and *šàš (the orthographic spelling of the Lipan word meaning bear)* (Hoijer, 1938: 85). However, all historical references to the Lipan word for bear spell the word as "shosh" or "shash," which is how the orthographic spelling is pronounced. Since the Spanish would not have been aware of Hoijer's Lipan orthography, the chief's name should probably be translated as "tailored shoe," which was an apt description of the high-beaked moccasin for which *Zapato Sas'* band was named.

6. The *Dapéshte* River was not the Rio Grande, Red River, Sabine, Mississippi, Nueces, Brazos, the Clear Fork of the Brazos, Pecos or Concho River.

7. Author's telephone interview with Mexican anthropologist José Medina Gonzalez Davila of *la Universidad Iberoamericana* in Mexico City, January 29, 2009. Mr. Medina is a native of northern Coahuila and the government's regional anthropological authority. Also see Cárdenas, 2008: 22-41.

8. This estimate assumes 700 warriors per Upper and Lower Lipans and a calculation of one female and one child for each of the 1,400 warriors.

9. 1886 is the first year in which tribal affiliations were noted.

10. Author's interview with Bernard Barcena (Chairman) and Robert Soto (First Vice Chairman) of the Lipan Apache Tribe of Texas, San Antonio. Author was appointed Tribal Historian of the Lipan Apache Tribe of Texas in September 2007.

Chapter 11   Political Organization: The Lipan Chief

1. For the Lipan word for "chief," see Gatschet, 1884: 53 and Rodriguez, 1995: 146.

2. All nineteenth century Mexican Lipans cited can be found in the 1885-1886 Mescalero Apache Reservation Census Rolls.

3. The translation of *Taguadas Chille* is based on the Spanish verb *chillar (to shriek or squeak)* and the noun *teguas (leather boots made in a particular style by the Tewa Indians but adopted for use by eighteenth century Spaniards).*

Chapter 12   Lipan Apache Raiding

1. The garrison was increased from 43 to 53 soldiers about 1720 in response to the onset of Apache raids (Bonilla, 1772: 11).

2. These horses can be assumed to have been taken from the saddle horse herd because of the quick response by the soldiers (Dunn, 1911: 206).

Chapter 13   Captives
 1. *Custaleta* was also known as *Costalites.*
 2. "Genealogy of Francis Monroe Buckelew and Nancy A. Witter." <http://www.worldconnect.rootsweb.com> (Accessed Sept. 18, 2006).
 3. Statement of Paula Whitworth Harris, "Genealogy of Jefferson Davis Smith and Julia Harriet Reed,"<http://www.worldconnect.rootsweb.com> (Accessed Sept. 17, 2006)

Chapter 14   Lipan Apache Warfare
 1. Email correspondence between author and Ruben D. Pastrana Guerrero, town historian of Los Aldamas (Nuevo Leon), January 2008.

Chapter 15   Lipan Apache Religion- Overview
 1. Author's email discussion with Robert Soto, First Vice Chairman of the Lipan Apache Tribe of Texas, June 1, 2007.
 2. Gatschet translated the word *tésä* as "Indian doctor," indicating a medical practitioner rather than a religious practitioner. However, in hunting and gathering cultures, the act of curing is inseparable from religious practice.

Chapter 16   Lipan Apache Religion- Mythic Shamanism
 1. Farrer's "shadow world" concept, developed after a study of the Mescaleros, can be applied to the Lipan Apaches as well. Evidence for this application lies in the Lipan emergence myth.
 2. Gatschet noted that this chant was a fragment of "a religious song."
 3. Author's email correspondence with Thomas Zermeno, an elder of the Lipan Apache Tribe of Texas, April, 2008.

Chapter 17   Lipan Apache Religion- Curative Shamanism
 1. The claim of the inheritability of Lipan shamanic practice was made by *Dinero,* a brother of *Chevato.* Although *Dinero* was a well-known peyote singer, his brother *Chevato* was the practicing shaman.
 2. For a good guide to herbal cures of northern Mexico, see *"México Descono-cido."* <http://www.mexicodesconocido.com> (Accessed June 11, 2007).

References Cited

Archives

Archivo General de Indies. The Center for American History, University of Texas at Austin

Archivo General de Mexico. The Center for American History, University of Texas at Austin

Archivo General de la Nación. Benson Latin American Collection, The Center for American History, University of Texas at Austin

Archivo San Francisco El Grande. The Center for American History, University of Texas at Austin

Béxar Archives. Texana Collection, San Antonio Public Library, San Antonio, Texas

Cassiano-Perez Collection. Daughters of the Republic of Texas Library at the Alamo, San Antonio, Texas

Harry Hoijer Papers. The American Philosophical Society, Philadelphia, PA.

Kiowa Agency Records. Oklahoma Historical Society, Oklahoma City, Oklahoma

National Anthropological Archives. Smithsonian Institution, Washington, D.C.

National Archives. Washington, D.C.

Saltillo Archives. The Center for American History, University of Texas at Austin

Sophienburg Archives. New Braunfels, Texas

Abbreviations

AGI- *Archivo General de Indies*
AGM- *Archivo General de Mexico*
AGN- *Archivo General de la Nación*
APS- The American Philosophical Society
ASFEG- *Archivo San Francisco el Grande*
BA(T)- Béxar Archives, Translated
BA(U)- Béxar Archives, Untranslated
BIA- Bureau of Indian Affairs
BLAC- Benson Latin American Collection
CAH- The Center for American History

CPC- Cassiano-Perez Collection
KAR- Kiowa Agency Records
MVS- Material from Various Sources
NAA- National Anthropological Archives
NA- National Archives
OHS- Oklahoma Historical Society
PI- *Provincias Internas*
RACC- Records of U.S Army Commands
SA- Sophienburg Archives
USS- U.S. Department of State

Unpublished Primary Sources

Almazán, Don Juan Antonio Pérez de

1733 Almazán to Viceroy, Feb. 10, AGN, PI, Vol. 32, fr. 347-351, BLAC. Anonymous citizen of Santa Rosa (Coahuila)

1878 Letter from anonymous citizen to Col. Ranald Mackenzie, June 12, RACC, *Letters Received by the Adjutant General*, microfilm publication #M666, Roll 207, NA.

Barreiro, Francisco Alvarez

1729 *"Plano corographico de los Reynos de Nuevo Estremadura o Coaguila y el Nuevo de Leon"* (Map of Coahuila and Nuevo Leon), Bryan (James P.) Map Collection, CAH.

Basterra, Don Prudencio de Orabio

1738 Basterra to Viceroy, June 25, Reel 2, Vol. 14, BA(T).

1739 Order of Governor Basterra, Feb. 16, Reel 2, Vol. 11, BA(T).

Béxar (San Antonio, Texas)

1769 Petition to Viceroy from the priests at San Antonio regarding Indian troubles, June 9, AGI, *Historia*, 2Q186, Vol. 383, CAH.

1783 Captain of Béxar presidio to Domingo Cabello, April 28, Reel 14, Vol. 118, BA(T).

Brown, Stephen S.

1868 Report on the Indians of Coahuila, Mexico, September, Explanatory Letter A, RACC, *Letters Received by the Adjutant General*, microfilm publication #M619, Roll 642, NA.

Buckelew, Frank

1868 Deposition of F.M. Buckelew, Mar. 21, in Winfrey and Day, *The Indian Papers of Texas*, Vol. 4.

Bustamante, Anastacio

1822 Treaty between Anastacio Bustamante and Lipan chiefs *Cuelgas de Castro* and *Poca Ropa*, Aug. 27, Eberstadt Collection, CAH.

Bustillo y Zevallos, Juan Antonio

1732 Report of Bustillo, Dec. 24, AGN, *PI*, Vol. 32, fr. 353-356, BLAC.

1733 Report to Conde de Galvé, Jan. 31, AGN, *PI*, Vol. 32, fr. 356-375, BLAC.

Cabello, Domingo

1779a Cabello to Viceroy, March 9, Reel 10, Vol. 75, BA(T).

1779b Report of Domingo Cabello, included in the *Expediente* regarding the abandonment of the Pueblo of Nuestra Senora del Pilar de Bucareli, April 24, AGI, *Historia*, 2Q179, Vol. 356, CAH.

1780a Cabello to Cavalier de Croix, Oct. 20, Reel 12, Vol. 104, BA(T).

1780b Cabello to Cavalier de Croix, Nov. 20, Reel 13, Vol. 106, BA(T).

1781 Cabello to Cavalier de Croix, Jan. 31, Reel 13, Vol. 106, BA(T)

1784 Cabello to Mathias de Galvez, Sept. 30, AGM, *PI*, 2Q204, Vol. 480, CAH.

1785 Cabello to Viceroy, Sept. 19, Reel 15, Vol. 133, BA(T).

1786a Cabello to Viceroy, March 18, Reel 16, Vol. 137, BA(T).

1786b Cabello to Jacobo Ugarte, June 12, Reel 16, Vol. 138, BA(T).

1786c Cabello to Jacobo Ugarte, July 2, Reel 16, Vol. 139, BA(T).

Cansio, Lorenzo

1763 "Diary of a Trip from New Mexico to San Sabá Mission," Feb. 20-28, AGI, *PI*, 2Q148, Vol. 92, CAH.

Carroll, James A. (Mescalero Apache Reservation Agent)

1908 Letter to Quanah Parker, July 13, KAR, *Indian History, 1875-1914*, microfilm #KA-48, OHS.

Castro Romero, Jr., Daniel

1854 Letter from William Davenport, Esq. to his sister Rachel Anderson, *The Castro Family History of the Lipan Apache Band of Texas*, 1996, SA.

Chevato

1889 Chevato to Quanah Parker, 1888 and 1889, attached to a letter from W.D. Myers, Kiowa Agent, to Commissioner of Indian Affairs, April 20, 1889, BIA, *Letters Received by the Department of the Interior*, Record Group 75, 11319-1889, NA.

Cuelgas de Castro

1822 "Notice of the captives that have been delivered by the chiefs of the nation *Lipana* and brought by Chief *Cuelgas de Castro*," undated fragment but list probably compiled ca. 1822, Reel 168, BA(U).

Cuervo y Valdez, Don Francisco
1699 "Testimony Regarding the Founding of the Mission," July 1, AGI, *Historia*,
    2Q178, Vol. 351, CAH.
De Anza, Juan Bautista
1786 De Anza to Jacobo Ugarte, Nov. 18, AGM, *PI*, 2Q205, Vol. 483, CAH.
De Castro, Ramon
1791a De Castro to Viceroy, July 21, AGM, *PI*, 2Q215, Vol. 529, CAH.
1791b De Castro to Governor of Nuevo Leon, Aug. 27, AGM, *PI*, 2Q215, Vol. 529,
    CAH
1791c De Castro to Viceroy, Sept. 14, AGM, *PI*, 2Q215, Vol. 529, CAH.
1791d De Castro to Viceroy, Dec. 4, 2Q215, Vol. 530, 285, CAH.
De Nava, Pedro
1791a Treaty between Pedro de Nava and Lipan chiefs *José Antonio, et al*, Feb. 8, AGM,
    PI, 2Q186, Vol. 530, CAH.
1791b De Nava to Viceroy regarding "the disposition of the Lipan who have entered into
    the peace," March 28, AGM, *PI*, 2Q186, Vol. 530, CAH.
1791c De Nava to Viceroy, March 16, AGM, *PI*, 2Q186, Vol. 530, CAH.
De Neve, Phelipe
1784 Order of Phelipe de Neve, May 17, Reel 12, Vol. 98, BA(T).
Depredation Reports
1867 Depredations attributed to the Lipan Apaches as reported by Texas counties, Win-
    frey and Day, *The Indian Papers of Texas*, Vol. 4.
Dolores, Fr. Mariano Francisco de los
1749a Dolores to Viceroy, Nov. 25, AGI, *PI*, 2Q177, Vol. 347, CAH.
1749b Dolores to Viceroy, Nov. 29, AGM, *Historia*, 2Q177, Vol. 347, CAH.
Ecay y Musquiz, Don Joseph Antonio
1734 Ecay to Blas de la Garza Falcon, Aug. 15, AGM, *PI*, 2Q147, Vol. 84, CAH.
Flores y Valdez, Nicolas
1723 Flores to Marquis de Aguayo, Oct. 21, AGM, *PI*, 2Q213, Vol. 522, CAH.
Galván, Juan
1753a Galván to Viceroy, June 18, AGM, *PI*, 2Q151, Vol. 105, CAH.
1753b Galván to Viceroy, Sept. 20, AGM, *PI*, 2Q151, Vol. 105, CAH.
Gatschet, Albert Samuel
1884 *Lipan Vocabulary Taken at Ft. Griffin, Texas, September- October 1884*. MS 81-a-
    b. NAA.
Green, Charles (Texas Indian Agent)
1844 Green to Commissioner of Indian Affairs, Dec. 14, in Winfrey and Day, *The Indian
    Papers of Texas*, Vol. 2.
Hoijer, Harry
1939a *The History and the Customs of the Lipans, as told by Augustina Zuazua*, Item
    #4473, Harry Hoijer Papers, APS.
1939b "Lipan Apache Field Notes," Item #4473, Harry Hoijer Papers, APS.
Hood, Captain Charles C.
1879 Hood to Lt. John L. Bullis, Jan. 29, RACC, *Letters Received by the Adjutant Gen-
    eral*, microfilm publication #M666, Roll 208, NA.
Irion, R.A.
1838 Irion to Sam Houston, March 14, in Winfrey and Day, *The Indian Papers of Texas*,
    Vol. 1.

Irvine, J.B. (Tonkawa Indian Agent)
1880 Irvine to Commissioner of Indian Affairs, Jan. 7, Pawnee Agency Letterpress Book,
    Vol. 1 (Special Tonkawa Agency), Pawnee Agency, *Letters Sent Jan. 31 to Nov. 5,
    1881*, microfilm #PA-30, OHS.
Jauregui Urrutia, Don Joseph Fernández de
1735 Jauregui Urrutia to Viceroy, Jan. 11, Reel 2, Vol. 6, BA(T).
1736 "Report on the Economic State of Nuevo Leon and its Indians," April 14, Reel 2,
    Vol. 6, BA(T).
Juntas de Guerra
1778 Minutes of four *Juntas de Guerra*, June 6 and Sept. 22. Reel 9, Vol. 69, BA(T).
Kinney, H.L.
1861 "Record of Evidence in Claim of H.L. Kinney against the United States," January
    1, in Winfrey and Day, *The Indian Papers of Texas*, Vol. 4.
La Bahía (Goliad, Texas)
1810 List of Individuals residing near Mission la Bahía del Espiritú Santo, January,
    Folder 40, CPC.
Lafuente, José
1798 Report from the Laredo presidio, March 17, AGM, *PI*, 2Q201, Vol. 457, CAH.
Lasaga, Diego de
1784 Lasaga to Viceroy, June 21, AGM, *PI*, 2Q205, Vol. 481, CAH.
Lipan Gifts
1807 "Report of articles given to four chiefs and 278 Comanche and Lipan Indians on
    Feb. 15-18 and Feb. 27," Reel 22, Vol. 17, BA(T)
Livestock Brands
1788-1828 Indian Livestock Brands issued by Spanish to *Lipanes*, Comanches, *Tan-
    cagues, Tahuacanos*, Undated fragment but probably dates from 1788-1828, Reel
    168, BA(U).
Lizarraras, Fr. Luis de
1770 Lizarraras to Governor of Coahuila, Mar. 31, AGM, *PI*, 2Q202, Vol. 463, CAH.
Memoria
1749 "*Memoria* of the gifts given by the Queretero missions in the Province of Texas for
    the pacification of the Apaches since the year 1749," AGM, *PI*, 2Q237, Vol. 768,
    CAH.
Menchaca, Josef
1790 Menchaca to Don Miguel de Emparán, Apr. 9, AGM, *PI*, 2Q202, Vol. 463, CAH.
Mescalero Reservation Census (New Mexico)
1885-1904 Apache Reservation Census Rolls, BIA, *Mescalero Apache Reservation,
    1885-1914*, microfilm publication #M595, Roll 254, NA.
Mexican Captives
1853-1854 "A List of Mexican Captives," *Letters Received by the Office of Indian Af-
    fairs*, Texas Indian Agency, 1853-1854, microfilm publication #M234, Roll 859, fr.
    404-414, NA.
Mission San José (San Antonio, Texas)
1805 "Census showing the number of Indians at the Mission of San José, and including
    the children and Spaniards in addition, January 1805," Reel 19, Vol. 5, BA(T).
Moffitt, R.E.
1879 Moffitt to Lt. John L. Bullis, Jan. 9, RACC, *Letters Received by the Adjutant Gen-
    eral*, microfilm publication #M666, Roll 208, NA.

Mooney, James

1897a *Tribal Names and Divisions of the Jicarillas, Lipans and Mescaleros*, MS 3785, NAA.

1897b *Comparative Vocabularies: Mescalero Apache and Lipan*, MS 425, NAA.

Moreno, Don José Ventura, Don Pedro Urrutia et al

1783 Moreno et al, Summary of Four Mescalero Campaigns of Juan de Ugalde, Mar. 26, AGI, *PI*, 2Q178, Vol. 349, CAH.

Neighbors, Robert S. (Texas Indian Agent)

1846 Neighbors to Commissioner of Indian Affairs, Feb. 4, in Winfrey and Day, *The Indian Papers of Texas*, Vol. 3.

Nuevo Leon

1791 "Report of New Enemy Occurrences in the Province of Nuevo Leon," Sept. 6, AGM, *PI*, 2Q215, Vol. 529, CAH.

Olivan Rebolledo, Don Juan de

1733 Olivan Rebolledo to Viceroy, July 18, Reel 1, Vol. 3, BA(T).

Pacheco, Rafael Martínez

1787 Pacheco to Juan de Ugalde, Dec. 24, 1787, Reel 17, Vol. 149, BA(T).

Perez, Matheo, et al

1732 Petition of the soldiers of Béxar, Dec. 24, AGN, *PI*, Vol. 32, fr. 354-356.

Picax-andé Yns-tinsle

1788 *Picax-andé* to Juan de Ugalde, April 5, AGM, *PI*, 2Q207, Vol. 494, CAH.

Piscina, Manuel Ramírez de la

1762 Piscina to the Governor of Texas, June 5, Reel 5, Vol. 35, BA(T).

Rabago y Teran, Don Phelipe de

1755 Rabago to Viceroy, Jan. 10, 1755, AGI, *PI*, 2Q151, Vol. 105, CAH.

1761 Rabago to Viceroy, Dec. 31, AGI, *Historia*, 2Q184, Vol. 373, CAH.

1762a Rabago to Viceroy, Jan. 23, AGI, *Historia*, 2Q184, Vol. 373, CAH.

1762b Rabago and Fr. Diego Ximenez upon the foundation of the Lipan mission of Santa Cruz, Feb. 7, AGI, *Historia*, 2Q184, Vol. 373, CAH.

Ramirez, Fr. Pedro

1762 Petition to Viceroy, June 5, Reel 9, Vol. 35, BA(T).

1778 Ramirez to Cavalier de Croix, Oct. 3, Reel 10, Vol. 75, BA(T).

Ramon, Diego

1718 Report to Viceroy, Apr. 28, Reel 1, Vol. 1, BA(T).

Ramon, Juan I.

1791 Juan I. Ramon to Ramon de Castro, Aug. 18, AGM, *PI*, 2Q215, Vol. 529, CAH.

Records of U.S. Army Continental Commands

1883-1886 "Record of Enlistments for the 20th Regiment of Infantry, 1878-1914," US Army, RACC, *Indian Scouts*, microfilm publication #M233, Roll 71, NA.

Republic of Texas

1838 Government Drafts in Winfrey and Day, *The Indian Papers of Texas*, Vol. 1.

Richards, H.J.

1868 Richards to E.M. Pease, May 18, in Winfrey and Day, *The Indian Papers of Texas*, Vol. 4.

Rodriguez, Vicente

1775 Rodriguez to Baron de Ripperda, June 6, Reel 8, Vol. 61, BA(T).

San Fernando de Béxar (San Antonio, Texas)
1762 Writ of the *Cabildo* of San Fernando de Béxar, June 5, Reel 5, Vol. 35, BA(T).
San Juan Bautista presidio (Coahuila)
1791 Report of "Flying Company" of San Juan Bautista presidio, Sept. 6, AGM, *PI*,
    2Q215, Vol. 529, CAH
Santa Ana, Fr. Benito Fernández de
1743a Santa Ana to Viceroy, March 3, AGM, *PI*, 2Q215, Vol. 531, CAH.
1743b Santa Ana to Viceroy, March 5, AGM, *PI*, 2Q215, Vol. 531, CAH.
1750a Santa Ana to the Viceroy, Feb. 19, 1750, 2Q177, Vol. 347, CAH.
1750b Santa Ana to Viceroy, Feb. 20, AGM, *Historia*, 2Q177, Vol. 347, CAH.
Sas, Juan María
1821 Report of *Juan María Sais* on a trip he made to Natchitoches to spy on the Caddoes,
    Dec. 20, AGM, *Relaciones Exteriores*, 2Q220, Vol. 552, CAH.
Schuhardt, William (U.S. Consul)
1869 Schuhardt to Secretary of State, June 1, Despatch #20, USS, *Despatches of the U.S.
    Consul at Piedras Negras, Coahuila, to the U.S. Secretary of State*, Vol. 1, micro-
    film publication #M299, Roll 1, NA.
1873a Schuhardt to Secretary of State, March 29, Despatch #101, USS, *Despatches of
    the U.S. Consul at Piedras Negras, Coahuila, to the U.S. Secretary of State*, Vol. 1,
    microfilm publication #M299, Roll 1, NA.
1873b Schuhardt to Secretary of State, May 8, Despatch #103, USS, *Despatches of the
    U.S. Consul at Piedras Negras, Coahuila, to the U.S. Secretary of State*, Vol. 1, mi-
    crofilm publication #M299, Roll 1, NA.
1878a Schuhardt to Secretary of State, May 7, Despatch #197, USS, *Despatches of the
    U.S. Consul at Piedras Negras, Coahuila, to the U.S. Secretary of State*, Vol. 2, mi-
    crofilm publication #M299, Roll 1, NA.
1878b Schuhardt to Secretary of State, May 14, 1878, Dispatch #198, USS, *Despatches
    from the U.S. Consul at Piedras Negras, Coahuila, to the U.S. Secretary of State*,
    Vol. 2, microfilm publication #M299, Roll 1, NA.
Serrano, Juan Antonio
1780 Serrano to Juan de Ugalde, Sept. 3, AGI, *PI*, 2Q141, Vol. 51, CAH.
Sierragorda, Conde de
1798 Sierragorda to Viceroy, Oct. 16, 2Q201, Vol. 457, BA(T):
1799a Sierragorda to Viceroy, Jan. 30, AGM, *PI*, 2Q201, Vol. 457, CAH.
1799b Sierragorda to Viceroy, June 3, AGM, *PI*, 2Q201, Vol. 457, CAH.
Starr, Samuel Henry
1853 Letter from Starr to his wife Eliza, May 19, Samuel Henry Starr Papers, *Personal
    Correspondence, 1848-1854*, Eberstadt Collection, CAH.
Tovar, Don Josef
1791 Tovar to Ramon de Castro, Sept. 6, AGM, *PI*, 2Q215, Vol. 529, CAH.
Ugalde, Juan de
1780 "Diary of Visit to Lipan Camps," Feb. 1780, AGI, *PI*, 2Q141, Vol. 51, CAH.
1781a Ugalde to Cavalier de Croix, Jan. 14, AGI, *PI*, 2Q141, Vol. 51, CAH.
1781b Ugalde to Cavalier de Croix, Feb. 8, 1781, 2Q141, Vol. 51, CAH.
1781c Ugalde to Viceroy, March 23, AGI, *PI*, 2Q141, Vol. 51, CAH.
1781d Ugalde to Cavalier de Croix, March 26, AGI, *PI*, 2Q141, Vol. 51, CAH.
1781e "Diary of News of the Lipans during August 1781," Sept. 17, AGM, *PI*, 2Q141,
    Vol. 51, CAH.

Ugalde, Juan de (cont'd)
1788a "Diary of Juan de Ugalde made upon his visit to the famous *Lipiyan* chief *Picax* in
    order to ratify the peace treaty signed on 10 July 1787," Diary entries for Feb. 27-29
    and March 1, 1788, AGM, *PI*, 2Q207, Vol. 494, CAH.
1788b "Diary of Juan de Ugalde of a Journey from San Antonio to San Juan Bautista,
    Coahuila," April 13 –June 12, 1788, AGM, *PI*, 2Q207, Vol. 494, CAH
1788c Ugalde to Viceroy, May 22, 1788, AGM, *PI*, 2Q207, Vol. 494, CAH.
1789 Ugalde to Viceroy, Apr. 1, AGM, *PI*, 2Q210, Vol. 509, CAH.
Ugarte y Loyola, Jacobo de
1775 Campaign diary of Ugarte against the Lipans on the Pecos River, diary entry for
    Nov. 6, AGM, *PI*, 2Q202, Vol. 463, CAH.
1776a Ugarte to Viceroy, July 9, AGM, *PI*, 2Q202, Vol. 463, CAH.
1776b Ugarte to Hugo O'Conor, Sept. 21, AGM, *PI*, 2Q205, Vol. 483, CAH.
Urrutia, Joseph
1738 Statement of J. Urrutia of Béxar presidio, June 26, Reel 2, Vol. 11 BA(T).
Urrutia, Thoribio
1750 Minutes of a meeting at Béxar presidio between Urrutia and Don Joachin de Ecay y
    Musquiz, June 20, AGI, *PI*, 2Q151, Vol. 105, CAH.
Valdez, Casimiro
1788 Valdez to Juan de Ugalde, Sept. 29, AGM, *PI*, 2Q207, Vol. 494, CAH.
Valdéz, Marcelo
1786 Valdés to Domingo Cabello, June 1786, Reel 16, Vol. 138, BA(T).
Valero, Marquis de
1719 Valero to Olivan Rebolledo, June 3, Reel 1, Vol. 1, BA(T).
Ximenez, Fr. Diego
1761a "Description of the Customs of the Apache Indians," ASFEG, *MVS*, 2Q256, Vol.
    407, CAH
1761b Ximenez to Fr. Manuel de Naxera, Nov. 4, AGI, *Historia*, 2Q177, Vol. 347,
    CAH.
1762 Ximenez, et. al., Report from the Mission of San Lorenzo de la Santa Cruz, Feb. 7,
    AGI, *Historia*, 2Q178, Vol. 349, CAH.
1763a Ximenez, *Consulta:* "Testimony re: planting missions on the Nueces," Feb. 25,
    AGI, *Historia*, 2Q148, Vol. 92, CAH.
1763b Ximenez to Lorenzo Cansio, Sept. 19, AGI, *Historia*, 2Q178, Vol. 349, CAH.
1764 Report on the State of the Missions under the Presidency of the Northern Rio
    Grande from Oct. 1758 to Dec. 1767, Fr. Diego Ximenez on the Texas missions for
    the Lipan, Dec. 26, AGI, *Historia*, 2Q178, Vol. 349, CAH.
Zaragosa
1763 Petition of citizens of San Fernando de Austria (Zaragosa), Mar. 21, Saltillo Ar-
    chives, 2Q313, Vol. 3, CAH.

Published Sources
Apuntes.
1998 *Apuntes para la Historia Antigua de la Mission Dulce Nombre de Jesus de Peyotes
    in el Anniversario 300 d.* San Antonio: Los Béxareños Society.
Aveni, Anthony F.
1980 *Skywatchers of Ancient Mexico.* Austin: University of Texas Press.
Ball, Eve.
1988 *Indeh: An Apache Odyssey.* Norman: University of Oklahoma Press.

Basso, Keith H., ed.

1971 *Western Apache Raiding and Warfare: From the Notes of Grenville Goodwin.* Tucson: University of Arizona Press.

Bedolla González, Miguel.

2001 "The Battle of La Rosita." *El Mesteño: A Magazine about Mexican-American Culture and Heritage in South Texas and Mexico* 4, no. 47 (August): 16.

Bolton, Herbert E.

1903 "Tienda de Cuervo's *Ynspeccion* of Laredo." *Southwestern Historical Quarterly* 6, no. 3 (January): 187-203.

Bonilla, Don Antonio.

1772 "A Brief Compendium of the Events Which Have Occurred in the Province of Texas from its Conquest, or Reduction, to the Present Date {1772}." *Southwestern Historical Quarterly* 8, no. 1 (July 1904): 9-78.

Brant, Charles S.

1949 "The Cultural Position of the Kiowa Apache." *Southwestern Journal of Anthropology* 5, no. 1 (Spring): 56-61.

Britannica

1992 *New Encyclopedia Britannica* Vol. 17. Chicago: Encyclopedia Britannica.

Brooks, James F.

2002 *Captives and Cousins: Slavery, Kinship and Community in the Southwest Borderlands.* Chapel Hill: University of North Carolina Press.

Campbell, Thomas N.

1996 "Yxandi Indians." *The New Handbook of Texas,* Vol. 6. Austin: The Texas State Historical Association.

Cárdenas, Carlos Villareal.

2008 *Mensaje de los Coahuiltecos, los Lipanes y los Catujanos.* Saltillo, Coahuila: *Escuela Normal Superior del Estado.*

Carlisle, Jeffrey D.

1996 "Apache Indians." *The New Handbook of Texas,* Vol. 1. Austin: The Texas State Historical Association.

Castaneda, Carlos, trans.

1926 "A Trip to Texas in 1828: José María Sanchez." *Southwestern Historical Quarterly* 29, No. 4 (April): 249-288.

Chabot, Frederick C. and Carlos Castaneda, trans.

1932 *Fray Juan Agustin de Morfi: Memorias for the History of the Province of Texas; Indian Excerpts.* San Antonio: Naylor Printing Co.

Chebahtah, William and Nancy McGown Minor.

2007 *Chevato: The Story of the Apache Warrior who Captured Herman Lehmann.* Lincoln: University of Nebraska Press.

Chipman, Donald E.

1992 *Spanish Texas, 1519-1821.* Austin: University of Texas Press.

Cobos, Rubén.

2003 *A Dictionary of New Mexico and Southern Colorado Spanish.* Santa Fe: Museum of New Mexico Press.

Comanche Language and Cultural Preservation Committee.

2003 *Our Comanche Dictionary.* Lawton: Comanche Language and Cultural Preservation Committee.

Coopwood, Bethel.
1900 "The Route of Cabeza de Vaca." *Southwestern Historical Quarterly* 3, no. 4: 229-264.
"Cross Timbers."
1996 *The New Handbook of Texas*, Vol. 2. Austin: The Texas State Historical Association.
Dennis, T.S. and Mrs. T.S. Dennis.
1925 *The Life of F.M. Buckelew, the Indian Captive, as Related by Himself.* Kerrville: Herring Publishing House.
Dunn, William Edward
1911 "Apache Relations in Texas, 1718-1750." *Southwestern Historical Quarterly* 14, no. 3 (January): 198-274.
1912 "Missionary Activities among the Eastern Apaches Previous to the Founding of the San Saba Mission." *Southwestern Historical Quarterly* 15, no. 3 (January): 186-200.
Ewers, John C., ed.
1969 *The Indians of Texas in 1830 by Jean Louis Berlandier.* WashingtonL: Smithsonian Institution Press.
1972 *Report on the Indian Tribes of Texas in 1828 by José Francisco Ruíz.* New Haven: Yale University Library.
Farrer, Claire R.
1991 *Living Life's Circle: Mescalero Apache Cosmovision.* Albuquerque: University of New Mexico Press.
Fikes, Jay C.
1996 "A Brief History of the Native American Church." *One Nation under God: The Triumph of the Native American Church.* Santa Fe: Clear Light Publishers.
Foster, William C., ed.
1998 *The La Salle Expedition to Texas: The Journal of Henri Joutel, 1684-1687.* Austin: The Texas State Historical Association.
"Genealogy of Francis Monroe Buckelew and Nancy A. Witter.
<http://www.worldconnect.rootsweb.com> (Sept. 18, 2006).
"Genealogy of Jefferson Davis Smith and Julia Harriet Reed."
<http://www.worldconnect.rootsweb.com> (Sept. 17, 2006).
Gerhard, Peter.
1920 *The North Frontier of New Spain.* Norman: University of Oklahoma Press.
Haas, Oscar.
1964 "Encounters with Local Indians Told by Early German Settlers." April 19, New Braunfels *Herald Zeitung.* Sophienburg Archives, New Braunfels, Texas.
Habig, Marian A., O.F.M.
1996 "Benito Fernández de Santa Ana." *The New Handbook of Texas*, Vol. 3. Austin: The Texas State Historical Association.
Hart, Brian.
1996 "Lipan, Texas." *The New Handbook of Texas*, Vol. 4. Austin: The Texas State Historical Association.
Hatcher, Mattie Austin, ed.
1919 "Juan Antonio Padilla: Texas in 1820, A Report on the Barbarous Indians of the Province of Texas." *Southwestern Historical Quarterly* 23 (July): 47-60.

Hester, Thomas R., ed.
1991 "Historic Native American Populations." *Ethnology of the Texas Indians*. New York: Garland Publishing.

Hickerson, Nancy Parrott.
1994 *The Jumanos: Hunters and Traders of the South Plains*. Austin: University of Texas Press.

Hodge, Frederick Webb, ed.
1912 *Handbook of American Indians North of Mexico*. Bulletin 30, Part I. Washington: Smithsonian Bureau of American Ethnology.

Hoijer, Harry.
1938 "The Southern Athapaskan Languages." *American Anthropologist* 40, no. 1 (Jan.-Mar.): 75-87.
1945 "Classificatory Verb Stems in the Apachean Languages." *International Journal of American Linguistics* 11, no. 1 (January): 13-23.
1956 "Athapaskan Kinship Systems." *American Anthropologist* 58, no. 2 (April): 309-333.

Hollon, W. Eugene and Ruth Lapham Butler.
1956 *William Bollaert's Texas*. Norman: University of Oklahoma Press.

Hoxie, Frederick E., ed.
1996 *Encyclopedia of North American Indians*. New York: Houghton Mifflin.

Jackson, Jack.
1986 *Los Mesteños: Spanish Ranching in Texas, 1721-1821*. College Station: Texas A&M University Press.

John, Elizabeth A.H.
1981 *Storms Brewed in Other Men's Worlds: The Confrontation of Indians, Spanish and French in the Southwest, 1540-1795*. Lincoln: University of Nebraska Press.
1989 *Views from the Apache Frontier: Report on the Northern Provinces of New Spain by José Cortés*. Norman: University of Oklahoma Press.
1991 "Views from a Desk in Chihuahua: Manuel Merino's Report on the Apaches Neighboring Nations, ca. 1804," *Southwestern Historical Quarterly* 155, no. 2 (October): 139-175.

Kavanagh, Thomas W.
1996 *The Comanches: A History, 1706-1875*. Lincoln: University of Nebraska Press.

Kenner, Charles L.
1969 *The Comanchero Frontier: A History of New Mexican- Plains Indian Relations*. Norman: University of Oklahoma Press.

Kidder, Alfred V.
2000 *An Introduction to the Study of Southwestern Archaeology*. New Haven: Yale University Press.

Latorre, Felipe A. and Delores L. Latorre.
1976 *The Mexican Kickapoo Indians*. Austin: University of Texas Press.

"Lipan Creek," "Lipan Flat," "Lipan Spring."
1996 *The New Handbook of Texas*, Vol. 4. Austin: The Texas State Historical Association.

Long, Christopher.
1996 "Helotes, Texas." *The New Handbook of Texas*, Vol. 3. Austin: The Texas State Historical Association.

McAllister, J. Gilbert.
1996 "Peyote." *The New Handbook of Texas*, Vol. 5. Austin: The Texas State Historical Association.
"México Desconocido."
  <http://www.mexicodesconocido.com> (June 11, 2007).
Mitchell, Mark.
2004 "Tracing Comanche History: Eighteenth Century Rock Art Depictions of Leather Armored Horses from the Arkansas River Basin, Southeastern Colorado." *Antiquity* 78, no. 299 (March): 115-126.
Moorhead, Max L.
1968 *The Apache Frontier: Jacobo Ugarte and Spanish-Indian Relations in Northern New Spain, 1769- 1791*. Norman: University of Oklahoma Press.
Nelson, Al B.
1940 "Juan de Ugalde and Picax-ande Ins-Tinsle, 1787-1788," *Southwestern Historical Quarterly* 43 (April): 438-464.
Ohlendorf, Sheila M., ed.
1980 *Jean Louis Berlandier: A Journey to Mexico during the years 1826 to 1845*. Austin: The Texas State Historical Association.
Olmstead, Frederick Law.
1978 *A Journey through Texas, or a Saddle Trip on the Southwestern Frontier*. Austin: University of Texas Press.
Opler, Morris E.
1938 "The Use of Peyote by the Carrizo and Lipan Apache Tribes." *American Anthropologist* 40, no. 2 (April-June): 271-285.
1940 *Myths and Legends of the Lipan Apache Indians*. Memoirs of the American Folk-Lore Society 26. New York: J.J. Augustine.
1945 "The Lipan Apache Death Complex and Its Extensions." *Southwestern Journal of Anthropology* 1, No. 1 (Spring): 122-141.
1975a "Problems in Apachean Cultural History, with Special Reference to the Lipan Apaches." *Anthropological Quarterly* 48, no. 3 (July): 182-192.
———. and Verne Frederick Ray.
1975b "The Lipan and Mescalero Apache in Texas." *An Ethnohistorical Analysis of Documents Regarding the Apaches in Texas*. New York: Garland Publishing.
Opler, Morris E. (cont'd)
1994 *Myths and Tales of the Chiricahua Apache Indians*. Lincoln: University of Nebraska Press.
2002 *Apache Odyssey: A Journey between Two Worlds*. Lincoln: University of Nebraska Press.
Ricklis, Robert A.
1996 *The Karankawa Indians of Texas*. Austin: University of Texas Press.
Rodriguez, Martha.
1995 *Historias de Resistencia y Extermino: Los Indios de Coahuila Durante el Siglo XIX*. Mexico City: Instituto Nacional Indigenista.
Salinas, Martin.
1990 *Indians of the Rio Grande Delta*. Austin: University of Texas Press.
Schilz, Thomas.
1987 *The Lipan Apaches in Texas*. El Paso: University of Texas.

Sjoberg, Andrée F.
1953 "Lipan Apache Culture in Historical Perspective." *Southwestern Journal of Anthropology* 9, no. 1 (Spring): 76-98.
Smith, Clinton L. and J. Marvin Hunter
2005 *The Boy Captives*. San Antonio: Cenveo Publishing.
Starnes, Gary B.
1996 "Juan de Ugalde." *The New Handbook of Texas*, Vol. 6. Austin: The Texas State Historical Association.
Stewart, Omer C.
1974 "Origin of the Peyote Religion in the United States." *Plains Anthropologist* 19, no. 65 (August 1974): 211-223.
Stogner, Charles Haskell.
1998 *Relations between the Comanches and Lipan Apache Indians from White Contact until the Early Nineteenth Century*. Privately bound, The Center for American History, University of Texas at Austin.
Tiller, Veronica E. Velarde.
1992 *The Jicarilla Apache Tribe: A History*. Lincoln: University of Nebraska Press.
Tunnell, Curtis D. and W.W. Newcomb, Jr.
1969 *A Lipan Apache Mission: San Lorenzo del Santa Cruz, 1761-1771*. Bulletin 14. Austin: The Texas Memorial Museum and the University of Texas.
Wade, Maria F.
2003 *The Native Americans of the Texas Edwards Plateau, 1582-1799*. Austin: University of Texas Press.
Weddle, Robert S.
1968 *San Juan Bautista: Gateway to Spanish Texas*. Austin: University of Texas Press.
Winfrey, Dorman H. and James M. Day, eds.
1995 *The Indian Papers of Texas and the Southwest*. Vols. 1-4. Austin: The Texas State Historical Association.

Index

About the Author

Nancy McGown Minor is an independent historical researcher with a Master's Degree from Texas State University. She specializes in archival research regarding the history and culture of the Lipan Apaches and is the Tribal Historian of the Lipan Apache Tribe of Texas.

Ms. Minor is also the co-author (with William Chebahtah) of *Chevato: The Story of the Apache Warrior who Captured Herman Lehmann* (University of Nebraska Press, 2007). This work contains the oral history and historical context of the life of Lipan Apache shaman *Chevato (1852-1931)*, one of the founders of the Native American Church.